THE GOOD-ENOUGH LIFE

THE GOOD-ENOUGH LIFE

Avram Alpert

PRINCETON UNIVERSITY PRESS

PRINCETON AND OXFORD

Published by Princeton University Press
41 William Street, Princeton, New Jersey 08540
99 Banbury Road, Oxford OX2 6JX

press.princeton.edu

All Rights Reserved

Library of Congress Cataloging-in-Publication Data

Names: Alpert, Avram, 1984– author.
Title: The good-enough life / Avram Alpert.
Description: Princeton : Princeton University Press, [2022] |
    Includes bibliographical references and index.
Identifiers: LCCN 2021038381 (print) | LCCN 2021038382 (ebook) |
    ISBN 9780691204352 (hardcover) | ISBN 9780691204345 (ebook)
Subjects: LCSH: Self-realization. | Ability. | Conduct of life. | BISAC:
    PHILOSOPHY / Social | SELF-HELP / Personal Growth / General
Classification: LCC BF637.S4 A5875 2022 (print) | LCC BF637.S4 (ebook) |
    DDC 158.1—dc23/eng/20211109
LC record available at https://lccn.loc.gov/2021038381
LC ebook record available at https://lccn.loc.gov/2021038382

British Library Cataloging-in-Publication Data is available

Editorial: Anne Savarese, James Collier
Production Editorial: Terri O'Prey
Text Design: Karl Spurzem
Jacket/Cover Design: Karl Spurzem
Production: Erin Suydam
Publicity: Jodi Price, Carmen Jimenez
Copyeditor: Jodi Beder

Jacket image: Japanese pottery restored using *kintsugi* technique.
Credit: Marco Montalti / Shutterstock

This book has been composed in Arno Pro and Clarendon BT Pro

Printed on acid-free paper. ∞

Printed in the United States of America

10 9 8 7 6 5 4 3 2 1

CONTENTS

THE GOOD-ENOUGH LIFE

Introduction

I used to aspire to greatness. When I was young, greatness meant wealth, and I wanted to find a way to be very rich. My first thought was to become a stockbroker, even though I didn't really know what that meant. Later, when I became obsessed with sports, I decided that my path to wealth should be as a famous athlete. I dreamed about playing basketball professionally, then tennis and baseball, but I never had enough talent for any of these.

Toward the end of high school and into my college years, I started to think of greatness as fame more than wealth. At first, I wanted to be a world-renowned fiction writer who was showered with prizes. Realizing how hard that would be to achieve, and (incorrectly) thinking that an academic life would be stabler, I went to graduate school, where I hoped to become one of those famous professors who was flown around the world to give prestigious lectures. I have come closer to achieving this goal than any of my previous professional plans, but it hasn't made me any more satisfied or happier. I think that's because while all of these different life goals have different values attached to them, they share the same basic aspiration: to become a member of the elite, sitting atop a social pyramid.

Over the last few years, I've come to think that this desire to be at the top is poisonous for ourselves, our relationships, our societies, and our planet—even for the individuals who do make it. And so, as much as I can, I've begun to work against these aspirations. I'm not saying I don't still find them appealing. Of course I do. I don't know if I'll ever set foot on an airplane without wishing I were sitting in the luxury of first class, or go to an event and not wish I were one of the luminaries on the stage. And of course I am still exercising and writing to the best of my abilities. What I have come to doubt is not the desire to do something well for its own sake, nor even the appeal of winning. Instead, I question the social order that takes our talents and turns them into a desire to win our spot at the top of competitive hierarchies. In fact, as I argue in this book, I have come to think that personal quests for greatness, and, perhaps even more important, the unequal social systems that fuel these quests, are at the heart of much that is wrong in our world.

I'll go into more detail about what precisely is wrong in the course of this book, but to get a rough sense of what I mean, consider a fundamental paradox of our present condition: there is too much, and yet there is not enough. We live amid unprecedented abundance and productive capacity, yet billions go unfed, unclothed, and uncared for. Thus, in a world that has a combined $399.2 trillion in wealth, more than 3.4 billion people still live on less than $5.50 a day, while 34.5 million people a year die from a lack of adequate healthcare, and around 9 million more pass away due to hunger.[1] Meanwhile, machines do more of the necessary work for sustaining life than ever, and yet we have so little leisure time. There are more people alive now than ever, and yet so many of us are alone. We benefit from centuries of wisdom and scientific advances for promoting happiness, and yet we are burdened by anxiety and depression. Indeed, not only is the number of people with depression rising, but so is the average number of years that people report feeling depressed. Anxiety and burnout are also on the rise.[2] We have the capacity to go all over the earth, to the depths of the oceans, and even into space, and yet those very means of exploration are depleting the sustainability of our home planet. Every year we are taking nearly double what the earth is able to regenerate on a yearly basis.[3]

These trends are all related. When we live in a world where some have too much and many have too little, there is tremendous pressure to either rise to the top or sink to the bottom. And in such a world, we will feel anxious at our prospects, depressed at our situation, alienated from our fellow competitors, and unconcerned with how we damage the environment if doing so feels like the only way to stay alive.

To get beyond the paradoxes caused by the pursuit of greatness, we have to understand where that pursuit itself comes from. I will consider various theories throughout this book—for example, the often-exaggerated claim that we are all hierarchical and competitive by nature—but my basic argument is that "greatness thinking" in fact begins as a meaningful response to the fact that life is imperfect. Accidents, tragedies, and failures befall us all. Greatness responds by saying, "Don't worry, we can overcome this: though the world as it is may be flawed, humans have the capacity to eventually remove the blemishes of our condition." To do so, we simply have to encourage the most talented among us—the great ones—to innovate and create and explore. They will push past the limits of our ecosystem and create a flourishing world for the rest of us. To incentivize them to do so, they should be given tremendous wealth and power. And in order to find out who these great ones are, we should have a fiercely competitive society where everyone is trying to prove why they are the greatest. To become great is to feel justified in being spared from suffering some real portion of life's calamities: because you are improving life for everyone (whether by creating wealth, entertainment, or inventions), all of your rewards are justified. Seeking that sense of satisfaction and security beyond the flux of life is how I now interpret the origins of my youthful desires for being great that I share with so many other people. Desiring greatness thus makes a lot of sense, but it also creates the anxieties and paradoxes of the world we live in.

Although there is a deep logic in our psyches and societies for the greatness worldview, we are not condemned to it. There is another way of seeing things that is full of potential today and that can bring us out of these frightening paradoxes. I call it "the good-enough life." I will also refer to it as "a good-enough life for all" and "the good-enough world." Good enough here does not just mean doing the bare minimum to get by—although I do argue for more leisure and relaxation. But more than this, I use the words to register an entire worldview dedicated to ensuring that all humans have both goodness (including decency, meaning, and dignity) *and* enoughness (including high-quality food, clothing, shelter, and medical care).[4] Further, because humans also have environmental, emotional, and social needs, goodness and enoughness are always linked. Our lives cannot be good if we do not have enough to survive, and we cannot have enough if our lives are not also suffused with the goodness of our relations.

Like greatness, the good-enough worldview begins with a recognition that life is imperfect. Unlike greatness, however, it denies the claim that only a worthy elite can help us improve our conditions. By supporting only the pursuit of greatness, we are not in fact advancing as much as we could because we are suppressing the vital energies and capacities of the bulk of humanity and wasting our time and passion competitively trying to prove that we are among the great few. There are almost always many more talented and qualified people for a job than the number of available positions. We can stop letting this circumstance lead to depression and unemployment, and shift our focus to working cooperatively, harnessing the abilities of 7.7 billion good-enough human beings. If we all try to be good enough, rather than great, we can individually do less while gaining as much, if not more.[5] Not only will the material quality of life for most humans improve, but so will their happiness and social cohesion.

To create this world for ourselves and future generations, we cannot take more from the earth than it is capable of producing. We don't need to live in perfect harmony with nature, but we also don't need to dominate it. Earth is not endlessly large, nor endlessly regenerating. It has its own limits, its own sense of well-being, its own material needs. What makes it miraculous is not its perfection, but the mere fact that it is good enough to sustain human life. We have to build our good-enough life within these good-enough conditions. The good-enough life is "for all," including, as much as possible, the many species and vegetal lives with which we share this planet, because when we recognize that none of us is so great as to be able to overcome the terrors of this life on our own, when we understand that the kinks in our condition can best be borne through connections to our infinite kindred, then we appreciate that the most meaningful life available is one that recognizes and fosters our essential interdependence.

The final difference between a good-enough worldview and the greatness worldview is that good-enoughness does not claim we will ever fully overcome the limits of our conditions. Life is only ever good enough: even in a wonderfully harmonious society, we would still have mistakes, tragedies, disagreements, betrayals, natural disasters. But in a good-enough world, there would be no great few who are spared the worst because of their status. We would all work to mitigate the suffering together. In the end, this is universally beneficial, because rather than existing in the anxious fear of either rising to the top or sinking to the bottom, everyone would have more time and leisure to appreciate the ordinary, good-enough pleasures of existence. Life at its best can never be more than good enough, but the way we live now, suffused with anxiety, inequality, and ecological destruction, is not yet good enough for all.

Rather than aspiring to versions of greatness, I now aspire to help create this good-enough life for all. Or, at the very least, I do my best to aspire. Like many people, I still feel the pull of desiring some slice of greatness for myself. As I'll discuss throughout the book, good-enoughness requires both a personal and political transformation. In a greatness-oriented world, trying to be good enough can ironically feel like you are *not* good enough, at least in the competitive terms presented to you. It is hard for any given individual to break out of this system. While I do believe that our personal aspirations matter—systems don't change without accompanying changes in our ideas about how the world should be—I do not think that this is just about finding singular good-enough heroes. It is about all of us working together to imagine, develop, and participate in a world in which we all have decency and sufficiency.

A few years ago, I made my first attempt to express this worldview in a public forum. I wrote a short article that focused on the philosophical and literary origins of the idea of a good-enough life.[6] Readers seemed to appreciate what I had to say, especially those who were tired of the inequalities that funnel so many resources to the few and so little to the many. But they also had a lot of questions. How could the ethical values of seeking a good-enough life translate into a social program? What counts as enough, anyway? If we succeeded in making a good-enough world, wouldn't that be a "great" accomplishment? Don't we need some people to seek out something more than the good enough in order for the rest of us to benefit? Can't life be great for some and good enough for everyone else? What will happen to motivation and incentives? Was I disputing the fact that some people are just more talented than others? Why the words *great* and *good enough*, anyway? Perhaps the most personal comment came from a fellow writer who asked why I seemed to be working so hard on my writing, even as I told others to slow down and embrace the good-enough life— wasn't I being hypocritical?[7] I realized that though the idea behind the good-enough life was based on a relatively simple set of values, explaining and defending its logic would take more than a short essay. That is why this book sets out to explain just what it means to move past a social order based on greatness and create instead a good-enough life for all.

It is because my concern is so universal that although my perspective in this book is largely formed by the experiences I've had as a (mostly) middle-class, able-bodied, White, cisgender male scholar in the United States, I have done my best to listen to and learn from those with other life stories, and I hope that the claims I make here are useful for people from many different backgrounds. I will often use the pronouns "we" and "you" in my writing in order to engage you, the reader, in what follows. Sometimes I will presume that you agree with me and are part of the "we" trying to make a good-enough world. At other points, I will use "we" in a more general sense for what I believe are broadly held beliefs. And sometimes I will address you as someone who probably doesn't agree with me at all and try to convince you that you should. You might at times, of course, think in response: "Stop saying we/you! I don't think that at all!" Given our diversity as humans, such miscues are inevitable, but I think it's worth the benefits of a more engaged manner of writing.

The four chapter titles ("For Our Selves," "For Our Relationships," "For Our World," and "For Our Planet") similarly embody this sense of inclusion. With the title of first chapter ("Why Greatness Is Not Good Enough"), they link together to form an exposition of a key theme of the book: "Why greatness is not good enough for ourselves, for our relationships, for our world, for our planet." The "for" in each of the chapter titles is also meant in the sense of being a benefit to something. The book is *for* our selves, our relationships, our planet, and our world because it is about creating a richer and more complex way of living than the focus on greatness enables. Through different lenses, each chapter argues that the ideology of greatness—that is, again, of thinking that each of us only has value so long as we are competing to be at the top of some hierarchy—is destructive for all the spheres of our life. *The Good-Enough Life* is an argument for revaluing all that is good, sufficient, and imperfect in us, in each other, in our societies, and in our natural world.

If you share the values of the good-enough life already, perhaps this book will help you articulate them better, see their coherence with each other, and understand their limited compatibility with the greatness worldview. If you share some of the values but still believe that supporting the greatness of the few is the best path to creating good-enoughness for the many, perhaps the book will convince you otherwise, or at least give you a logic against which you can explain your position. And if you don't share any of these values now, perhaps I can convince you by the end of this book that they are worth considering. Perhaps you will even take the time to think with me about what the good-enough life is and how we can achieve it. I want this book to be part of a larger, continuing conversation (one that started long before my writing this) because a good-enough life for all is a complex, dynamic, and evolving ideal that is most meaningful when we all work toward it together. The events that surrounded the writing of this book have only made this point about interdependence more fundamental to my analysis. I began writing during one of the most epochal events of our era—the early days of the COVID-19 pandemic—and continued working during a second—the uprising against racism and state violence spurred by the police killing of George Floyd in Minneapolis, Minnesota, in May 2020. As many commentators have noted, these events have been like an X-ray of the contemporary world, revealing the truth of our condition for anyone who had not previously seen just how unequal and unjust our societies are.[8] The world built around greatness has left billions of people without adequate income, food, or healthcare, while the fortunes of the world's wealthiest have grown by billions of dollars. This is not an accidental flaw; it is the direct result of a world built to reward the few at the expense of the many.

The German-Jewish writer Walter Benjamin wrote an essay on the philosophy of history as he was fleeing the Nazis in 1940. One line in his essay has always resonated with me: "The tradition of the oppressed teaches us that the 'state of emergency' in which we live is not the exception but the rule."[9] The upheavals during which I wrote this book will be followed by others throughout our history until we recognize that an unequal social order creates unbearable tensions between those deemed great and those deemed expendable in the pursuit of greatness. The good-enough life offers a vision of a world beyond this state of emergency. It will still have problems, of course. There will still be pandemics, accidents, betrayals. But we can work toward a world in which, when problems arise, our society—built on care, trust, and decency for all—is able to come together to face them.

Some will undoubtedly respond that my vision of humanity is sentimental. It sounds nice, sure, but it's not how the world works, and it's not possible because humans are hardwired by evolution to competitively pursue hierarchical positions. Moreover, you might be thinking, this vision is a potential blow to progress: Isn't the remarkable revolution of the modern age that it took a species once ruled by warrior strength and created a civic culture open to anyone with the right talent and effort?

While these arguments make some sense, they are not entirely accurate: we have always been defined as much by cooperation as by hierarchical competition, and meritocratic ideals have existed for thousands of years. Nor do they speak well to how we might progress as a species. There is increasing evidence today, for example, that progress is made not by getting the "best and brightest" in the room, but rather by cooperative reflection among diverse, well-informed viewpoints.[10] There is also good evidence to suggest that "collective intelligence" is more fundamental to human progress than individual genius.[11] And even when a singular genius appears, their work always depends on vast networks and institutions that have supported them. We will see later in the book why this is true for everyone from Albert Einstein to Lebron James and Steve Jobs.

To arrive at this better world for all, we don't just need more minds; we need more good minds. So instead of dumping resources (including respect and attention) *on* the few, we should work continually and cooperatively *as* the many. This won't be easy, and it requires good training and good institutions with clear forms of both solidarity and non-oppressive hierarchy. Mistakes will undoubtedly be made. But creating this good-enough life for all is worth the effort, because, ultimately, this is about our fundamental values, and this is the kind of world toward which our ideals of equality, liberty, and justice have always guided us.

You may rightly wonder if human societies can ever truly create a good-enough life for all. I will try to show not only why we can, but why it is necessary to do so. Ultimately, what is unrealistic is not the hope that we might live in a world that is good-enough for all, but rather the belief that we can keep surviving in our greatness culture, with all the hatred, inequality, and destruction that tear us apart day by day.[12]

I will not, however, insist that I have all the answers on how to create this other world. My point, after all, is that good-enoughness is not about one person's idea of how the world should be—it's about all of us working together. I suggest a baseline goal, not a specific set of contents. This is a democratic offering for all of us to keep thinking together about how to create a more encompassing social value system. This system aims to make a world that is good, that provides enough goodness for all, and yet still appreciates that life is unavoidably filled with accidents and tragedies, and that we have to work within the limits of our natural resources. (Once again: it's only ever good enough.)

It is only fitting, then, to have begun writing this book in circumstances that threaten to overturn everything we think of as normal: this is precisely the kind of situation that leads us to question our greatness-oriented society and to understand what the good-enough world we should be building would look like. Our ongoing crises push on the frailty of our individual powers, showing us that though none of us can survive very well on our own, all of us together can build and thrive. This vision is well captured in thoughts like these from "Jester D," a sanitation worker, shared on Twitter one morning in early March 2020, when I began writing during a pandemic:

> I can't work from home and my job is an essential city service that must get done. It's a tough job, from getting up pre-dawn to the physical toll it takes on my body to the monotonous nature of the job, at times it's hard to keep on going . . .
>
> Right now though, I am feeling an extra sense of pride and purpose as I do my work. I see the people, my people, of my city, peeking out their windows at me. They're scared, we're scared. Scared but resilient . . .
>
> Us garbagemen are gonna keep collecting the garbage, doctors and nurses are gonna keep doctoring and nurse-ering. It's gonna be ok, we're gonna make it be ok. I love my city. I love my country. I love my planet Earth. Be good to each other and we'll get through this.[13]

Being good to each other and providing enough for each other; not asking too much of each other and not taking too much for ourselves: We do not need more than this for humanity to flourish.

1

Why Greatness Is Not Good Enough

There is no single cause for our dire situation in which too few have too much and too many have too little. And good books come out almost daily to explain some vital aspect of the problem and propose a way to resolve it: criticisms of particular value systems, such as elitism, or caste, or winner-take-all capitalism, or the false promises of meritocracy, or perfectionism, or humans as masters of nature. I build on the ideas of many such criticisms. But one of my central claims is that a common value system unites these seemingly distinct regimes of personal, political, and ecological organization. It is what I am calling greatness. If we look at greatness only in particular systems or moments of belief, we miss out on this broader, interlocking network of concerns that stem from the idea that some people, families, nations, or species are simply better and more deserving than others.

In choosing the word *greatness*, I want to expand on a long-standing distinction between "the great" and "the good."[1] In John Milton's epic poem *Paradise Lost* (1667), for example, Jesus proves himself worthy by "being good, / Far more than great or high."[2] In this distinction, "great" refers to those who have power and significance in determining the course of many human lives, while "good" refers to those who act with ethics and dignity. In practice, greatness and goodness often are opposed. Many great entrepreneurs, entertainers, or political rulers may not be particularly good people. The United States, meanwhile, often asserts an exceptional status as a nation because it claims to be able to reconcile this opposition. This is why politicians across the political spectrum will say, "We are great because we are good."[3] In other words, we have come to our position of power because of our decency.

While one individual may very well be both great and good, however, the general system of greatness is detrimental to creating a world that is good-enough for all. This claim might seem out of touch in a meritocratic world. Many people would agree that wealth and power should not follow from heredity or prejudiced notions about the superiority of certain genders or races or religions. But those same people might believe that a just society provides genuine opportunities for everyone to show their talents and incentivizes that process through rewards of wealth, honor, and power. Moreover, they might say, such a system works to the benefit of all: incentivizing and rewarding the great should eventually help the rest of us to live in a better world.

There is undoubtedly a certain logic to this argument, and we are all the beneficiaries of many such great people. We can watch the remarkable talents of athletes and entertainers, see the masterworks of artists and musicians, or use the inventions of leading scientists and entrepreneurs. Across the pages of this book, however, I will attempt to show why the focus on promoting the individual triumphs of the few ultimately comes not only at the expense of the many, but at a tremendous cost to everyone's psychic and personal lives, while also damaging our social cohesion and natural world. Unpacking the specifics of this argument will take some time, but the gist is that while greatness is a zero-sum game, good-enoughness enables all of us to succeed. There can only be so many winners, no matter how many talented people or nations compete. The gap between those deemed great and those deemed ordinary will never be closed. Such is the paradox of top-down versions of progress: as things improve for some, they become relatively worse for others. Thus even when basic needs are met, this enoughness for all does not equate to goodness for all. People are still left out of enhanced life expectations and having a meaningful say in their lives.[4] A majority of humanity—such as the billions who live in poverty in the midst of a world flush with wealth—remain excluded, their potential contributions to general uplift lost forever. This is not a meaningful way to ensure human progress. Rather than placing the promotion of the best at the center of our values, we should focus directly on the development of the decency and sufficiency (the good-enoughness) of the many. This does not mean flooding the halls of power in a cacophony of voices, but instead developing systems that can meaningfully organize, integrate, and respect everyone, even as we recognize that no system can be perfect enough to supply each person with all of their desires.

The sociologist Michael Young, in his book criticizing the idea of a meritocracy (a term he in fact invented), gives us a glimpse of what such a world would offer. He speaks of equal opportunity not as offering the possibility to rise up in the social scale, but rather the chance to subvert the scale entirely: "equal opportunity for all people, irrespective of their 'intelligence,' to develop the virtues and talents with which they are endowed, all their capacities for appreciating the beauty and depth of human experience, all their potential for living to the full."[5] As I understand it, this kind of equality is based on the conviction that "living to the full" does not mean maximization, but rather a meaningful appreciation for being human, including its tragic dimensions. It is hard from within our present condition to even imagine a world like what Young is describing, one in which kindness and empathy are considered talents as worthy of cultivation as computer coding or making money, and one in which the point of cultivating any talent is to enrich your life and that of others, rather than gain fame, wealth, and power.

Thus, when I say I want us to create a world beyond greatness, I do not mean that we should abandon our personal efforts or strivings to pursue what we love. Indeed, the idea that we have to compete to be the best can inhibit us from pursuing our passions because it so narrowly defines what is valuable that it inevitably excludes much human potential. And I certainly don't mean you should abandon the very word "great," as in "he's such a great father," or "she's a great athlete," or, "this book is great!" I have nothing against the use of superlative adjectives to describe tremendous accomplishments. What I do oppose is any vision of life that ignores the values and capacities of most human beings in the name of selecting and excessively rewarding the few.

Some people I've talked to about these ideas have asked why, instead of trying to move past greatness, I don't instead try to redefine greatness to mean treating each other well, respecting each other's abilities, and helping each other to flourish. That's a fair question, and if you prefer to understand what I'm doing in this book as redefining greatness, I won't (indeed, I can't) stop you. But, besides my stubbornness, there are reasons that I don't just want to redefine greatness. However much we might improve the world and ourselves and each other, the worldview I offer here is premised on the fact that life can only ever be good enough—that there are inevitable tragedies, accidents, and imperfections that we need to learn to live with. Even if we built the kind of good-enough world I am arguing for here—one in which everyone has a good life in which they can find meaning and purpose, in which we value each other's unique abilities and appreciate each other's faults, in which our social order works to ensure decency and sufficiency for all, and in which our natural world is cared for and thus enabled to sustain life—we would still have to deal with the potential for melancholy, the likelihood of unrequited love, the possibility of political betrayal, the inevitability of natural disasters. The world simply cannot be great all the time; but it can and should be good enough.

The Origins of "Good Enough"

Like many people who have thought about the idea of the good enough, I first came across the philosophical use of this term in the work of Donald Winnicott, a British psychoanalyst best known for his work on childhood development and psychic relations within the family. In one of his essays, he developed the idea of the "good-enough mother," or what I prefer to call the good-enough parent.[6] The good-enough parent has a specific and difficult role to play. It begins with "an almost complete adaptation to the infant's needs." In other words, the path to the good enough begins with a bit of excess (the constant care required to keep an infant alive) in *only* the earliest stages of life. This is just part of our somewhat unique human evolution that requires us to receive special attention in infancy. The problem occurs when this extra care essential for survival continues past the point of necessity. And there is a strong and logical temptation to do this—to overindulge our children with unceasing care.[7] Of course we want to provide everything for our child and give them more of ourselves than we possibly can. But, according to Winnicott, this is bad for both the parent and the child. For the parent, it places an overwhelming burden on their time and energy. For the child, it deprives them of their "growing ability to deal with . . . failure." Among other things, a child's ability to cope with failure at an early age sets in motion their future capacities for creativity.[8] Through our appreciation of difficulty grows our imaginative and creative powers. A parent who gives their child too much thus winds up taking these vital capacities away.

What I appreciate in Winnicott is the idea that being good enough is both relaxing and difficult. It forces us to question our deep instinctual desires to be ceaselessly loving and protective. But it also eases our anxieties and burdens—both the ones we feel in our hearts and the ones we place on others in our relentless pursuit of perfection. Winnicott shows that overcoming these pressures does not mean that we are giving up on our duties to each other, but rather that we are working toward a more meaningful way to inhabit our relationships.

His work also shows us that when we are speaking about what is enough, we are not just discussing material matters. As psychologists Roy Baumeister and Mark Leary argued in their famous essay "The Need to Belong," "human beings have a pervasive drive to form and maintain at least a minimum quantity of lasting, positive, and significant interpersonal relationships."[9] This drive rises to the level of "need," they argue, because we cannot understand human history from a purely material perspective. To be sure, we cannot live without food and shelter, but, the "belongingess hypothesis" maintains, we cannot secure our material needs without each other, nor can we experience the fullness of human flourishing.[10] Research along parallel lines has led policy makers at the United Nations to reconsider how we understand what constitutes human development. It's not just material goods, but also things like our capacities to form social connections, develop our imagination, and use our reason freely.[11]

Clearly, then, I am not alone in making this case, and I rely on many other writers and social movements to sculpt my vision of the good-enough life. I do depart from one standard path, however. Some writers in the self-help genre focus their solutions on our individual capacities to change our desires. They offer a mostly personal ethic of wanting less and becoming more comfortable with failure.[12] Writers like Ada Calhoun tell us that our crises would be eased by "letting go of expectations," or, in Mark Manson's more colorful expression, by learning the "subtle art of not giving a fuck."[13] This isn't bad advice—in fact, it's pretty good advice—but it doesn't change the social or political contexts that make following it so difficult.[14] When this personal transformation becomes linked to social movements—as we may be witnessing in 2021's "lying flat," "low-desire life" movement protesting the commercialist success ethic in contemporary China—it has the potential to ripple out and create profound transformations.[15] But when it remains at the personal level (as may also happen with the lying flat movement), it tends to have limited efficacy because the changes recommended are too incompatible with social pressures. Decreasing expectations and learning when to let go are important personal transformations, but they don't offer us a vision of a world in which everyone can live a decent, meaningful, and materially and emotionally sufficient life.[16] Nor do they force us to come to terms with the difficulty of creating such a world.

A Long History of Overcoming Greatness

Indeed, as greatness advocates readily point out, building a world that provides enough goodness for all is a monumental task. Not only that, but it seems to go against human nature. Some say that there are just too many out there who are driven by dreams of personal success. Our inherent selfishness is an insuperable block to developing collective goals. Calhoun or Manson or I can write our paeans to good-enoughness all we want; there are humans who are just going to amass great power and dominate the rest of us. The sociologist Robert Michels called this "the iron law of oligarchy."[17]

But as much as human societies exhibit a tendency to oligarchy, so they also showcase a perpetual push for decency and sufficiency for all. Indeed, for as long as we have evidence, the drive to equality has been part of the human condition. As the evolutionary biologist Christopher Boehm has shown, one can trace this lineage back at least 5 million years, when a particular group of African apes began to "whittle away" at the power of alpha leaders by forming "political coalitions" among equals.[18] Since at least the time of these ape ancestors, we have been marked by the duel between the promotion of and submission to the great on the one hand and the egalitarian coalition that respects all on the other. We are not bound by one or the other of these histories. Even if some degree of competition and hierarchy will always remain, we at least have the ability to orient ourselves more fully toward equality and cooperation.

Adam Smith, in his work on moral philosophy, gave us one of the most important accounts of the split between these two horizons of human motivation. Smith's theory of the origins of the desire for greatness is different from mine, or so it appears at first. Where I see it in the hope to avoid suffering, he sees it in the desire to be loved: "Man naturally desires not only to be loved, but to be lovely; or to be that thing which is the natural and proper object of love."[19] And what we see constantly is that great people receive that love: "The man of rank and distinction . . . is observed by all the world. Every body is eager to look at him, and to conceive . . . that joy and exultation with which his circumstances naturally inspire him." Seeing this, we seek it for ourselves, even though we know that doing so will increase our anxieties and burdens: "[This] renders greatness the object of envy, and compensates, in the opinion of mankind, all that toil, all that anxiety, all those mortifications which must be undergone in the pursuit of it."[20] Contrary to what people usually assume about Smith and his theories of self-interest, he does not actually think this is a good thing: it is for him "the great and most universal cause of the corruption of our moral sentiments."[21]

For Smith, then, it would appear that greatness is a burden to bear, not an escape from suffering. But if we follow his theory through to the end, we see the basic outlines of the justification of greatness as something that will decrease the suffering of all. Thus, although Smith rails against the corruption of our morals, he still comes to accept it and develop a theory (now called capitalism) for why this pursuit of greatness still works out in our favor. The basic idea is that even though greatness poorly distributes esteem and reward in society, there is an "invisible hand" that works to redistribute the benefits to everyone else.[22] By the visible hand, the quest to be at the top of society ruins us; by the invisible hand, our moral decency is restored. We all become better because some people take on the burden of rising to the top.

Looking at the difficulties of overcoming greatness, Smith capitulates. He sees how greatness corrupts, but he does not push through to the point of asking us to overcome it. Rather, he makes a Faustian pact, hoping that we can use greatness to our advantage, rather than being corrupted by it. I argue that we can do better than the accidental benefits of the corruptions of greatness. We can, with the collective hands of communal life, avoid the depredations of domination.

This, in part, is why I disagree with the idea that a good-enough world will strip us of our motivations. Many people worry that in a world that ensures decency and sufficiency for all, most humans will become lazy free riders who do nothing but benefit from the continued hard work of others. Some of this might happen, of course—we're aiming for a good-enough world, not a perfect one. But the idea that we will lose our motivation ignores the deep human passion to create and sustain a world that is decent and dignified for all. There is a profound human yearning, stretching across millions of years, to create a just community of equals in which we all find love, care, and dignity. Many of the most motivated acts in human history—the big political revolutions and nonviolent social movements—have been precisely about assuring such communities. Thus, although the good-enough life may seem at first glance less inspiring than greatness, the achievement of justice, equality, having a say in our own lives, and being prepared to confront life's inevitable tragedies together is one of the most abiding passions in the human experience. And once we have that world, we would still have to be motivated to maintain it. The difference is that rather than waiting for the great few, we would all have to be actively engaged.

Recalibrating

All the same, I understand very well what Smith means when he discusses the allure of greatness. I am no less susceptible to it than anyone else. I grew up with joint custody split between a suburb in Philadelphia—Jenkintown—and a neighborhood on the edge of the city—East Mt. Airy. Because I went to public schools in the suburb, much of my world vision was shaped by the ideals of this pretty standard slice of the suburban United States: the biggest house, the fanciest car, the highest salary. My parents had met in rabbinical school and divorced when I was young. My father remained at a local congregation while my mother became a professor of women's and religious studies.

They each remarried—my father to a woman who works primarily with otherly abled children in Philadelphia public schools, and my mother to a woman who works in social justice philanthropy and early childhood education.

I thus had plenty of models around me of people who had chosen to live lives geared toward community and solidarity rather than climbing the social ladder. Although for a brief period after my parents' divorce we didn't have much money, I generally grew up solidly in the middle class. But I also grew up around a lot of wealth and saw precisely the kind of esteem that Smith talked about as it trickled down to the kids of the wealthiest in the neighborhood. They had the latest technology, the best playrooms, and took the most luxurious beach vacations. Other kids in the neighborhood would rather have the rich kids' parents drive them with their fancy cars, or go with them to sporting events with box seats. And of course, this immediate surrounding was just a small part of the general cultural and advertising assault telling me that the best lifestyles were those of the rich and famous. My parents did good work, but my early teenage ambitions were set on getting to the top of the economic hierarchy, in a very conventional way.

By the time I was five, all of my grandparents had passed away, and so my great aunt and uncle on my mother's side were as close as I had to grandparents growing up. My great uncle claimed—and it seems true—that his company had been the first to take butter and put it in little aluminum foil packets. Not great for the environment, but good for his retirement. I was around thirteen when he passed away and left some money to us—not much, but enough for my mother and me to take a trip to Costa Rica for a Spanish language immersion program.

I had envisioned that trip, in line with my suburban dreams, as something luxurious and by the beach. But my mom had booked for us a course with the Institute for Central American

Development Studies, a social justice–oriented program based in the capital, San José. We lived with a working-class family, and in the Spanish language courses I was introduced to something called globalization, which was not talked about much in the suburbs then. It was only a year later (1999) that protests against the World Trade Organization happened in Seattle. When the protests erupted, I, who had quickly earned a reputation as a young radical, was asked by my friends' wealthy parents, "What exactly are *your* people doing in the streets?" It was largely this trip, and this learning, that shattered my belief in the pursuit of economic greatness and indeed made me feel like "my people" were the ones in the street, trying to disrupt the deals designed to help the very wealthy get very much wealthier.[23]

In high school I began going to protests, started a "No More Prisons" club at my school, and tried, unsuccessfully, to form a student union. I also had the undue privilege of interning at two organizations that fundamentally shaped my worldview: United for a Fair Economy (UFE) in Boston and Art Sanctuary in Philadelphia. At UFE, under the guidance of Betsy Leondar-Wright and Chuck Collins, I learned about the problems in wealth distribution and how to change them through creative actions. And at Art Sanctuary, with the perpetually sage advice of Lorene Cary, I got to see how a community arts organization could transform lives without infinite resources. Inspired by these experiences, I transferred my energies to intellectual life instead of making money. I started writing a novel, reading history and philosophy, and taking night courses at a local university. I wanted to learn as much as I could, travel as much as I could, and write as much as I could. I now wanted to be a famous writer, not a wealthy stockbroker.

I didn't yet realize it, but I had made one of the mistakes that plagues our culture today: I had criticized material wealth, but

I had not given up my obsession with greatness. After all, my desire was not to be a good writer, or an excellent writer, or a writer who contributes knowledge about how to ensure a good-enough life for all. I wanted to be a *famous* writer. I wanted, in other words, not just to pursue my craft, but to climb to the top of a hierarchy of social status.

This is, of course, still *very* different than becoming wealthy as, for example, an oil executive who knowingly despoils the planet in their pursuit of wealth. But there is a risk that in comparing oneself to the worst, it excuses the problems of one's own aspirations. Being wealthy or being a famous writer—both are about being at the top of the pyramid. Neither are about calling the pyramid into question.

And as William Deresiewicz argues in his book *The Death of the Artist* (2020), that pyramid is crushing most creative types: "The system, yet again, rewards the few and leaves the rest to fight for scraps. It's virality or bust, stardom or oblivion." People like Deresiewicz, or me, who want to be recognized as writers or artists, have to clamber our way up these pyramids. In the society in which we live, I cannot help but want my book to receive recognition and awards, because my getting one of the few jobs available in my field depends on it. I'd rather sit atop a crumbling pyramid than get crushed at the bottom. But if these are the only options for intellectual work today, then our situation is far from good enough.

And if you're thinking, "Well, the stars are stars for a reason; they truly are the best," you might pause to consider the words of the poet Donald Justice, himself a winner of prestigious awards: "There may well be analyzable causes behind the oblivion some good writers suffer, but the causes, whatever they are, remain elusive. There is a randomness in the operation of the laws of fame that approaches the chaotic."[24] Whether the people at prestigious universities, or at the top of the bestseller list, or headlining Carnegie Hall, are talented is not, in the end, the real question here. The trouble is that in a world of scarce opportunities, repeated recognition of one writer or thinker or artist crowds out opportunities for others. It creates competitive cycles. Inner cliques. Power centers. It changes writing from an earnest desire to use language to express or transform the world to another system of greatness, where the few are rewarded and the many struggle. Some of those who are rewarded are extremely talented. But so are many of those who never get the opportunity.

The Two Economies

Many people who want to see a more decent and equal world are less concerned with fame and social status than I am. They view our problems primarily through the lens of the material economy. There is something wrong, they say, with our current economic system, which creates concentrations of wealth and power. As I'll discuss in the fourth chapter, I largely agree with these criticisms. But one of my concerns is that simply moving past any given economic system is not enough. Following Smith's logic, we need to understand that these economic ideas about the value of concentrating wealth at the top of the pyramid have significant corollaries in other elements of our worldview. Our dire situation is not just about material wealth. It is also about the often-related inequality of who gets a voice, honor, respect, and attention in society. Indeed, even if we achieved a more materially egalitarian society, we might still live in a world in which only a few people had power and esteem.

Such a maldistribution of what are sometimes called "positional goods"—material and nonmaterial benefits that derive from one's relative position in a social order—can in turn drive material inequality and social instability. This is something that Michael Young satirized poignantly in his critique of meritocracy. Although everyone in his hypothetical society has the same level of income, that income is set extremely low, and those with the highest IQs are rewarded with seemingly infinite perks and benefits. In actual history, this was also the case in the Soviet Union, where they managed to reduce material inequality but still gave extensive power and privilege to a small and corrupt elite cadre.[25]

The general idea of positional goods can be traced back to at least the writings of Aristotle in the fourth century BCE, who spoke about both "inequality of property" and "inequality of honor."[26] The term "positional goods" itself was coined by the economist Fred Hirsch in 1976. Among his key insights was that a dangerous feedback loop exists between the material and the positional economy. In his analysis, positional goods range from specific kinds of material goods (there is only so much property in Manhattan) to precious intangibles, like leadership positions in one's profession, prizes and awards, and access to governmental power (at least in most social orders). When a society grows materially but not positionally (when only a few are rewarded and esteemed even as general quality of life improves), "the distributional struggle returns, heightened rather than relieved by the dynamic process of growth."[27] In other words, part of why material growth does not get properly distributed is that it is undone by an increased scramble for the money to acquire positional goods. Some of this scramble will occur through what are effectively auctions, such as real estate markets and access to politicians for those who can pay the most. Others will require increasingly selective and expensive qualifications, such as the need for an advanced degree for jobs that do not in fact require them. But as material growth (and debt) expands and more people have access to education, the number of available slots does not also increase.

This creates the situation in which people either pursue positional power as a means to material wealth, or material wealth as a means to positional power. And this has a damaging effect across society. As Hirsch points out, for example, as living in cities like New York or London becomes a positional good, there is a scramble for the material wealth to live where one's family and friends are. In this situation, people who might otherwise thrive in the city, like teachers and artists and plumbers, are forced to take on more jobs, or to fight their own way to the top of their positional hierarchy. For plumbers, this may mean offering 24/7 service and constant customer attention to ensure five-star online reviews. For artists, it means networking and clawing their way to the limited slots in blue-chip galleries or tenured teaching posts.

But since not everyone can or wants to make the sacrifices required, and because, even if they did, the limited number of slots means that there are more qualified applicants than positions, the scramble for positional goods creates increasing dissatisfaction and inequality across all spheres of social life. The individual is left with the rational choice of embarking on the irrational hierarchical struggle in the positional economy of their chosen field: "However small the favored minority, no individual knows that [they] will be excluded from it; all can therefore set their sights on participating in it."[28] And yet, "what is possible for the single individual is not possible for all individuals—and would not be possible even if they all possessed equal talent."[29] Even the good-enough jobs my parents had—in universities, congregations, and civil service—are threatened by increasing competition. It is often not enough today to do want to do good. One has to be the best at doing good, or risk winding up with many degrees and no job. This kind of irrational social order, in which well-being depends on becoming the one who sneaks through to the top of the material or positional pyramid, is central to what I am calling "greatness."

Hirsch's idea of positional goods, I should note, is more limited than the one I use here. He did not appreciate, for example, that patriarchy and racism and ableism can function as positional goods by allowing some people to place themselves (or imagine themselves) higher up than others because of their identity. W.E.B. Du Bois famously called this a "public and psychological wage" paid to whiteness—a wage that cost even white people more than they realized, because it effectively stopped them from forming cross-race coalitions to democratize the economy.[30] Hirsch also did not discuss what the implications of positional goods were for our social esteem, or why it mattered that some people in society—not necessarily of any particular talent—took up a larger slice of our "attention economy." Nevertheless, his work helps us understand the basic contours of the two economies.

While most of Hirsch's book is about economics, he concludes in perhaps a surprising place. He warns that "we may be near the limit of explicit social organization possible without a supporting social morality."[31] I *do* think we have a supporting social morality: it is the values that many of us share that underlie the vision of a good-enough life for all. But Hirsch is right that this morality is still undone by the usurpation of decency by greatness that Smith noted centuries ago. In the world we live in, pursuing the best for oneself simply fits the logic of the pyramid, even if it goes against our morality. Our morality thus needs to be accompanied by a social transformation that gives a new logic to our social order—a logic that recognizes that good enough for all makes more sense than great for some.

Lost Einstein Myths

To arrive at that other, more logical system of values, we'll have to get over our myth of the value of greatness, in every sphere of life. Even if we know that success depends greatly on luck, we still tend to think, implicitly or explicitly, that the greatest talents in politics, sports, music, and even intellectual life should be supported and rewarded for what they produce. And we likely do so because of a belief in "trickle-down culture," if not trickle-down economics. For the assumption is that if we find and support the greatest talents—the Albert Einsteins, the Toni Morrisons, the Frida Kahlos—then society as a whole will become greater through the fruits of their efforts.

This seems to make sense. If we could get the greatest—or even just a few among the best—to the top of whatever field, wouldn't we all benefit from their inventions, ideas, discoveries, and performances? Again, such a system of course can benefit some, but it ultimately deprives us of much more. Consider the case of Jeff Bezos's plans for interplanetary development. Bezos has argued that his tremendous wealth allows him to accomplish other things to benefit humanity. At our current rate of growth, we will soon break through the ecological limits of the planet. The most important thing to do in response, Bezos said in 2018, was to colonize other planets for their resources.[32] (He has since committed to saving this planet from climate change first, so long, it would seem, as it does not interfere with Amazon's business model.[33] And it seems likely that his space exploration plans are less about benevolence than capturing the potentially lucrative "low-earth orbit economy" of satellites, tourism, and minerals.[34] But I digress.)

What is particularly interesting in this context is one of the benefits Bezos claimed would result from his work in space. With the resources of the solar system, we could support a population of 1 trillion people, and "if we had a trillion humans, we would have a thousand Einsteins and a thousand Mozarts."[35] Bezos the great entrepreneur seeks to produce the population that will create more great scientists and artists, and the rest of humanity will, in this theory, benefit from the resources generated by these new thousands.

The first glaring error here is one that Raj Chetty and his collaborators at the Equality of Opportunity Project have rigorously documented: there are potentially thousands of "lost Einsteins" already here on planet Earth. We don't find them not because they don't exist, but because they are poor, or women, or people of color who have not had the resources or encouragement to become innovators.[36] Stephen Jay Gould made this point poetically some decades ago: "I am . . . less interested in the weight and convolutions of Einstein's brain than in the near certainty that people of equal talent have lived and died in cotton fields and sweatshops."[37] What Bezos does not seem to realize is that if we increase our population but keep our same social structure, this only means we'll be missing out on a greater number of Einsteins.

But my claim is not the same as Chetty's, either. It is important to promote the talents of all children, of course, but to focus simply on lost innovators is to miss the point. Innovation, like disruption, is a neutral term. Bernie Sanders and Donald Trump are both political innovators, but that observation tells us little about their politics. What matters are the values of the innovation. As Einstein himself put it: "Science . . . cannot create ends and, even less, instill them in human beings; science, at most, can supply the means by which to attain certain ends."[38] In short: science needs morality.

That quote is from Einstein's essay "Why Socialism?" in the inaugural issue of the socialist magazine *Monthly Review* from May 1949. My concern for the moment is not his economic platform. It's the moral reasoning that underlies it: "The education of the individual, in addition to promoting his own innate abilities, would attempt to develop in him a sense of responsibility for his fellow men in place of the glorification of power and success in our present society." Einstein himself, in other words, would oppose the glorification of Einstein. He is less interested in finding the next great version of himself, and more interested in how scientists can get past competition and learn how to work together to promote the general benefit of the planet. He isn't concerned with lost Einsteins; he is concerned with the lost energies of 7.7 billion humans as all the resources go not even to the few extremely talented like him, but to the even rarer few whose talents get recognized. The point is not about demoting Einstein. It's about Einstein's understanding that he became who he was based on the contributions not only of the great minds who preceded him, but also those of the "ordinary" people who made sure he had the equipment he needed to do his research, who ensured his workspace was clean and well-maintained, who ordered whatever materials he needed on time, and who supplied the moral ends for which his scientific research sought the practical means. He recognized, in other words, that because of our fundamental interdependence, everyone deserves to live a good-enough life, no matter who they are—even an unknown patent clerk.

But, Come On, Aren't There Good Forms of Greatness?

I should clarify something at this point, because it is often where I get the greatest resistance to my argument.[39] People often understand why Bezos's wealth is too much, but a world that doesn't reward and support Einstein as much as possible—how is that good enough? Am I also trying to get rid of the idea that people like Gandhi or Martin Luther King Jr. were great? And other examples are more forceful still. I received an email once from a community organizer who asked me something like the following: "I help organize people living in poverty, who work multiple, tough jobs to put food on the table, and still every night, after helping their kids with their homework, they take the time to go talk to their neighbors, attend meetings, and help fight for their community's betterment. Do we really want to say these people are just good enough? Aren't they great?"

The short answer is: of course they are great. Again, I am opposed to greatness as a regime for structuring society, not the word itself. And I fully understand and acknowledge that in a world as unjust as ours, we may need to rely on people doing much more than should normally be expected in order to improve our shared conditions. But the questions for me are: Should it be this way? Should we live in a world in which people have to work so hard just to get by, and then work even harder to make a better world for others? The work these people are doing may be great, but their work is not about greatness; that is to say, it's not about them being the best or their society being the best or their nation being the best so that they can sit atop the pyramid. It is about everybody having the decency and sufficiency they need—in other words, it's about good-enoughness.

Indeed, in the pursuit of justice, as in anything else, the regime of greatness can become a problem. We see this across the world as revolutionary leaders who promise to make a decent life for all instead enrich themselves and those around them. And we see it every day in social movements whose regular participants and leaders experience burnout.[40] The path to overcoming this is not for individuals to push themselves harder— it's to find ways to share the burdens of the transformation by bringing ever more people into the movement. "Come join our cause and get burnt out fighting the powers that be" is not a good slogan. As social justice organizer adrienne maree brown related in a blog post: "right now i feel like i don't want the rest that comes . . . [after] burnout. i want to intentionally bring my attention to my well being, and make adjustments so that i can sustain. i want all of us who are tired to learn how to stagger our efforts with each other." She writes of "staggering" as what geese do in their V formation flights. Geese rotate into the forward point of the V, since leading is the hardest position to maintain. Activists, too, should stagger, she says, rotating in ever more "ordinary" people whose capacities otherwise remain hidden behind the leadership. This doesn't mean there won't be leaders—leadership is a skill, and some may have more aptitude for it than others. But it is often a teachable skill that many more people share than are enabled to practice it. By opening up a more rotational structure of leadership to those who show willingness and ability, the movement will not depend on the greatness of the (often about to burn out) leader so much as the good-enoughness of all members, all of whom (if they want) will take turns leading the flock.[41]

This point of view is part of a long-standing lesson of the Civil Rights Movement in the United States. While this movement is often remembered for its charismatic leaders, it was equally dependent on the extraordinary base of support from Black people from all walks of life. This part of the movement, according to the historian Charles Payne, is better understood by turning to women like Ella Baker and Septima Clark than to leaders like Martin Luther King Jr. These women were "radical democrats, insistent on the right of people to have a voice in the decisions affecting their lives, confident in the potential of ordinary men and women to develop the capacity to do that effectively, skeptical of top-down organizations, the people who led them, and the egotism that leadership frequently engendered."[42] (Indeed, King was one of the leaders whose egotism they challenged.[43]) This type of movement building, like everything in the good-enough life, is not easy. Sometimes, as maree brown notes, what is most difficult is to slow down before burnout even though the cause is just so important that you don't want to stop. As with Winnicott's good-enough parent, the challenge for the good-enough organizer is to learn the right balance of supporting and withdrawing to enable the movement to flourish. So while we may rightly say that some people's actions or achievements are great, that is no defense for building a world around the ideology of greatness.

Cold, Broken, But Still Hallelujah

Such troubles with the greatness regime have long been recognized. In the chapters that follow, I will discuss the history of the ideology of greatness alongside the parallel movements that have fought back against it. Greatness is a standard paradigm of many social orders. They use it to justify castes, hierarchies, and the privileges of the few. And within each of these orders, thinkers and social movements rise up to contest the regime of greatness and present alternative models for how to create a world that works for the many.

Part of what makes creating a good-enough life for all such a challenge is that, on our path to overcoming greatness, we may come to think of ourselves as the new deserving elite—the new greats around whom society should be structured. We can see this with movements like Buddhism, Christianity, and Marxism. Each began with a critique of power and a desire to remake the world in an egalitarian image, and each in turn produced new cliques of power and new forms of hierarchy. Although some Buddhists fought against the caste system and argued that all were capable of salvation, others aligned themselves with violent emperors and used monastery slaves to till their land while they recited religious hymns. Although Jesus of Nazareth railed against the inequality and violence of the Roman Empire, his followers would go on to found some of the most violent and unequal kingdoms of the last two millennia. Although Marxists set out to make a free and equal world, the leaders who claimed to take up the communist ideal have been as brutal, violent, and greedy as almost any of history's worst villains.

The gap between the theory of the good-enough world and its enactment is not uncommon. Reflecting on the failures of states that claimed to pursue communism in the twentieth century, many on the political right today use this fact to disparage egalitarian movements as "inevitably" leading to authoritarianism. But it is important to remember that Adam Smith also envisioned what became the capitalist system as a means of creating "nearly the same distribution of the necessaries of life, which would have been made, had the earth been divided in equal proportions among all its inhabitants."[44] His method did not exactly produce the desired results, either. If there is so much demonstrably wrong with unequal situations and so much to recommend a decent life for all, why do we keep failing to create such a world? Part of the answer is simply that over-coming elite domination is very difficult. Being in power means that you can build the structure to keep you in power. But it is also the case that the best parts of all of these movements *have* helped diminish elite domination and our internal greatness motors, and each will be part of the story I tell.

Furthermore, we can learn from the ways in which these movements veered away from their quest for good-enoughness. Perhaps the most common mistake is simply to believe that you are replacing greatness with a new kind of perfect world, rather than understanding that part of what it means to be human is to confront inevitable failures. Leonard Cohen wrote and sang once of love: it "is not a victory march. It's a cold, and it's a broken Hallelujah." Most movements trying to get beyond greatness have wound up replicating it by believing that they were on a victory march. They imagined utopias of blessedness and redemption. Unfortunately, as the philosopher Isaiah Berlin clearly grasped in the years after World War II, "If one really believes that such a solution is possible then surely no cost would be too high to obtain it: to make mankind just and happy and creative and harmonious forever—what could be too high a price to pay for that?"[45] And in their willingness to pay that cost, movements will often rush into their own hierarchies, creating new circuits of power in the name of subverting a former elite while they themselves become the new one. The proper response to this situation is not cynicism. It is not to believe in the iron law of oligarchy and succumb to the permanent dystopia of the present's failures. It is to articulate a vision akin to Cohen's: there is love, and it deserves our joyous praise, but its own limitations must be borne in mind. Cold and broken, yes. Hallelujah and love, yes. This is the wisdom of the good enough.

A Good-Enough Life for All

Good-enoughness, as I hope is clear by now, is not a synonym for "just OK." It is not an excuse to give up and accept intolerable conditions. Although good-enoughness begins by accepting that human beings cannot entirely avoid tragedy or difficulty, thinkers of the good-enough do not stop there. They follow James Baldwin in understanding that this is only one of two opposing needs: this need of "acceptance, totally without rancor, of life as it is," but also the demand of "equal power: that one must never . . . accept these injustices as commonplace."[46] The good-enough life accepts human failings—it appreciates that we are only ever good enough—and, *because of these failings*, it demands both decency and sufficiency for everyone. Because the world is good enough, we should be good enough to each other. But this is not a capitulation. It is a call to reimagine the world as a place brimming with meaning, access, and creativity for all. It is a call to think of who we are as irrevocably bound up with the destinies of all our fellow humans on this elegant and delicate sphere. And it is a call to appreciate that much of what is valuable in our world is overlooked by the regime of greatness—from the ordinary acts of labor that sustain our lives, to the ordinary caresses of intimacy that bring us home to ourselves.

In the coming chapters I will look at how all of these elements are related: how being good enough to ourselves requires good-enough relationships with others, which in turn requires social policies that encourage good-enoughness both for all humans and our shared planet. Since we are shaped by our social and natural worlds as we shape them in turn, each of these relations informs the others. In briefest form, the case I will make for the good-enough life across these linked spheres of our existence is as follows. As good-enough individuals, we will accept our limitations and embrace our humility, but we will also insist on our right to a voice, to equal power, to the recognition that we are decent and deserving of a world that appreciates our contributions. Our primary aspiration will not be to rise to the top of the social order, but to help create a world in which rising to the top hardly matters. We will find our virtue in our ability to work together to ensure decency and sufficiency for all. Having embraced the possibility of failure, we will be creative and adaptable, and we will have the security that allows us to engage with the full complexity of being human.

This complexity includes learning how to provide for each other's social and emotional needs. Because we are making a world where one's well-being is not overly dependent on reaching the top of a social hierarchy, we can have relationships that do not involve pressuring each other to achieve success above all else. And because we understand that even good people might betray and harm one another, we can begin to have relationships that are not about being perfect partners or friends, but about providing for each other the kind of everyday love and care that we need to feel at home in this world. Regrounded in this everyday reality, we can better appreciate the ordinary labors and small acts of care that actually sustain and affirm our social fabric. We can have both a tragic sense that prepares us for misunderstandings, and an overwhelming levity that rises above the potential fractures.

Our social systems, then, will support this vision of the kinds of selves and relationships that we want to help flourish. In many ways, this resembles the best of social democratic governance, but it still goes beyond social democracy by focusing more on the development of cooperative economic, political, and social progress. In this model of society, we do not await the great entrepreneurs, leaders, and disrupters to innovate an ethically numb future rife with violent competition for market shares and political power. Instead, we work together to develop socioeconomic progress that more equally benefits everyone by drawing on the lost energies of those who have fallen out of our greatness-oriented societies. This is not utopian; this is not an argument that doing these things will result in a perfect equality or an edgeless, harmonious social world. It is a claim that we can better circulate and distribute the value and goodness and decency of humanity to buffer ourselves collectively from the treachery and errors that are also part of our condition.

None of this progress will be possible without a deeper understanding of our natural condition. We are not determined by evolution to seek a place on the top of the hierarchy. We are the inheritors of a cooperative history that we bequeath to future generations. To ensure decency in this futurity, we will need to understand culturally what science already knows: that no group of humans is greater than any other, and that humans as a whole are not greater than nature. Humans and nature are both good-enough systems working in symbiosis. The natural world is not some perfected harmony to which we can and should return; it is as full of brutality as human history. But it is nevertheless something amazing and rare: it is good enough to sustain life, something that we have yet to find anywhere else in the universe. Our planet will only be able to keep sustaining us within specific resource and climate conditions. Living within these planetary conditions means appreciating that the earth is good and has enough, but only if we recognize that it is only good enough, that it is not an endless resource to exploit.

You should not have to be great to live a good-enough life. Indeed, the culture that tells us that we must be great at something in order to be of value undoes the possibility of a good-enough life for all of us. The ideology of greatness damages our psyches, our relationships, our societies, and our environment. In overcoming this destruction, good-enoughness does not thereby become perfect. To the contrary, it embraces and appreciates our imperfections, all the while insisting on the goal of ensuring decency and sufficiency for all. In the good-enough life we do not lose progress; we gain a new power for progress through the cooperative labor of otherwise ignored billions. Less anxiety and more meaning, less distraction and more care, less inequality and more democratic cooperation, less destruction and more alignment with nature—these are the elements of the good-enough life.

2

For Our Selves

What kind of person should you aspire to be? To answer this fundamental question about our lives we rely on a variety of sources, consciously or implicitly, including: our personal inclinations and dispositions (which result from our genetic and evolutionary inheritance); our family and its values; any religious or philosophical traditions we might ascribe to; our friends and peers; and the suggestions of our social, economic, political, and cultural structures and norms. These are all connected with one another: the family we are born into might influence how religious we are (either because we follow or we rebel), and the religion itself might change over the years as it is affected by popular culture, which itself is likely shaped by economic interests.

One of the most powerful influences on our aspirations today, which cuts across all of these spheres, is the pressure to be great, which is to say, to maximize our potential and be at the top of our field. Where does this pressure come from? Part of it, I have suggested, is from a desire to avoid suffering. This desire is compounded by personal pressures, cultural pressures, economic and political pressures, and pressures from our biology. This chapter outlines how philosophical ideas may drive one to compete for greatness, but also shows that there are vibrant philosophical systems that encourage a more egalitarian alternative.

I have chosen to focus on philosophy here because it grounds our conceptions of the good life. Philosophy is usually the discipline most fundamentally concerned with the question, what should I do with my life? Of course, whichever philosophy we choose, we have to contend with the cultural forces in which we try to live out its ideals. Philosophy has competition for claims to grounding what we should think of as the good life, especially from the belief that our life's value is tied to our economic gains. Indeed, given the structural difficulties I outlined in the previous chapter, working on ourselves at all may seem pointless. But while there are limits to what we can do on our own, it remains important for us to try to shape the normative horizon of our aspirations—that is, the ideas about the right thing to do that help shape our sense of how we should live.

The ideal of the good-enough life for all asks us to orient our goals toward making ourselves into the kind of people who can promote and participate in a world that is decent and sufficient for everyone. Importantly, the ideal encourages us *as individuals*. This is not about our giving up our wills and desires in perpetual sacrifice to some higher calling. Indeed, that is the very problem of a society that focuses so much on the competitive growth of profit: we are asked to define ourselves by our ability to produce economic value.[1] In a good-enough world, freed from this singular demand, we might be able to pursue things because we actually care about them, not simply because they satisfy our need for a job. This is the sense in which the ideal is both good and enough: it is not about mere enoughness but about actively meeting our emotional and psychic need to pursue our abilities and passions. Of course, a good-enough world still won't be perfect. There may be some socially necessary labor to perform that nobody really wants to do. But instead of that work falling to the least fortunate, it would be our shared social burden to distribute it more or less evenly.[2]

This is why, even as the good-enough life affects us as individuals, it is not simply about self-help. In his half-enlightening, half-infuriating book *The Subtle Art of Not Giving a F*ck*, the popular blogger Mark Manson encourages his readers to realize that "not giving a fuck is key. This is why it's going to save the world. And it's going to save it by accepting that the world is totally fucked and that's all right, because it's always been that way, and always will be."[3] Manson's point is not that we shouldn't care at all, but that we should learn to "reserve [our] fucks for what truly matters. Friends. Family. Purpose. Burritos. And an occasional lawsuit or two."[4] There is some genuinely good advice here about not getting worked up about pointless things and about finding meaningful concerns to engage. But there are also some obvious problems with the items on Manson's list: they are all about getting what you and yours want. There is no broader mission here. And without such a broader mission, it is almost impossible for any one of us to direct our "fucks" toward anything but our own interests.

We need an ethical system that takes Manson's wisdom about the difficulties of being alive and redirects it into a social vision. Whether we do this because we believe we are equal under God (or gods) or because we believe in materialist interdependence is not my concern. I am arguing for what we could call "good-enough universalism," with a double entendre intended— it's a universalism about being good enough, but it's not a complete universalism. This is not about the impossible and antipluralist goal of having everyone do and think the same things. It's about all of us using our unique capacities and potential to engage in the shared project of making the world good enough for all. To do so we can rely on aspects of the world that we already know—our attitudes toward cooperation and connectedness and care—but do not always emphasize. Foregrounding these in our worldview can help establish decency and sufficiency for all as our normative horizon.

The philosophies that I discuss in this chapter—versions of virtue ethics, Buddhism, and African American philosophy—are all oriented toward this normative horizon. They suggest the radical idea that life is not about what the most talented and successful among us can contribute to the rest of society, but about how, in a meaningful world, each and every person can be considered successful and meritorious. From virtue ethics, especially as it is showcased in the wonderful TV show *The Good Place*, we can learn that virtues are teachable, and that enabling our own flourishing means enabling that of others. From Buddhism we can learn that although some suffering in life is inevitable, the best path to decreasing it is through embracing our interdependence. And from African American philosophy we can learn that overcoming greatness is a battle that needs to be waged on multiple fronts, and that the end of the struggle is not a new hierarchy of peoples, but a universal establishment of decency, sufficiency, and imperfection for all.

Some may protest before I even begin that individuals are driven to pursue their own happiness, and that such virtuous visions will fail. But if we've learned anything from the scientific study of the psychology of happiness, it's actually that this individualist pursuit is what fails to provide joy in our lives. We fool ourselves into thinking that wealth and success will make us happy. Most research shows, however, that winning is a leaky cup: the more we get, the more we want. There's always another promotion or accomplishment around the bend. Community and kindness, however, tend to have long-lasting benefits.[5] Greatness really might not be so good after all.

In the Beginning

The book of Genesis begins with the story of how God took the "formless void" that was the world, and fashioned it into the heavens and the earth, the land and the sea, the light and the dark. And each time that God made something, They stood back and appraised. And They saw that it was . . . perfect? No. Great? No. Excellent? No. It is none of these things. It was "good."[6] In context, the Hebrew word here, *tov*, likely does not mean morally good, or even particularly special. It means something like good enough—it is adequate for its purpose, and its purpose is to sustain life.[7]

According to some contemporary anthropologists and archaeologists, early human life around 10,000 years ago in some parts of the world was indeed "good" in this sense. It had pain and violence, but, in sustenance and leisure, things were perfectly sufficient. The anthropologist Marshall Sahlins called this "the original affluent society," because there was an abundance of food, which meant that there was relatively little work to do, and social norms were geared toward maintaining this leisurely life. The average workday was just a few hours, with the rest of the time reserved for leisure, play, and rituals. A hunter-gatherer life might not be good enough for many people today (even contemporary hunter-gatherers, who are frequently imperiled by various outside forces), but it was in some ways the "original good-enough society."[8]

Adam and Eve live in this world. They receive the bounty of the land, even as they remain ignorant of its operations and meanings. When they eat from the tree of the knowledge of good and evil, by some accounts, they exit the original good-enough society where they do not have to do backbreaking labor to have basic sustenance. Some scholars now believe that the Garden of Eden story is an allegory of the transition from the easier food-collecting practices in the hunter-gatherer life to the difficult labor of grain cultivation.[9] This explains the punishment that Adam received for his part in eating from the tree: "Cursed is the ground because of you; in toil you shall eat of it all the days of your life."[10] No longer will the land be giving and abundant. Humans will now have to toil to reap its reward. And as political scientist James C. Scott has argued, this new society of scarcity is an origin of the zero-sum competition for hierarchy. The Fall, in this account, allegorizes the origin of the greatness-oriented society, where survival is competition.[11]

Underlying much of the philosophical history of the world is a battle between two views of this history. On the one hand, there is a call for us to live more simply, more in tune with nature, and less anxiously trying to make our way to the next big thing. We might associate this position with thinkers like Siddhartha Gautama, Jean-Jacques Rousseau, and Henry David Thoreau. On the other, there is a belief that an individual's singular goal on earth should be to break free from our limitations and become as great and powerful as possible. This might be associated with Confucius (Pinyin: Kongfuzi), Plato, and Adam Smith. (None of these associations are entirely accurate, but the common understandings can help illustrate the two types.) The simplicity group cannot understand why the perfectionists are willing to take on all the misery of labor and anxiety of excellence when the world can be bountiful and decent without the stress. The perfectionist group cannot understand why others are so insensibly indolent, when the possibilities for human potential are infinite. For the former, the departure from hunter-gatherer life was a tragic fall that we still have not overcome. For the latter, it is a "happy fall" that ripped us out of the idyll of nature and set us on the true path of our human vocation.

But this either/or view threatens to obscure a third option: that we can come up with *better ways of being good enough*. We don't have to long for prelapsarian times of leisure and natural abundance, nor do we have to toil endlessly in pursuit of an intrinsically unachievable perfection. (If the whole point is striving, after all, then the goalposts will always be pushed back.) Instead, we can think that how we were in the beginning—at least as imagined in Genesis—is a template for how to proceed. The hunter-gatherer life probably does not lie ahead for most people reading this book. But some new form of good-enoughness just might.

It's Not Just the Economy, Stupid[12]

One major impediment to achieving new forms of good-enoughness is the deep desire of many people to have more money than everyone else—that, we should remember, is the meaning of wealth; it is only a relative measure. This desire is not reserved to the greedy few, however. Economic interests increasingly shape our visions of the good life. The idiosyncratic economist Kenneth Boulding, writing in the 1960s, called this "economics imperialism."[13] Social scientists today, like the political scientist Wendy Brown, tend to speak of "neoliberalism."[14] The basic idea is that economic rationality increasingly has a monopoly on values. One example of this is that governments literally set a price on human life when considering regulations. In the late 1960s and early 1970s, for example, lives were valued by the Nixon and Ford administrations at around $200,000 each. In 1967, the actress Jayne Mansfield died in a car crash after her car slid under the back of a trailer truck. In response to a proposal to require bars on the underside of trailer trucks to prevent such accidents in the future, analysts tallied the numbers and determined that adding the bars would save 180 lives a year in the United States. That meant the value of lives saved would be $36 million, but the cost of adding the bars would be $310 million. No regulation was put in place.[15] (Democrats in the United States tend to raise the value of human life in such calculations, and thus justify more safety regulations. One reason to vote Democrat is thus that it might literally save your life.[16]) And it is not just in such regulations that economics is surpassing other value systems. As Brown shows, the way that we think about education, free speech, and even love increasingly occurs in economic terms. Where to go to school and what to study, who gets to speak and how much, and what person to marry—all of these decisions get made with at least some reference to economics.

What happens to our sense of aspiration in such a culture? One result is that jobs that pay more tend to be more sought after. As a teacher at Princeton, I sometimes feel that I work at a pre-professional school for business. Although many of my students detest inequality, feel overwhelmed by stress and familial pressures, and would like to contribute meaningfully to society, many wind up seeking employment based solely on how much it pays. I once overheard a brilliant student from a wealthy family who danced ballet, railed against inequality, and wrote a paper for my class on the radical philosopher Michel Foucault say that if they weren't going to make $200,000 a year when they graduated, they were not sure why they were attending an Ivy League university. Of course, not all of my students have this goal, and many students I have taught from low-income backgrounds also want to do financially well after college, sometimes for reasons related to family debt or other crises. But the solution to these problems is not for a select few to do well; it is to overcome the conditions that lead to such troubles.

I don't think my students would entirely disagree. When I described the message of this book to my class one semester— how the world had too much anxiety and stress and inequality and destruction, and how we could live more sustainably and caringly—they all stared intently at me, nodding along to every word. Many of them want to live a good-enough life and find work that aligns with their values and interests. But everything in society is pushing them in another direction. And so I see students compete ruthlessly for internships at large tech companies and big banks, even though they oppose the very effects these companies have had stoking inequality and injustice. They may have justifications: for example, that they will give all their money away, or that they want the experience of corporate life before moving into work that means more to them, or that economic growth is good for society as a whole. But while some feel the need to justify their choice, for the most part they do not have to. It is culturally accepted that making as much money as you can is not only an acceptable thing to do, but a morally justified aspiration.

Although the power of economic logic has been intensifying in the past few decades, it has earlier roots. They do not, however, stretch as far back as we might suspect. Max Weber, in his classic book *The Protestant Ethic and the Spirit of Capitalism* (1905), suggested that thinking of monetary gain as united to the good life was in fact a revolution from only a few centuries ago. In a discussion of the sayings of Benjamin Franklin, Weber noted that Franklin tended to associate thrift and economic gain with wisdom. To be sure, people throughout history have sought wealth and power. The difference here is that whereas previous cultures had tended to separate being wealthy and being good, often to the point of using wisdom to condemn the pursuit of gain, Franklin insisted on their fundamental relation. To be wise, in Franklin's view, was to save and make money: A penny saved is a penny earned, and so on.[17] Around the same time that Franklin was writing, Adam Smith was providing the moral logic for this argument in his *Wealth of Nations* (1776). Smith's point was quite simple: everyone does better when there is more money around, so growing the economy is a moral imperative. Smith did not, by any means, suggest that growing money was the *only* value. But by suggesting that it was perhaps the highest value, he helped pry the lid off Pandora's box.[18] Now that wealth was the highest value, everything else, even a human life, would have to justify itself in the name of economic value.

This is not, of course, an uncontested story, and not everyone at every moment is consumed with these kinds of economic rationales. We often still do things that make no or little economic sense in the name of other values. We marry for love; we give generously more than we have, especially in times of crisis; we choose careers that we think are socially valuable—like nursing or aged care or teaching (if I may)—even if the pay is not as good as we might make in other fields. But opting out of the economic race has its consequences. Public school teachers across the United States, for example, launched a massive series of strikes in 2018. In part, they struck over inadequate funding for their students, which led some teachers in states like West Virginia to spend more than a thousand dollars of their own meager salaries every year on basic school supplies.[19] They struck over low wages, which on average had *decreased* over the past two decades.[20] And they struck over the sense of injustice that they had chosen careers in the public service, cared about their students and worked hard, and yet found themselves earning "seventeen per cent less than comparably educated workers in other professions."[21] This circumstance results in burnout, high turnover, and a decrease in teacher morale, which in turn deprives future generations of opportunities to grow and develop their potential.[22]

The solution here isn't only higher pay for teachers, as the example of Finland shows. Finland is generally considered to have some of the best public education in the world. Teachers there make somewhat more than teachers in the United States, but, more than this, they enjoy the general benefits of a more egalitarian society and high regard for their profession. As such, teachers can live good-enough lives while enjoying a high amount of social esteem.[23] Finland is no utopia, but it still respects its teachers more, and the country's shared provision of social goods means that it values high salaries less. How might countries like the United States escape the grip of economic logic and its demand that the pursuit of great wealth should be our highest aspiration? And how might countries like Finland ensure that the logic of wealth, which has made inroads in the past few years, does not overtake their social values?[24]

The Return of Virtue

One of the most important answers to these questions from a philosophical perspective was set out by scholars who sought to revive the Aristotelian tradition of virtue ethics in the twentieth century.[25] Prominent figures here are Alasdair MacIntyre, Michael Walzer, and Michael Sandel. I will discuss this revival at some length, because I believe that although it is promising, it shows the limitations of any model that only looks at one aspect of greatness (in the economy), and does not consider greatness as a problem across the various domains of our lives.

According to Aristotle (384–322 BCE), virtue is a habit that can be taught. Through pedagogy and contemplation, anyone can develop their capacities for virtuous action.[26] For Aristotle, virtue has nothing to do with wealth—indeed, Aristotle was part of the tradition of wisdom that placed moral growth above economic growth. And this moral growth centers on the perfection of a series of attributes such as courage and temperance. These virtues are golden means to be found between "defect and excess." So one should want to be courageous, but not foolhardy (excess) or timid (defect); one wants to be temperate, but not self-indulgent (excess) or insensible (defect).[27] As a visual representation:

Defect	Moderate Virtue	Excess
Timid	Courageous	Foolhardy
Insensible	Temperate	Self-indulgent

Aristotle argues that achieving such virtue requires a lot of training. "It is no easy task," he tells us, "to be good." And he goes further. To know how angry to get, or how to lend money efficaciously, or how to act appropriately in any circumstance, is *very* hard: "to do this to the right person, to the right extent, at the right time, with the right motive, and in the right way, *that* is not for everyone, nor is it easy; wherefore goodness is both rare and laudable and noble."[28] Aristotle, we have to remember, is an avowed aristocrat—not in the contemporary sense of an elite powerbroker, but in the traditional sense of someone who believes that the most excellent (*aristos*) should have power (*kratos*). Although he admits the limits of humans to achieve a perfect excellence, he still believes that we should give everything we have to achieving it: we "must, so far as we can, make ourselves immortal, and strain every nerve to live in accordance with the best thing in us."[29]

In spite of Aristotle's aristocratic bent, however, today's virtue ethicists have argued that his ideas can help hold back the tide of neoliberalism. One straightforward reason for this is that Aristotle was critical of the pursuit of wealth. He argued that the aim of life was contemplative and civic flourishing, not material progress. A more unique reason is that Aristotle asked us to think about how each field of life had its own goal, or teleology. This goal could be debated about, but it could not be the same in all spheres of life. So we might argue about whether the goal of education is to become a better citizen or to have deeper thoughts about life, but it cannot be to make money. That would be the goal of the economy taking over the goal of education. If the problem is that economic thinking threatens to overtake all other forms of value, then one solution is to enforce this kind of separation between what Walzer calls "spheres" and MacIntyre calls "practices."[30] The basic idea is for each sphere or practice to produce its own metric for value. For example: the best doctor would be the one who performs the best surgery, not the one who makes the most money for the hospital by doing many surgeries quickly and regardless of their quality. As Walzer puts it, "Good fences [between spheres] make good societies."[31]

In his popular book *Justice* (2009), Michael Sandel states the case for this social vision very clearly. He begins his discussion of Aristotle with the example of how to distribute flutes. Who should get the best flute? Why, the best flute player. This seems obviously correct, and with consequences that would upend the marketization of life. Consider a situation in which there was one kind of flute that was vastly superior to all others but was no longer made. As such, it has become very expensive. If spheres collapse, the rare flute will go to the highest bidder. In "virtue ethics," it will go to the best flute player. And as for flutes, so for politics. Who should govern? Not the wealthiest, but those who are best in guiding the people toward the good life.[32] The obvious consequence for the individual is to strive to be the best at whatever they pursue—not to make money, but to achieve the highest goals of their chosen field.

For Walzer, this means that some degree of inequality within spheres is acceptable: we "live with the autonomy of distributions [of different spheres] and . . . recognize that different outcomes for different people in different spheres make a just society."[33] Like Aristotle's ethics, then, there is a sense of aristocracy here: it is about excellence and ensuring that the most excellent are at the top of each sphere or practice. As I argued in the first chapter, this moves us away from the material economy but may keep us constrained within the positional economy. And, as Fred Hirsch warned us, when there is great competition in the positional economy, it eventually creates inequalities in the material economy.

This is perhaps not obvious at first. Like the best flute example, the basic virtue ethics argument *sounds* very good. Of course we want the best flutes to be played rather than displayed, and of course we want our politicians to be guided by the common good, not their stock portfolios. But the problem with virtue ethics in this form is that it tends to undo the very thing it sets out to establish. To understand why, we just need to ask a simple question: How do we find the best flute player? Or politician, for that matter? It turns out that there is no good answer to this question, and that trying to find the best in every sphere tends to recreate the very economic problem that virtue ethics claims to solve.

Let's take one common route to finding the best player: training and competition. (I'll consider this more as a thought experiment than an actual description of finding talented flute players. It is not meant to be specific to this profession, so much as a general reflection on the logic and values of seeking to reward those deemed best within any given sphere.) We'll teach anyone who wants to learn how to play. Whoever has the most aptitude will be selected for an academy, and whoever is the best player at the academy will be in the number-one orchestra. Seems plausible. But let's look at this generic "teach anyone who wants to learn how to play." How would everyone know about this opportunity? And do they all have teachers of the same quality? Does everyone in the world learn how to play the flute? And if learning how to play the flute is something that, like virtue in Aristotle's account, is teachable, then how much does the quality of the teacher matter? Social scientists (and common sense) tell us that practice and teaching matter a great deal, but some degree of natural aptitude and ability are irreplaceable.[34] But how do we find such natural talents without practice and teaching? Most musical training starts early, but very few people know what they want to do at an early age. What if the flautist born with the most aptitude wants to be a ballerina or a chef for the first twenty years of their life, and thus never fully develops their potential? Or what if that person never even plays a flute?

So let's concede these points and say, fine, we won't get the absolute best flautist, but of those who, for whatever range of reasons, find their way into the opportunity, then, of those remaining, we can surely choose the best. This is a pretty big concession, but fair enough for now; let's play it out. We have our random selection of top flute talent. And to choose who gets the world's best flutes, and who gets to play in the most prestigious orchestra and become one of the few musicians in the world who can make a full salary from their work, we bring them all out for a competition. The flautists at our academy come out one by one; they're assessed by rigorous and transparent standards;

a decision is made. We have our winner. The best flautist has been found. Case closed.

Or is it? Let's start with the very premise: a competition. There is little evidence that competition brings out the best in us. In fact, according to some studies, competition decreases our performance, because it distracts us from doing the thing we want to do—play our instrument—and instead focuses us on an *exterior* goal: winning.[35] In the very act of seeking the best, we are already no longer talking about the best flautist; we are talking about the person who plays the flute best under conditions of pressure and performance. We are finding the best *competitor*, not the best flute player. These are not the same thing. One study of children making art, for example, found that those who were told they were in a competition to win made much more formulaic and staid art, because they thought it was more likely to win. Those who were just told to paint made more creative and aesthetically powerful projects.[36]

The distinction between winning a competition and pursuing excellence is important, in part because it reminds us that the problem here is not with talent, and that our aim is not to reduce or constrain anyone's talents. There is a difference between skill or excellence, on the one hand, and greatness or being the best, on the other. Skill is not zero-sum: in theory, anyone can be an excellent flautist. But only one person can be the best flautist and be recognized and rewarded as such. The problem with Walzer's argument about different rewards in different spheres is that while it potentially overcomes the material wealth problem, it keeps in place the positional wealth problem. After all, in a world full of excellent flautists, how are we to choose the few who receive all the rewards—be they material or positional? What are we to do with all those who are excellent but for whatever reason don't rise to the top because they are simply not good at competitions?

A traditional virtue ethicist might respond by saying, well, that's the point. Being the best flute player in your room is no better than being the best politician in your room. Doesn't being the best flute player imply not getting nervous during competition? As Ralph Waldo Emerson put it, "It is easy in solitude to live after our own; but the great man is he who in the midst of the crowd keeps with perfect sweetness the independence of solitude."[37] This is a fair point, but we have to register what it actually means. If we think about politicians for a second, it implies that we will often wind up with people who are charismatic in presenting their personal views in front of cameras regardless of whether they are skilled at finding the common good. And it may mean that rather than cultivating the talents of nervous but capable flautists, we focus on people who have confidence and aplomb. Talented people who enjoy playing their instrument but do not like competition may very well drop out rather than continuing on this path. This phenomenon has been especially noted in youth sports. According to Charles A. Popkin, a pediatric surgeon and child sports researcher, "Children who specialize in one sport early in life were found to be the first to quit their sport and ended up having higher *inactivity* rates as an adult."[38] Competition may in fact drive away excellence.

If these competitions take place in our present society, there are also inequalities that may affect the results. For example, it is much easier to do your best if you can fall back on your inheritance at the end of the day. It is much harder if not getting the best flautist position means that you will not be able to feed your family. It is also much easier to be the best flautist in public if you grew up with enough money to have the best teachers;

opportunities to compete at an early age; access to psychologists to help ease the anxiety of competition; and the ability to focus on the flute full-time, without a job on the side to earn extra money. (Although, of course, family wealth isn't necessarily a benefit here—after all, a wealthy parent might encourage their child to make money instead of becoming a flautist, or they might pay less attention to their children because they have other pursuits, or they might have higher expectations for perfection, which can lead to anxiety beyond what a psychologist or pill can fix.) Perhaps after years of practice, the person who did not win would turn out to be an equally good flautist, even in public. But in this kind of system, we'll never know.

Given these arguments, we can return to my original concession and see what's wrong: we cannot simply get rid of the question of equality of opportunity here. Of course, none of our Aristotelians would disagree. They would readily say that these issues need to be dealt with if we are to find our best flautist. But here's the rub: Can an ethical system that promotes being the best be part of the movement for equality of opportunity? Quite simply, no, because any society with an aristocracy will inevitably enable that aristocracy to give its children tremendous advantages.[39] (As Michael Young correctly showed in his satire of meritocracy, the only path to meritocracy would involve the ruthless separation of children from their families based on their talents.) Unless the world's best flautist and worst flautist are to be paid the same (or nearly the same) *and* have the same (or nearly the same) social status and value in the eyes of the world, then the child of the world's best is going to be able to get a lot more training and support in whatever profession they choose to pursue. (This is one reason why "equality of opportunity" without any accompanying focus on ensuring a decent life regardless of what one does with that opportunity is generally impossible. The previous winners will always give their kids more opportunities.[40]) Counterintuitively, then, the pursuit of maximal excellence and its accompanying rewards does not, in fact, give us the best. It gives us a skewed system in which a few are rewarded too much for reasons not necessarily of their own making, and the vast and edifying talents of the many go to waste.

But not only does the pursuit and reward of excellence fail to deliver on its promises; it also brings real psychic damages along with it. For the past several years, one meta-analysis after another has shown that perfectionist tendencies lead to psychological difficulties.[41] Two psychologists recently summed up the research as follows: "Perfectionists need to be told that they have achieved the best possible outcomes, whether that's through scores and metrics, or other peoples' approval. When this need is not met, they experience psychological turmoil, because they equate mistakes and failure to inner weakness and unworthiness."[42] This has led to a spike in burnout, anxiety, depression, and eating disorders.[43] As with most psychic and social phenomena, this pressure is experienced very differently across race, class, and gender groups.[44] Because of this, as I'll discuss more at the end of this chapter, there is no single response that can turn back the tide of perfectionism and its tendency to drown out our good-enough selves.

Nevertheless, with these general insights we can sketch a system to transform our aspirations. What we need instead of an ethics of aristocracy—even an aristocracy of virtue—is not a philosophy that encourages us to strive for our personal place in a competitive hierarchy, but rather one that encourages us to improve our abilities, whatever they may be, to cooperatively increase the general pool of material and social resources. Our goal would not be to achieve our own success, nor to make the world perfect, but to create a good-enough world that we can all enjoy. In this world, our inevitable imperfections would be understood and worked through, rather than considered irredeemable blemishes. Then, after we create a good-enough world, we would aspire to maintain it and continue its dynamism. We would achieve and grow this good-enough world in a few ways:

1) By ensuring that there are good people in the right places. We would not be giving up on talent or expertise; we would simply be trying to move past the system that, in seeking the best, perverts the whole social order.

2) By recognizing that those who receive extra attention or acclaim are—and can only ever be—good enough, and that many others could have been in their positions with different luck or circumstance. Because of this, we would not reward them excessively in either money or prestige. And we would properly give credit and ensure a good quality of life to everyone who makes that possible—from the person who cuts down the tree or mines the metal to make the flute to the janitor who cleans the concert hall.

3) And by recognizing, with Aristotle, that virtue is a teachable habit, we would still accord everyone not in positions of leadership the respect and value that they deserve not only as human beings, but as humans who in different circumstances could have themselves risen through the ranks.

As a result, without the pressure to be the best, people would be able to pursue their passions and talents in unprecedented ways. We would also reduce our anxiety, remove the social resentment and envy that comes through excessive reward, and blunt the fraying of the social fabric caused by inequality. It would have the further potential of increasing respect for expertise, because experts would be viewed as those diligently pursuing knowledge for the common good, not as part of an out-of-touch elite. Moreover, while we might miss having the best leader or flautist ever, we can virtually guarantee that we will no longer be subject to the whims of having the worst one.

Meritocracy, No. Greatness, Maybe.

Reimagining the world in this way does not mean doing away with virtue ethics; it just means preserving its central insight into the teachability of the virtues while discarding its aristocratic bent. Sandel's recent work is especially strong in this respect as he continues to redevelop virtue ethics through a criticism of meritocracy. This can also be seen in some similar writing by another contemporary public philosopher, Kwame Anthony Appiah. The analysis of virtue ethics so far has shown why we need to keep in mind both the positional and material economy, and why focusing on greatness in just one sphere of our lives (the economy) is not enough. The critique of meritocracy, especially by Sandel, further advances the general critique of greatness, and asks us to consider how the obsession with finding the talented few is fragmenting our personal and political lives. It's worth looking closely at what these contemporary philosophers have written, because they will help us understand the limitations of any system of greatness, even as they themselves make claims that I think still fall into the greatness model. While I will thus have some critical things to say about their arguments, my remarks are intended as an allied attempt to keep thinking through the challenges their philosophies pose to meritocracy. Sandel and Appiah find serious fault with the meritocratic logic of rewarding those who rise to the top, but they also seem to accept some of the haphazard luck of success stories as inevitable.

Sandel's book *The Tyranny of Merit* (2020) is a sustained exploration of why meritocracies fail not only in their stated mission, but also in their concept of justice. It is a book very much aligned with what I am arguing here. Sandel is a good public interlocutor, and so is generous to the meritocratic ideal, noting that it makes a fair amount of sense. He appreciates the obvious fact that we should hire people who can do the job well, not just—as the saying in the United States goes—give everyone a trophy. And he appreciates the moral logic: arguments for meritocracy suggest that everyone should be free to pursue their talents, and that whatever rewards they reap from this pursuit are justified.

But Sandel's argument is that meritocracy's flaws do not reside simply in the fact that inequality makes such a system difficult to achieve. Meritocracy, he claims, is not an argument against inequality but a justification for it—if everyone has a fair chance to show their talents, then it would seem to be perfectly fair for those with the most talent to get the most reward. Sandel doubts whether this justification itself is justified—that is, whether a society that works to establish unequal regimes of wealth and power is one that has legitimacy. He argues that such a society rests on a confusion about the moral value of talent and effort. Talent is a product of hereditary luck, and effort, while venerable, is insufficient without that primary hereditary luck. He further argues that the ability to put forth effort has roots in both nature and nurture, and thus capacity for effort is subject to not one but two forms of luck.

As I noted above, Fred Hirsch's ideas about the positional economy have some analogies in Aristotle's writings about the "inequality of honor." Sandel, influenced by both Aristotle and Hirsch, is deeply concerned about what happens to a society that creates vast inequalities in material and positional goods. These "inequalities of wealth and esteem that are defended in the name of merit . . . foster resentment, poison our politics, and drive us apart."[45] This means that rectifying our current system will require a focus on not just "distributive justice" but also what Sandel, following others, calls "contributive justice."[46] It is simply not enough for us as human beings to have our material needs met. We also need to be able to contribute meaningfully to the world—to have a recognized voice across the spheres of our existence. According to Sandel, achieving contributive justice would lead to "a broad equality of condition that enables those who do not achieve great wealth or prestigious positions to live lives of decency and dignity—developing and exercising their abilities in work that wins social esteem, sharing in a widely diffused culture of learning, and deliberating with their fellow citizens about public affairs."[47]

I very much appreciate Sandel's work here, and the vision of a just society oriented toward the common good that he offers. And as I'll discuss in chapter 4, I am especially in agreement with his proposal for the use of a lottery to diminish the prestige and insanity of college admissions. I do have some reservations, however, that in focusing on meritocracy per se and not the system of greatness more broadly, he may leave too much of our current problems intact. For example, Sandel's focus is almost exclusively on the United States and creating a common good for its citizens. It's unclear how such a nationally focused system can sustain itself if it must still fight for international supremacy. If one only annuls the justification for meritocracy at a national level, one risks that it will return through an international competition. Sandel similarly does not address the problem with greatness when it comes to the limits of our natural world. Although he is of the political left, Sandel is thus willing to endorse—if rather tepidly—the "productivist" proposal of conservative economist Oren Cass. Cass shares with Sandel a concern that we only see ourselves as consumers and not producers—that is, economic contributors. But he sidesteps the problem that Cass's proposal is both anti-immigrant and largely unconcerned with ecological damage.[48]

Finally, as I've said repeatedly, there is nothing wrong with Sandel using the word "great." But it is not clear precisely what he means by the relationship between those who still have "great wealth and prestigious positions" and the common good. If the whole concern is that the concentration of wealth and prestige damage both distributive and contributive justice, then how do we reconcile the continued existence of "great wealth" with the "broad equality of condition" that Sandel urges in the same sentence?[49]

For Sandel, the answer seems to rely on people recognizing that their advantages in life are not deserved, and that they derive from grace or luck. As he writes in the book's final sentences, "A lively sense of the contingency of our lot can inspire a certain humility. . . . Such humility is the beginning of the way back from the harsh ethic of success that drives us apart. It points beyond the tyranny of merit toward a less rancorous, more generous public life."[50] I very much appreciate this sentiment. But it's noteworthy that Sandel criticizes the *ethic* of success, rather than what *counts* as success. And it's hard to see how, once we recognize the arbitrariness of success, people would be content to say: "Well, gee, I know it could have been me who had great wealth or a prestigious position, but it's you instead for no particularly good reason. But since you recognize my dignity, I have a sustainable if not exciting quality of life, and you appreciate what I have to say about civic matters, no worries."

We need more than an appreciation of contingency; we need an actual set of practices to ensure distributive and contributive justice, as well as a corresponding set of personal aspirations that guide us to create such a world. This means that being humble at one's success is good, but it's not enough. Success itself has to mean helping to create a world that ensures decency and sufficiency for all. Achieving a good-enough world, not personal wealth or power, should be the goal on our normative horizon. I don't think that transforming our desires in the midst of a world that so highly values wealth and power is easy, and I don't think we should be hard on ourselves if we sometimes have fantasies of the ease and power of greatness. But I do think that guiding ourselves to new aspirations can take these desires and help channel their energy toward making a good-enough world for all. Our personal and social transformations must go hand in hand.

My other concern with focusing on the embrace of humility is that there is no necessary link between appreciating luck and actually changing unfair conditions. Consider here the recent criticism of meritocracy by Kwame Anthony Appiah. Appiah advances an argument that is largely similar to Sandel's, although he focuses less on the economic and political questions, and more on Michael Young's idea about what it means for a life to have value. Recall that Young proposed a world in which everyone has equal opportunity not to prove their intelligence, but to develop whatever is profound and meaningful in them. This would be, he wrote, a world of "plural values," where kindness matters as much as intelligence.[51] Appiah notes that this view of life can sound "quixotic," but he argues that it answers to the "central task of ethics." By this he means that it answers the question of what it means for a human life to go well. A good life, he says, lies at the intersection of the talents you are born with, the historical circumstances you grow up with, and decisions you make about what matters.[52] Because each of these things is so specific, it means that there can be no general measure of how well one lives. In Appiah's words, there is "no single scale of human worth."[53]

Like Sandel, Appiah appreciates the basic idea of merit, and also the equalizing potential of it. He notes, for example, that in a merit-driven society we indeed should see that some jobs once reserved for people of particular identities are now generally available to those who qualify.[54] But he also notes that what that means is not always so clear: "to prepare the next Einstein, you'd need to know what talents it will take to make the next great breakthrough in physics. If we knew *that*, we wouldn't need the next Einstein."[55]

The world that appreciates all this complexity would not be one without "great wealth or prestigious positions," but only one where such a position is not a requirement of a good life. While "the social rewards of wealth and honor are inevitably going to be unequally shared, because that is the only way they can serve their role as incentives for human behavior," Appiah maintains those who miss out on rewards still deserve to be recognized in their basic human dignity. But, he continues, with less concern for economic or political inequality than Sandel, "The goal isn't to eradicate hierarchy and to turn every mountain into a salt flat. . . . The circulation of social esteem will always advantage the better novelist, the more important mathematician, the savvier businessman. . . . But . . . it remains an urgent collective endeavor to revise the associated labels, norms, and treatments in service of what we can call moral equality."[56]

Appiah's argument begins from essentially the same position as Sandel about what's wrong with meritocratic societies. And yet, he does not discuss the real problems in political and economic inequality. In fact, in spite of their contingencies, he largely says that they are not only inevitable, but should be so. To get at what's wrong with the meritocratic argument, again, we can't just say what's wrong with meritocracy. We have to explain what's wrong with the vision of life that suggests there is something logical and proper with having steep hierarchies, even when we know, as Appiah himself says, that those hierarchies are the product of a great deal of circumstance.

Appiah's argument rests on three assumptions that are worth examining in detail because they are so widespread. The first is his claim that inequality in reward is necessary to incentivize human behavior. Appiah might be saying that we need some *very limited* inequalities in order to generate such incentives, in which case I would happily agree. But the rest of his comments suggest that such limits are not his concern. In any case, it's worth pausing on this claim about incentives. Appiah states here a common belief that unequal rewards incentivize excellence without going into more detail. For many, the claim might not seem to require much evidence. Why get up in the morning and try to write a book if the end result is that I'm not going to get anything for it? But Appiah himself, citing Young, has told us why: in the social order Appiah seems to endorse, we would do things for the sake of doing them, not for the incentive of wealth or honor. Appiah appears to be saying that wealth and honor should be unequal because otherwise they won't function as incentives. But if the activity itself should provide incentive, it's unclear why incentives matter.

Perhaps that sounds a little too utopian. It does seem to me logical to suggest that we might get a little bit of reward for what we do—a *little* extra acknowledgment or money, so long as there is something like a continually progressive tax to keep wealth from piling up in too few hands. But if that's the case, what kinds of activities should we incentivize? We might want to give extra esteem or rewards to those who do jobs like Jester D, the sanitation worker we met in the introduction, or people who care for the aged. We might also note that what actually motivates human beings to do things is not just about honor or wealth: people do things because of the very plurality of values that Appiah maintains. We might work in sanitation because we think it's an important civic service, not because we'll be paid more to do it, and as long as we're paid well enough to do it.

This is what perplexes me about Appiah's claim about the logic of incentivizing. On the one hand, he is saying that we should give honor and rewards in order to motivate people. On the other, he is saying that we should ensure that everyone has dignity whether or not they are successful in this classical sense. But doesn't the one point undercut the other? What is the basis for dignity if we are explicitly telling people that, in the system of social esteem and reward, they have lost out? To achieve the moral equality that Appiah rightly wants, it seems we might have to think more about the material and positional equality he seems to brush aside.

Appiah's second assumption is that social esteem "always" goes to the "better" person in whatever profession. In my discussion of the flute player, I showed why this is clearly not the case, and why many "better" people might in fact get lost in the process. Donald Justice's remarks on success in writing are worth quoting again: "There may well be analyzable causes behind the oblivion some good writers suffer, but the causes, whatever they are, remain elusive. There is a randomness in the operation of the laws of fame that approaches the chaotic."[57] It is simply not the case that more talented people get more esteem. Indeed, I'm sure that anyone reading this right now can rattle off a list of people who get more esteem for no good reason than someone else they know. Some people might get more attention because of their power or privilege. Or, as political theorists have noted about electoral politics, they might have won their election simply because they are taller or more charismatic[58] (neither of which has much to do with crafting good policy). Rather than heaping the same praise on the same people again and again, we should acknowledge that talented individuals often go unrecognized, and find ways of incorporating that fact into our social and economic systems.

But this does not mean, as Appiah puts it in his third assumption, that the opposite of a hierarchical system of reward is a world of barren "salt flats." We can have *some* differentials in society. It's not a question of eliminating them. It's a question of limiting them because, to extend the logic of Sandel and Appiah, we recognize the arbitrariness of who becomes recognized and who doesn't in a world of limited attention and limited positional goods. And the logical conclusion of doing that is to shift our own aspirations from becoming one of the few people who gets esteem, or who climbs to the top of whatever hierarchy, to becoming someone who can meaningfully participate in the formation of the good-enough life for all. If we do *that* well, perhaps we deserve a little bit of recognition. But not too much. We don't have to strain our eyes into some distant future to see what this would look like. We can just turn on our TVs.

Virtues beyond Greatness

From 2016 to 2020, the TV show *The Good Place* offered viewers a rare glimpse of what happens when philosophers and comedy writers get together to think about what the world could be like if we got beyond greatness. (If you haven't watched the show, and if you don't like spoilers, feel free to skip ahead. Or even better: take a pause from reading to watch it—it really is both profound and entertaining.) The show is about four humans—Eleanor, Chidi, Tahani, and Jason—who have died and believe that they have gone to "the Good Place." It turns out that they are not actually in the Good Place, but an experimental version of the Bad Place, designed by the demon Michael. The aim is for the four of them to torture each other mentally instead of physically because they are all such frustrating individuals.

The central character is Eleanor, who we know from the beginning "does not belong" in the Good Place. She is made to believe that she is "the wrong Eleanor," and should really be in the Bad Place. Another principal character, Chidi, is a professor of moral philosophy who seems perfect at first, but whose inability to make decisions—because he always wants to make the best one—makes him an impossible person to be around. Eleanor hopes that if she studies with him and can learn to be good, she might be able to stay in the Good Place. He offers to give her lessons in moral philosophy. Eventually Tahani and Jason join Chidi's courses, too. Through a series of plot twists, so does Michael, who joins the group in fighting against other demons.

As they learn about what it means to be good, they move past Eleanor's original focus on learning to be good enough to stay in the Good Place. They realize that this whole system of dividing humanity into good and bad, winners and losers, deserving and undeserving, is a fundamental misunderstanding of the potential and value of human life. Together they launch a revolt against heaven and hell and a create a new system in which there is no more Good Place or Bad Place, but only an endless series of opportunities to become a better person through moral learning. Everyone is given the opportunity and support to keep improving themselves—no matter how many times they fail. Once they reach their full potential, they move on to what was once the Good Place, where they have as much time as they like to pursue a plurality of meaningful pursuits. Tahani the socialite learns various forms of manual labor. Eleanor the party girl continues her study of philosophy. The Good Place is no longer about rewards, but about the gift of time that is extended to everyone. In Chidi's words, "It's not even a place, really. It's just having enough time with the people you love." It is good, and it provides enough, but still, it is not about perfection or endless eternal bliss. Indeed, when they finally get to the original Good Place, they discover that everyone is miserable there because it is too good all of the time. To make the Good Place meaningful, they realize that it needs a bit of limitation. When someone has had enough time, they can walk through a special door and go out of existence. What makes it special, what makes it enough but not too much, is that it, too, can now end.

To fully appreciate the show's message, we have to realize the extraordinary premise that four deeply flawed humans and one seemingly irredeemable demon overthrow and vastly improve the entire judgment system of the afterlife. Rather than judging people based on what they've already done, the show suggests that we are better off finding creative, pedagogic ways to encourage them to improve in the future. (Obviously, it's not just about the afterlife.) Our four main characters do this not because they are the best people to do it, or the only people to do it. Nowhere is it written that four bumbling heroes will become the saviors of humanity. They do it because they cooperate to improve one another and make their lives better. Even Chidi, the moral philosopher, must learn to stop trying to make the best decision. What is important in his character is not that he embodies the ideal, but that he encourages everyone to study together to learn how to improve. In so doing, he plants the seed: life should not be a game of judging who is best and worst, but of enabling everyone to *work together* to achieve their full potential. Since we all live in one shared system, that system will work best if it works for all of us.

Perhaps surprisingly, one of the show's key inspirations was Aristotle. In an interview at the show's end, its creator Michael Schur was asked if the writers had come up with an answer to the question of the good life. After joking, "Yep, nailed it," he continued: "I don't know that we have an answer, but the show ended up taking a position, and it's something close to Aristotelian virtue ethics." He then clarifies: "Because you're doomed to fail, what matters isn't that you do everything right. What matters is that you try. When you make a mistake, you apologize and then you try something else. The show is suggesting that the real victory of being alive is just putting these things in the front of your brain and attempting all the time to be a better person than you were yesterday."[59] This is not, I have suggested, Aristotelian virtue ethics in their original articulation, which really were about the few who could achieve their demanded excellence. But Aristotle's virtue ethics, like any other system of thought, can evolve and modernize. There can be virtue ethics without hierarchy—a system that recognizes our failures, and foregrounds that, because of our personal limitations or historical conditions, we all deserve to be given not only the opportunity to reform, but the educational and caring encouragement to do so.

Some versions of virtue ethics guide us into a kind of "trickle-down" virtue culture. By ensuring that we have the best leaders, best teachers, best musicians, it assumes that we will all benefit from their innovations and ideas. But what *The Good Place* exposes is that such a system is actually torture for anyone not in the Good Place. It creates an elite few who have boundless resources while the rest of us must struggle to keep afloat—torturing one another day by day. While we may indeed enjoy and appreciate the elite's moments of creativity or insight, we also must suffer the constant pressures and losses of not feeling that we are among the best, of trying to cram ourselves into the boxes that past aristocrats have deemed appropriately excellent, of struggling in the same unjust economic system that virtue ethics was meant to overcome. A good-enough virtue ethics offers us something much more wondrous and valuable: a world in which the anxieties of perfection are lost, but the joys of pursuing our talents for their own sake are gained; in which aristocratic demands are annulled, but new creative powers flourish; in which everyone has a decent quality of life, no matter what nature- or God-given talents they might be born with.

The World As It Already Is

Perhaps such a world sounds, on the one hand, too good to be true, and, on the other, like it would deprive us of too much. I think it sounds too good to be true only because we haven't tried it yet. But is there a good reason we haven't? Does this Good Place world ignore the simple fact that some people just are more talented? Lebron James is better at basketball than I am or ever will be or ever could have been. What would the point be of not rewarding his natural talents alongside the work ethic and coaching systems that allowed him to expand on those gifts? And who would want to live in a world in which we could not watch such performances of excellence?[60]

There is nothing wrong with striving, or pursuing one's craft, or trying to continually progress in the development of one's talent. What I am arguing against is a world in which our well-being depends on having such a specific talent. Those who support the greatness orientation of our current world might readily agree, but they have yet to prove that their world—a world where a handful of billionaires own more than billions of people—can make it possible for everyone to have what they need regardless of their talents. Indeed, our current system so narrowly distributes value that, in the early 2020 pandemic days, mere access to a test to know if one was sick required a degree of celebrity, even though the real heroes were "essential workers" like the underpaid nurses, aged-care workers, and delivery people.[61] If we believe that being at the top of the hierarchy in particular domains is the path of virtue, we will inevitably subvert our ability to recognize worth and excellence in other spheres. In a good-enough system of virtue ethics, our concern is not with the excellence of a given sphere or practice. It is with understanding the *interrelatedness* of practices. Lebron James can only do what he does because there are janitors, concession workers, people who farm and produce the food sold at the concessions, trainers, and stadium builders, not to mention all the people who build, run, and maintain the public roads and modes of transportation that get people to the games. The good-enough life is not in the least about minimizing the talent of someone like James. It is about seeing that talent as one node in a world shot through with meaningful connections. It is about recognizing everyone who makes a talent like his possible.

One of the most eloquent spokespeople for this is James himself. In a remarkable TV advertisement, "Lebron: Beginnings," James offered a full-on assault against the idea that what defines character is having to rise through terrible circumstances to become successful. James, who grew up with a single mother in public housing in Akron, Ohio, narrates what appears at first like a clichéd repetition of the American Dream: "We always hear about an athlete's humble beginnings. How they emerged from poverty or tragedy to beat the odds. They're supposed to be the stories of determination that capture the American dream. They're supposed to be stories to let you know these people are special." Suddenly, James twists the narrative, calling into question this whole social order: "But you know what would be really special? If there were no more humble beginnings." The point isn't to rise from poverty; it is to end it. Not everything that James has done in his life quite aligns with this vision—nor does the company he did it for, Nike, have a particularly good track record on creating a more just world.[62] Nevertheless, it is a powerful statement working to shift some of the values that define US culture.

And it is a powerful response to the idea that creating a good-enough life for all would dishonor past sacrifices and triumphs. Those who have risen as James did through tremendous difficulties deserve tremendous credit. But so do those who have not risen. Such a person, after all, could have been James himself. We do not know how many Lebron James–level talents have been lost because we do not provide sufficient opportunities. Equally, we do not know how many such talents would go unrecognized even *with* such opportunities because of whatever else might go wrong in a person's life, or because they just did not realize their particular gift until too late, or because of the simple fact that there are, in Fred Hirsch's phrase, social limits to growth—there will always be more talented people than there are positions. The point is not just opportunity; it's about ensuring, as James says, that there are no humble beginnings, that everyone has a good-enough life, whether they are recognized for having a great talent or not.

To create such a world is also to recognize that individuals who are often isolated and upheld as great are the products of broader systems. In a remarkable research synthesis, the economist

Mariana Mazzucato has shown that literally the entire infrastructure of an iPhone—multi-touch screens, micro hard drives, GPS, Siri, and nine other technologies—would not exist without decades of public investment.[63] What Steve Jobs and others at Apple did was to seize on these technologies and integrate them in consumer-friendly and sleekly designed ways. No small feat. But an impossible one without all of society pitching in. Rather than regret not being an early investor in Apple, remember that you were. You just don't get any of the rewards.

Virtue ethics attempted to solve the neoliberal problem of having economic value define everything by erecting fences between spheres while still enabling the pursuit of hierarchies within the spheres. But this did not get at the whole problem. It left intact too much of the system of greatness and the relentless pursuit of excellence for reward. That this happens to occur in the economy and spread from there in the era of neoliberalism is a secondary issue. We will do no better if we have a world in which philosopher-kings (or IQ leaders in Young's story) have no money but endless power to control other people's lives. Walzer relies on the old adage "Good fences make good neighbors" for his riff, "Good fences make good societies." But good fences do not make good neighbors. Good neighbors are made by how they treat one another with respect and appreciate their fundamental dependence on each other. A good fence won't do you much good when your neighbor's house is on fire. It will just provide tinder for the flame.

Virtue ethics without hierarchy, however, has something profound to teach us about our aspirations. It encourages us to be a good-enough member of a collective effort trying to make decency and sufficiency available to all. It is by doing this work *on the system* that we enable it for ourselves. This is a dynamic relationship. We change our aspirations from seeking our own perfection to seeking good-enoughness for all, and in so doing we make it possible for us to be good enough ourselves. This is what Eleanor learns throughout *The Good Place*. It is not enough to change her ethical habits; she has to make the world around her a place in which those habits can find their groove. This kind of virtue ethics, then, is not about creating separate spheres of excellence to pursue alone, but about working together to build interdependent systems of material and spiritual sufficiency.

Satisfaction Not Guaranteed

While virtue ethicists turned to expanding the spheres of excellence in order to overcome the overreach of economics, other schools of thought popular today worked to redirect our desire away from outward forms of success. Mostly associated with "Eastern" religion (so-called—cardinal directions are of course relative to one's location), techniques like yoga and meditation have skyrocketed in popularity. In the United States, for example, between 2012 and 2018 the number of people reporting that they meditated tripled, while those doing yoga doubled. About ten percent of the general population, or 35 million people, reported practicing one or both.[64] And it's not just in the United States. The popular forms of meditation and yoga that we know today were largely restricted practices in the histories of Buddhism and Hinduism. Up until the late nineteenth century, the vast majority of their practitioners would have been monks and ascetics who dedicated their lives to perfecting religious insight. It was only in response to the developments of modern science and technology, as well as the force of European colonialism, that these techniques were expanded to the laity. As monasteries were destroyed, traditions derided as backward, and foreign domination enforced, ascetic practices became ways to preserve the teachings in the bodies of the general population, while also allowing the practices to be promoted as ways to deal with the problems of excessive materialism and uncaring rationality.[65]

At first glance, much of what we see today in these practices is the opposite of the virtue ethics appeal to excellence. Meditation is said to be about getting in touch with your body and breath, letting go of your materialist concerns, decreasing your desires, and learning to love and appreciate yourself and others. This is certainly true. But it's important to remember that these practices do not take place outside of their broader cultural orbit. Just as during the anticolonial era they took on a new meaning as a stance against empire, so today they are being transformed by their use within a greatness-oriented culture.

Consider, for example, Mark Manson's take on the matter in his *Subtle Art* book (not to pick on him; he is just a helpful example because he is one of the clearest expositors of this worldview). In his first chapter, Manson invokes the work of Alan Watts, a mid-twentieth-century British popularizer of a hybrid form of Zen Buddhism, Hinduism, and Taoism. Watts was a charismatic writer and lecturer who expressed complex ideas in clarifying, even electrifying ways. His *The Wisdom of Insecurity* (1951) and *The Way of Zen* (1957) were among the first books to introduce me to Buddhism and Taoism, and they had a profound impact on my own life when I read them in college. According to Watts, most of our strategies for self-improvement backfire. When we feel insecure, for example, we assume that the best way to overcome this is through confidence and power. But in fact, according to Watts, it is by embracing our insecurity and not trying to overcome it that we, paradoxically, can become secure. (That's on a long list of things I wish I'd been told in high school.) Watts called this the "law of reversed effort" or "the backwards law." It is as much Christian as Zen or Taoist, which

Watts signified by giving as its primary explanatory quote this line from the Christian Gospels: "Whoever would save his soul shall lose it."[66]

Manson mentions Watts in relation to the following hypothetical question from a reader: "'What about the Camaro I've been saving up for? What about the beach body I've been starving myself for? . . . What about the big house on the lake I've been dreaming of?'"[67] Manson's response is that he is not actually asking you to give up on any of these pursuits. While for Watts the backwards law was about psychological security, for Manson it's a roundabout route to material success. "Ever notice that when you care *less* about something, you do better at it? Notice how it's often the person who is the least invested in the success of something that actually ends up achieving it?"[68] Manson is smart enough not to suggest that we will achieve our desires simply by not caring about them. He really does want people to understand and appreciate failure. But that failure is often ultimately rerouted into success. Because we fail, and because we don't "give a fuck" about failing, we will eventually succeed. I would rather say, though, that Buddhism teaches us something about failure as a value for its own sake, something that teaches us not how to succeed next time, but that success in a competitive system has its own flaws and is only one metric of a good life.

But Manson is not alone in his interpretation of figures like Watts. Many people today think of "Eastern wisdom" as a path to helping them succeed in today's competitive marketplace. The philosopher Slavoj Žižek has gone so far as to diagnose what he calls "The Taoist Ethic and the Spirit of Global Capitalism."[69] According to Žižek, the whole idea of "letting things go" always puts us back into a space like Manson's. He traces the rise of practices like "corporate yoga" and Zen meditation retreats for business executives. While Žižek is willing to concede that some Buddhists and Taoists out there may genuinely fight for social justice, he believes that the basic philosophical structure of things like the "law of reversed effort" ultimately serves to provide justification for us to keep striving for material success and personal achievement. Meditation in this sense does not fight back against ceaseless striving; it simply enables a less anxious path to the same end.

It would be inaccurate to blame these things simply on capitalism, colonialism, and modernization. Throughout history, Buddhists and Taoists have been as susceptible to the pursuit of great wealth and power as any other group of humans. But to focus only on these aspects of the traditions overlooks a lot of what we might learn about the good-enough life from each of them. I will focus my discussion here on Buddhism and return to Taoism in the next chapter.

Buddhist philosophy provides some fundamental insights for understanding how our world and our lives can be meaningfully good enough. Some of the earliest Buddhist texts speak directly against the Aristotelian idea that living virtuously is the possession of an elite few. The relationship between Buddhism, Brahminism, and caste is complicated, and we need not get into the details about its historical accuracy here.[70] But in some texts of the Buddhist canon, Siddhartha Gautama is shown speaking against the idea that only those born into the Brahmin (priestly) caste are capable of salvation. In the *Assalāyana Sutta* (date unknown, probably from around the same time as Aristotle[71]), for example, several Brahmins gather together and discuss if it is true that the "recluse Gautama describes purifications for all of the four castes." When no one knows for sure, one of them, Assalāyana, decides to approach the Buddha and ask if he really teaches this. The Buddha gives a series of reasons why yes, in fact, he does. They include our shared condition as children; the fact that there are other cultures which do not have castes; a querying about the Brahmins' knowledge of genetics; and, perhaps most importantly, an assertion that whether born high or low, one can act despicably or morally, and that is what matters. Assalāyana becomes a follower of the Buddha.[72]

Why did Gautama preach this openness to all? Perhaps one reason is that it follows logically from his rather unique theory of *dukkha*, a Pali word usually translated "suffering," but which may be better rendered as "unsatisfactoriness."[73] The point is not that every moment of our lives is full of suffering. Indeed, suffering as a translation for *dukkha* has sometimes led to the false vision of Buddhism as unnecessarily pessimistic. Rather, Buddhism has an insightful idea about the limits of pleasure.

Doubts about whether the world was able to give humans pleasure were not uncommon in diverse philosophical schools. Aristotle, for example, even felt it necessary to insist: "It *is* possible to be pleased." But in so saying, he is forced to explain something obvious yet surprising: while pleasure is possible, we are still unpleased much of the time in our lives, even in the midst of what should be pleasurable activities. For Aristotle, pleasure is "complete," that is, it is entirely self-contained and admits of no negative feelings.[74] This complete feeling is the result of a pleasurable *activity*. So it is when we are immersed in activity that we experience pleasure. Thus the reason we lose pleasure has nothing to do with pleasure itself, but rather simply because we cannot be active all the time. Aristotle's theory anticipates and gives a logic for what today are called "diminishing returns": what gives us pleasure when we first do or see something is from a stimulation of activity in the mind about the newness, which relaxes on later encounters.[75]

Gautama has a different theory about pleasure, and it is somewhat radical. He argues that pleasure *itself* is unsatisfactory: "The Blessed One . . . has stated that sensual pleasures are time-consuming, full of suffering, full of despair."[76] Pleasure is full of despair? What kind of sense does that make? According to Buddhism's subtle psychology, the cause of our suffering is not pleasure itself, but the fact that we cling to pleasure. So anytime that we experience something nice—which is said in the Buddhist canon to include just about everything, including the mere facts of being able to see, hear, feel, smell, taste, and think—it makes us want to experience it more.[77] In a way, in Buddhism, life has the potential to be *so* pleasurable that it overwhelms us. We crave it. We become addicted to it. So pleasure, *pace* Aristotle, is not complete in itself. Every time we experience it, we want more of it. That's why *dukkha* is better translated as "unsatisfactoriness," and why it has an important point about greatness: even in those moments where we think we have reached the top, the chain reaction of dissatisfaction will inevitably kick in. If we cling to greatness, we will keep trying to recreate and hold onto a feeling that we can never ultimately sustain.

Current evidence (not to mention our own experience) suggests that Gautama and not Aristotle got this one right. The evolutionary psychologist Robert Wright has written an engaging book—*Why Buddhism Is True* (2017)—about why this insight from Buddhism maps onto the effects of natural selection. If the aim of natural selection is to get us to propagate our genes, then it needs to do two things. First, we should get pleasure from activities that keep us alive and help us procreate. Second, these activities should leave us feeling a bit dissatisfied after and wanting more so that we keep trying.[78] Our very survival depends on our seeking satisfaction and then finding it unsatisfactory. The result is that we have become creatures who experience suffering that we foolishly try to cure with pleasures rather than acknowledging the impossibility of total satisfaction.

Wright thinks that "Buddhism is true" not only because it understood this basic problem, but also because it gave us a solution: mindfulness meditation. In the *Mahāsatipaṭṭhāna Sutta* (*The Greater Discourse on the Foundations of Mindfulness*), the Buddha lays out his argument about the cause *and* the cessation of suffering (what is known as the Four Noble Truths). The basic idea is that we can overcome our craving by following a series of ethical precepts and meditative activities. These meditations begin with a simple recognition that one is breathing in and out. One then follows this breathing through a series of steps and into one's daily activities like walking. The claim—and it seems to work pretty well in both classical and modern contexts[79]—is that by this focusing on what we are doing rather than the chain of our thoughts, we can become present and lose the grip of mourning for the lost pleasure or yearning for the future one.

At the conclusion of the *Sutta*, the Buddha seems to offer a glimpse of a feeling greater than what we have known as pleasure: "Having given up pleasure and pain, and with the disappearance of former gladness and sadness, he [the meditator] enters and remains in the fourth *jhāna* [the highest state of meditation], which is beyond pleasure and pain, and purified by equanimity and mindfulness."[80] That fourth *jhāna* certainly sounds like something better than the good-enough life! Indeed, in classical Buddhism, there appears to be no end to the tenacity with which people will meditate and practice in order to achieve the ultimate perfection—nirvana. And, in modern Buddhism, we get secularized versions of such ideas in figures like Watts—on the other side of enlightenment is a life free from anxiety, coupled with exquisite and otherwise unimaginable pleasures. Such claims are at the heart of what has led an entire generation of mindfulness meditators to think that Buddhism offers something like a great life, if only one can meditate enough. But this understanding takes Buddhism out of its broader soteriological (salvation-oriented) context. Steven Collins, one of the most important academic interpreters of the Pali Canon, repeatedly affirmed that, indeed, an individual could experience a remarkably good life within Buddhism. *But*, he cautioned, Buddhism is fundamentally not just about individuals. It is also about an entire system of interconnected persons who are the accrual of forces and processes that have spun around the universe for endless millennia (this is the meaning of "karma"). If *I* am a successful meditator and manage to diminish some of my personal suffering, that is all well and good. But "I" am not separable from the entire cycle of existence that has formed me and that continues to exist. What is at stake is not just your or my suffering, but suffering as such—the suffering of the universe. And that *cannot* end, because if it did, it would mean there would be no more life, because life itself is the product of unsatisfactoriness propelling us forward. The world, because it is the world, will always have elements of unsatisfactoriness, even if the concretion of causes that is our individual self is able to put them at bay.[81] Buddhism asks us to aspire to improve the world, even though the world can never be fully improved.

To return to where we began the discussion of Buddhism: this is why the critique of caste is related to the idea of unsatisfactoriness. For whether or not Buddhists have always fought back against caste, and despite the fact that they sometimes create hierarchical castes within their own formation, their canonical texts offer one of the most profound formulations of the good-enough life that I know. Life always has some elements of dissatisfaction. That dissatisfaction cannot be removed, but it can be ameliorated. And since I am connected to you, it is just as important for me to help you overcome your negative emotions as it is for me to overcome my own. And, furthermore, since our negative emotions are not just about our personal feelings but also the way that the world affects us, then improving the world itself—making sure it provides decency and sufficiency for everyone—is a necessary part of a good-enough life. The subtle art of this version of Buddhism is not about giving up our desires on the front end in order to receive them by an indirect route. It is about realizing that *even if this were to happen*, we could not remove the unsatisfactory parts of life. The subtle art of not giving a fuck can only help us so much, because it can only help our own individual psychologies, which are only a small part of who we are. We need a different kind of subtle art of what to strive for—one that is about giving a fuck about making a good-enough world.

Philosophies Born of Struggle

Aristotle was an aristocrat. Siddhartha Gautama was a prince. I was born to loving parents in a middle-class suburban US family. If one has lived a good life already, it may seem easier to think about living a good-enough one. But for people who have grown up in struggle, in poverty, in violence, in despair, does the good-enough life sound like somebody saying, "I had my run at the top, and it really stressed me out, so now I know nobody should have it"? Writer bell hooks has suggested that Buddhism often sounded this way to someone who, like herself, grew up in poverty, racism, and patriarchy in the US South. In an interview in the early 1990s, hooks discussed how many teachers talk about Buddhism as directed toward giving things up. She noted: "This has communicated that the teachings were for the materially privileged and those preoccupied with their own comforts. When other black people come to my house they say, 'Giving up what comforts?'"[82]

Nevertheless, hooks found meaning in Buddhist practices from teachers like Thich Nhat Hanh, a Vietnamese monk whose earliest writings on Buddhism were part of his response to the US invasion of his country. Nhat Hanh preached a form of "engaged Buddhism," in which Buddhism was not about disconnected meditation, but rather an ethic of activated compassion to diminish the anguish of modern warfare, politics, and economics. This modern Buddhism was not an eternal philosophy of the inevitable dissatisfaction of life. It was, to borrow a phrase from the African American philosopher Leonard Harris, a "philosophy born of struggle."[83] In her life and writings, hooks has combined Nhat Hanh's ideas with her own critiques of patriarchy, capitalism, and racism in order to develop an ethics of love and presence. This ethics helped ground her in the struggle against the damages of everyday life. She uses Buddhism as part of her work "making a world where all people can live fully and well, where everyone can belong."[84]

hooks is part of a long tradition of African American philosophy that criticizes the ideal of being an equal part of a corrupted US society. Rather than join in the pursuit of excess, leading African American thinkers like W.E.B. Du Bois implored Black Americans to be leaders in a different struggle. In fact, Du Bois argued, it was from the very position of having been marginalized in the United States that he and others could see the need to transform society so clearly. At the NAACP's 1926 conference, he offered one of the most finely worded critiques of greatness, and visions of the good-enough life, that I know:

> If you tonight suddenly should become full-fledged Americans; if your color faded, or the color line here in Chicago was miraculously forgotten; suppose, too, you became at the same time rich and powerful;—what is it that you would want? What would you immediately seek? Would you buy the most powerful of motor cars and outrace Cook County? Would you buy the most elaborate estate on the North Shore? Would you be a Rotarian or a Lion or a What-not of the very last degree? Would you wear the most striking clothes, give the richest dinners, and buy the longest press notices?
>
> Even as you visualize such ideals you know in your hearts that these are not the things you really want. You realize this sooner than the average white American because, pushed aside as we have been in America, there has come to us not only a certain distaste for the tawdry and flamboyant but a vision of what the world could be if it were really a beautiful world; if we had the true spirit; if we had the Seeing Eye, the Cunning Hand, the Feeling Heart; if we had, to be sure, not perfect happiness, but plenty of good hard work, the inevitable suffering that always comes with life; sacrifice and waiting, all that—but, nevertheless, lived in a world where men know, where men create, where they realize themselves and where they enjoy life. It is that sort of a world we want to create for ourselves and for all America.[85]

It is no mean thing for a prince to give up his privilege. But it is quite another for someone like Du Bois to be offered a seat at the head of the table and respond: "No thank you. This whole table and head-of-table thing is the problem in the first place." And Du Bois goes further still: he suggests that the history of oppression does not lead him to strive for greatness, but rather illuminates these other values. Linking his profound understanding of the inevitable tragedies of life to an appreciation of a creative and mutually caring response, Du Bois offered the history of struggle as a path toward good-enoughness. Of course, that Du Bois says this does not mean that he never felt the allure of greatness. We all feel the temptation at times. This allure manifested in his equivocations around the idea of "The Talented Tenth," or the belief that ten percent of Black men would uplift the rest of the race. As he wrote in 1903: "The Negro race, like all races, is going to be saved by its exceptional men."[86] Over the next few decades of his life, however, Du Bois began to sense the contrast between this position and his espousal of a good-enough life for all. In 1948, he gave a "revised" version of the Talented Tenth speech, in which he acknowledged that his ideas had been corrupted by an aristocratic elitism. He now saw that such elitism was more likely to produce men disconnected from the realities of the struggle than to actually uplift and equalize everyone else. Nevertheless, he continued to claim that centuries of oppression had limited the prospects for many talented youth who simply had not been given the proper opportunity. He said that he now believed that the main task for African American society was to develop a global alliance that could transform these political conditions so as to allow everyone to "work according to gift and training."[87] It would be led by a "Guiding Hundredth," a select committee of some 30,000 formerly colonized peoples worldwide whose aim would not be their own excellence, but the general welfare of all the world's peoples.[88] Coming out of conditions of oppression, Du Bois claims that some reliance on the top of the hierarchy may be necessary.

I have heard this meaningfully expressed in other contexts. After one public lecture I gave on the good-enough life, for example, a Black woman came up to me and said something to the effect of: "I appreciate what you're trying to do, but for Black people, especially Black women, we can't just be good enough. We have to be great." I quickly acknowledged the point but had my ready response: "I don't think this is just a White thing. We can find it in hooks, Du Bois, others. There are resources in Black thought . . ." She cut me off: "I'm not talking about Black thought. I'm talking about waking up every day as a Black woman." I didn't know how to respond then except to say that I would have to think about it.

I have kept my promise and have continued to think about this moment. I realize now even more deeply that my response was not good enough. I tried to have an answer rather than listening to what she was saying. I did not accept that my ideas would always need to be reformed as I listened carefully to others. I should have asked more questions. In retrospect, I do not think she was not advocating the system of greatness as a general goal. Rather, I hear her as making at least two points: one, that sometimes a struggle for equality requires people trying to rise to power to make change (a post-patriarchal version of Du Bois's Guiding Hundredth); two, that it is often a kind of White privilege to be able to succeed in society without giving every ounce of one's energy. BIPOC men and women, trans and nonbinary people, people of all races and genders living in extreme poverty, and people with disabilities frequently have more demanded of them than middle- and upper-class White men, to receive fewer rewards.[89] With respect to Black people in the United States, Ta-Nehisi Coates has powerfully noted the damage this does to normal human life: "Urging African-Americans to become superhuman is great advice if you are concerned with creating extraordinary individuals. It is terrible advice if you are concerned with creating an equitable society.

The black freedom struggle is not about raising a race of hyper-moral super-humans. It is about all people garnering the right to live like the normal humans they are."[90] I don't think, in other words, that she was defending the hierarchy: she was trying to get me to see that by not discussing racism in my talk, I was not doing enough to tear greatness down.

Heather McGhee has brilliantly made an argument along these lines in *The Sum of Us* (2021). There she shows, in instance after instance, how racism has undone the United States' ability to provide a decent life for all of its citizens. Her central example is public swimming pools. Cities once vied to create ever more beautiful and elaborate pools, some reputedly able to hold up to 10,000 people.[91] After civil rights advocates sued to integrate these pools, however, cities shut them down rather than allow everyone to swim. This is largely forgotten or unknown by most Americans today—including, until I read her book, me. McGhee argues that this explicit racism similarly went underground, and increasingly manifested itself as "colorblind" opposition to public goods. The lack of decency and sufficiency for all, she shows, was frequently the result of racism. As James Baldwin once put it: "The price of liberation of the white people is the liberation of the blacks—the total liberation, in the cities, in the towns, before the law, and in the mind."[92] Achieving such liberation may mean that, in an unequal world, people who have been oppressed, devalued, and marginalized will feel compelled to strive for greatness—to be atop the pyramid—as a means not of uplift, but of mere survival. But as Coates says, this is a condition of oppression, *not* a normative goal.

While we learn from good-enough philosophies born of struggle that conditions of oppression sometimes force us to change metrics for individual striving, they also provide a warning against allowing those changed metrics to stray too far from the good-enough ideal. Often this lesson has come from Black women writers who have had to respond to male leaders claiming their own greatness. In 1886, for example, Anna Julia Cooper noted that Martin Delany, a leading abolitionist and writer, had sometimes claimed that he was the representative of his people, and thus when he entered a room the "whole Negro race" entered with him. Cooper wrote that this was like saying, "by pointing to sun-bathed mountain tops do we prove that Phoebus warms the valleys." If we wanted to see the condition of the race, we had to look to the average working people: "then and not until then will the whole plateau be lifted into the sunlight." She then gave her famous retort to Delany's claim: "Only the BLACK WOMAN can say 'when and where I enter, in the quiet, undisputed dignity of my womanhood, without violence and without suing or special patronage, then and there the whole Negro race enters with me.'"[93]

A century later, in a 1970 interview about her role in the Civil Rights Movement, the organizer Ella Baker suggested that the great leader model similarly limited the progress of that movement. "I have always felt it was a handicap for oppressed peoples to depend so largely upon a leader," she said, because the leader was often chosen more by the media than by the people.[94] This meant that the media could just as quickly crush the leader, and also that the leader could easily become disconnected from the movement. On the ground, while men are usually credited with leading the fight for equality, "the movement of the '50's and '60's was carried largely by women."[95] Baker placed her hope in future leaders: "Every time I see a young person who . . . could profit from the system . . . but who identifies more with the struggle of black people who had not had his chance . . . I take new hope."[96]

Baker might have taken heart in young leaders today like adrienne maree brown, who cites this interview from Baker in

her own "Confessions of a Charismatic Leader in Recovery."
brown lives in an era where a young, queer woman of color like
herself can take the kind of leadership role that in Cooper's and
Baker's times was largely reserved for men. brown quickly dis-
covered that the attraction of being a charismatic leader—she
calls it "charismitis"—can be powerful to anybody, regardless
of their background or social identity.[97] It is an affliction that
anyone can catch if given the opportunity. But it remains different for those coming from different positions. brown explains that when she first got recognized, it was "healing . . .
I went from being a nerdy fat girl in glasses to a fabulous! brilliant! badass! nerdy fat girl in glasses."[98] All the same, the healing eventually faded and was replaced with anxiety, burnout,
and separation from the movement's goals in the work of maintaining her own status. brown notes that when dealing with
funders or large gatherings, she still uses her charisma, but she
has used her awareness of it to ensure that her skills remain
part of the movement's resources to help develop decency for
all, rather than part of her own story of uplift into greatness.
She summarizes the lessons: "I am socialized to seek achievement alone, to try to have the best idea. . . . But that leads to
loneliness and, I suspect, extinction. If we are all trying to win,
no one really ever wins."[99]

One risk in the game of greatness is that, if you win, you will
begin to justify your place atop the hierarchy. When Martin
Luther King began thinking about a universal guaranteed income later in his life, he was, in spite of his own success, attempting to ensure that he helped lead a movement beyond
greatness. As he put it: "The contemporary tendency in our
society is . . . to compress our abundance into the overfed
mouths of the middle and upper classes until they gag with su-
perfluity. If democracy is to have breadth of meaning, it is

necessary to adjust this inequity. It is not only moral, but it is also intelligent. We are wasting and degrading human life."[100]

The path to ending this waste and degradation of life will be different for everyone. As the differences across personal histories discussed in this chapter have shown, good-enough striving is not an absolute universal position. It will mean different things for different people, and our paths to it will also be diverse. But as these writers have reminded us, each path is part of a broader mission, to repeat hooks's phrase, of "making a world where all people can live fully and well, where everyone can belong."[101]

Making this world where everyone belongs also means raising questions about how we treat each other interpersonally. How does a good-enough orientation in one's own life lead one to treat others differently? What does a good-enough relationship look like? Can good-enoughness as a normative horizon meaningfully transform both our sense of self-worth and our capacities for love and care for others? In the next chapter I argue that to create a world in which good-enoughness flourishes, we have to look at the cultural norms that create and sustain greatness culture, and how these are contested by good-enough visions of interpersonal relationships.

3

For Our Relationships

It can be awkward to talk to friends and family about my work on a book about the good-enough life. They understand the principle and the values, but, they insist, I can't possibly be referring to *all* aspects of life. Aren't they "better than good-enough" friends and loved ones? How would it sound if someone asked about my wife and I responded, "She's good enough"? The person would probably think that I had "settled" in my marriage for a mediocre relationship, and they might even pity me.

Such a colloquial conception of good-enoughness is not what I am talking about here. Indeed, a good-enough life that meets our social and emotional needs should be understood rather expansively. For example, the philosopher Kimberly Brownlee, building on the work by Baumeister and Leary about the need to belong that I mentioned in chapter 1, offers a long list of such needs, including "physical closeness, caring touch . . . interactional inclusion, interactive play, physical and mental protection . . . companionship, persistent association, and meaningful opportunities to sustain the people we care about."[1] Good-enough relationships in this sense, then, are those that are good (they promise meaningful and robust connections between persons); that are enough (our essential needs and yearnings from each other are met); and that are good enough (we have the capacity to appreciate how much everyday acts of care matter more than grand gestures, and have the creative adaptability to survive and even thrive together in the midst of inevitable tragedy, betrayal, or ordinary unrequited desire).

Brownlee offers further important insights into the nature of good-enough relationships. She speaks of relationships and time as resources that can be as poorly distributed as any other. This can happen, for example, if everyone wants to hang out with the same person, or if everyone decides that they want to avoid a given person. Brownlee encourages us to see that everyone has something meaningful to contribute to social life, and that excluding someone has deleterious effects both on that individual and on social relationships more broadly.[2] The problem she describes is much like what I think we see in greatness-oriented thinking more broadly: too many social resources (attention and care especially) go to too few people, while the possible contributions of the many are ignored. Bringing in those people does not mean that we will suddenly have an endlessly satisfying social life. Indeed, some part of our lives is now and always will be spent in the company of people whom we do not particularly enjoy being around. While cruelty in relationships should never be excused, the need to provide a degree of care for people we don't always care to spend time with is simply part of inhabiting a social world.[3]

When we seek greatness for ourselves, we are trying to become maximized individuals who are the best at whatever we do not for its own sake, or because it contributes to the general welfare, but because it secures us a place atop any given social hierarchy. I have suggested that this desire in fact works against us—creating undue burdens and anxieties, forcing us into metrics that don't match our own worth, and depriving us of the ability to grow our capacities for ordinary decency and cooperation. When we seek greatness in our relationships, it means that we are imposing these same pressures on both our intimate partners and the relationships themselves. That is to say, the greatness model gets doubled: we push our spouse or child or friend to make it to the top of the pyramid, and we want our relationship with them to be considered as the most socially desirable. We don't just want to be best friends with the best person; we want to have the best possible kind of best-friend relationship. In so doing, we make too little room for appreciating our differences and limitations.

Greatness manifests differently in ourselves and in our relationships, but in both instances it is the product of a world that teaches us that in order to overcome suffering, we should value rising to the top above all else. And, in the other direction, visions of perfection in our relationships can seem to justify hierarchical social orders. If we think of our love life as a quest to find the most perfect, absolute, best match, then what is to stop us from thinking that we should also find such things in ourselves, in our job, in our homes, in our society, or from our natural world? Although these kinds of pursuits of greatness are distinct, they feed into each other.

The pursuit of greatness manifests in our relationships in different ways depending on the kind of relationship we are talking about. In parent-child relations, for example, a greatness-orientation is about making our children into people who strive for winning in the social hierarchy and positional economy. We want our children to achieve positions in the world that reward them within the competitive system. In so doing, we try to become great parents who will do absolutely anything for our children so that they can be the best. The trouble is that when we try to be great parents, we put too many pressures on ourselves and create unrealistic expectations for our children; and further, we disrupt other people's abilities to make their own good-enough lives. When an ambitious teenager hears that the father down the street sleeps four hours a night so that he can use the extra time to teach his son Latin and the viola so he can get into Harvard, she may wonder why her own decent, caring, and attentive father is so selfish as to insist on getting a full night's sleep.[4] Meanwhile, when the child down the street still doesn't get into Harvard because too many of the thousands of applicants also know Latin and are star viola players, he will likely be unprepared for the crushing blow to his expectations. Even though the young man will by most accounts still lead a fantastically privileged life, both father and child will feel themselves to be failures.

What's worse is that, even if either child *does* get in to Harvard, how could they possibly live up to all the expectations now heaped on them for greatness? Their lives—like all lives—can be no better than good enough, no freer of accident or tragedy, no less blemished by the contingencies of errors and catastrophes not their own making. They will have no resources for this, no way to cope when, late at night, in their well-appointed home, the panic for perfection pushes them to take yet another sleeping pill to quiet the voices in their head ceaselessly demanding improvement.[5]

Many of us know that the stress and anxiety we place on our relationships is part of the whole set of problems fueled today by greatness culture. And as with how we treat ourselves, we know that part of the problem is that we have hollowed out the middle. If we are not the best parent or lover, we can come to think of ourselves as the worst one. But we don't have to choose between seeking Prince Charming and "Mr. OK, I guess," or between the perfect father and the dad who deigns to occasionally drive us to soccer practice, or the friend who would give their life for ours and the one who remembers to call and say hi every two years or so. We can offer an entirely different goal: to act toward our loved ones in such a way as to enable both them and us to promote and participate in a good-enough world.

Instead of the mutually destructive arms-race of parenting (or the parallels in friendship and love), we can reimagine the types of people we want to be for each other. We can realize that being the good-enough parent or friend or lover is difficult and unparalleled in its offering. If I have been a good-enough friend or lover or son in my life, it is when I have managed to resist the various temptations of greatness. I have given what I can of myself without doing so much that I burn out. I have accepted the failings of my loved ones and been open and honest about my own limitations. I have recognized those moments when more than ordinary care is called for, and I have been able to ask for or offer extra attention without expectation of incessant increase. I have not imagined that I alone have the perfect solution to every problem we confront, but a humble position that will only be meaningful if it speaks to everyone's needs and concerns. I have encouraged those around me to find meaning and purpose in creating a good-enough world for all, not seeking to get a piece of greatness for themselves.

I fear, as I write this brief list, that I have often failed, succumbing to the temptations of greatness. Greatness in relationships is a tortuous dance of imbalanced passions. It is a seesaw of excessive energies that leave each person overworked, overexpectant, and inevitably unfulfilled. Good-enoughness in relationships, on the other hand, is an imperfect harmony of pleasant connections and mild mishaps. It leaves each person energetic, respectful, and feeling appreciated and cared for. If I say that my family relations, or my friendships, or my marriage, is good enough, I am being so bold as to claim that we have managed, enough of the time, to be these kinds of people for each other.

Romantic Stories

In the previous chapter I used the history of philosophy to help me think through how individuals can understand themselves in relation to the goal of good-enoughness. In this chapter, I use a variety of stories—personal, literary, and cinematic. Why stories? Because how we think about relationships and the kinds of parents, friends, and partners that we want to be comes, in part, through the stories we are told and tell ourselves about how people should treat each other. Like philosophies, these stories will change over time, and their meanings will transform as we confront them in different contexts. I want to understand how storytelling can help us see the problems with aiming for greatness in our relationships, and the values of achieving good-enough ones.

In his essay "The Storyteller" (1936), Walter Benjamin suggested that part of what storytelling does is to "provide counsel." But, he warned, we cannot simply go to stories for such wisdom. There is a kind of paradox at the heart of receiving wisdom from storytelling: "Counsel is less an answer to a question than a proposal concerning the continuation of a story which is just unfolding. To seek this counsel one would first have to be able to tell the story."[6] In other words, we can only hear the wisdom of the story if we are able to narrate our own lives in the first place. If we do not know where we find ourselves, we will have no way to incorporate the wisdom we receive into our lives. We need to analyze the stories we are telling ourselves in order to open up to new possibilities.

I know this to be true from my own past. I used to tell myself a story about how my parents' divorce when I was very young affected my desire to be in a relationship when I got older. Throughout much of my life, I had an intense—and annoying to my friends—desire to be in a relationship. I always interpreted it as an attempt to heal the fracture of the divorce. And so I kept getting into relationships too soon and staying in them too long, even when it was clear that they would not last. I would do everything in my power to keep from breaking the relationship apart. It was a fantasy of my own greatness as a partner, a belief that I could be so wonderful that I could heal the obvious failures of my connection to someone. I have, for example, an embarrassing memory of a time when a partner betrayed me. I told her on the spot that I forgave her—and then asked, almost in the same breath, if that made me her best partner ever.

The inaccurate story I was telling myself is well described by the philosopher Alain de Botton in his writing on love. He argues that many of us are stuck in "the Romantic idea . . . that a perfect being exists who can meet all our needs and satisfy our every yearning." Equally, I would add, we sometimes imagine ourselves as just such a perfect being. De Botton encourages people to swap this view for a "tragic (and at points comedic) awareness that every human will frustrate, anger, annoy, madden and disappoint us—and we will (without any malice) do the same to them."[7] By telling myself a Romantic story about myself and the kind of relationship I could create, I was blocking myself off from this wisdom about the limits of any relationship. Throughout the relationship-craving stage of my life, friends tried to give me counsel about either my general attitude or the particular relationship I was in. But because I had a bad story—a faulty narrative about what I was looking for—I could not receive that counsel.

But, you might say, isn't falling in love supposed to be one of those perfect moments in one's life? Aren't we meant to be struck by Cupid's arrow and get pulled out of our narrow selves and into the grandeur of union? This was another story I was telling myself. It is an old one. We can see it in Plato's *Symposium* (fourth century BCE), for example. One interlocutor, Aristophanes, tells a myth (with echoes of the story of Babel) of how humans were once androgynous orbs who were growing too large and powerful for the gods, and so Zeus cut them in half. We are all now these halved souls. A few of us are so lucky as to reunite with our other half. These are the people who are so bounded to each other that they would prefer to be melted into one and go into the afterlife as a single soul.[8] The Roman poet Ovid (first century CE) tells a version of this story in the myth of Baucis and Philemon, two humble landowners who offer excessive generosity to two anonymous travelers, who turn out to be the gods Zeus and Hermes. In return (with echoes of the biblical story of Noah), the gods spare the couple from a flood, and later allow them to die in the same instant, bound together as they become perpetually blossoming trees.[9] A decent gloss of these myths can be found in the phrase made famous by the movie *Jerry Maguire* (1996): "You complete me." Who could not want to find a love like this?

The journalist Lori Gottlieb, for one. In her book *Marry Him: The Case for Settling for Mr. Good Enough*, Gottlieb comes to terms with what her search for the perfect mate has left her: she has wound up perpetually dissatisfied and alone. As she looks back on her dating life, she sees that she passed up on a number of perfectly good men in search of "the one." And she finds that she is not alone. Interviewing other women her age, she discovers that most of them believe they would be happier now if they had just married that nice guy they met through a friend a decade ago, instead of blowing him off for a one-night stand with the sexiest person at the party. Gottlieb concludes: "Marriage isn't a passion-fest; it's more like a partnership formed to run a very small, mundane, and often boring non-profit business. And I mean this in a good way."[10] Or as Bridget Fonda's character says in the 1992 film *Singles*: She just wants someone who says "bless you or at least gesundheit" when she sneezes.

As she was writing her book, Gottlieb came across the research of Paul Amato, a sociologist who coined the concept of the "good-enough marriage." Amato has shown that divorce rates are highest not among people who really hate each other, but among people who think that they are just missing a bit of spark. These people tend to divorce, remarry, and then find themselves dissatisfied yet again. Average divorce rates for second marriages are thus higher, and third marriages higher still. Moreover, unlike children of actually bad marriages who suffered through the heartbreak and anger, children of sparkless-driven divorces tend to suffer higher rates of depression, and similar misguided hopes for their own relationships. The evidence would seem to suggest clearly: if you rate your marriage a 7 or 8, then you're doing as well as one can, and if you can't find satisfaction there, you won't find it anywhere.[11]

But as Gottlieb also notes, settling itself is not a particularly clear concept. Even once she commits to settling for Mr. Good Enough, she still wonders, *Maybe I can settle for better.*[12] The ambivalence here strikes at the heart of why we need a more robust understanding of what "good enough" actually means. Is there something between settling for a guy who meets the basest criteria of saying "bless you" and someone to whom you are so perfectly fitted that you are literally the other half of your partner's soul?

We can start by going back to the stories in Plato and Ovid. I certainly think that part of a good-enough relationship means we will feel this intense desire for oneness *some of the time*. There are times when I hug my wife and it feels so completing—to use Jerry Maguire's language—that I never want to let go. I will even, in a cute mood, whisper "merge." But the truth, of course, is that neither of us wants to merge. Neither of us wants to give up our individuality, our alone time, our different interests or friends or pursuits. What makes our marriage work is not that we want to merge in perfection. It's that we know when to say such merging is enough; we've had this beautiful moment, and, OK, now we have other elements of our lives to explore.

The problem with most romantic theories of love is that they ignore time. I don't just mean what marriage counselors call the "natural ebb and flow of lasting relationships," that is, the ways in which healthy relationships go through cycles that relate, in part, to different chemical processes in our brain.[13] I mean that romantic love stories exist at the level of legend rather than history. I take this distinction from the literary critic Erich Auerbach, who explains it as follows: "[Legend] runs far too smoothly. All cross-currents, all friction, all that is casual, secondary to the main events and themes, everything unresolved, truncated, and uncertain, which confuses the clear progress of the action and the simple orientation of the actors, has disappeared. The historical event which we witness . . . runs much more variously, contradictorily, and confusedly."[14] When we think about the moment of melting together in Plato, we forget about all the little skirmishes along the way—the bad tempers aroused by too little sleep, the inability to read a glance or grimace, the distraction that causes us to ignore a plea for aid. And because we have a vision of perfection that contradicts such realities, we grow frustrated by them and neglect to treat them as the pedagogic events that they are. There are limits, to be sure, to how much we can reduce our irritability when exhausted, but we can certainly improve our ability to recognize exhaustion and not our partner as the cause. But to do so, we have to study our relationships as histories, not legends: full of miscues, mistakes, and melioration, not limitless oneness.

This is what it means to settle for better. It is not "good enough" in the sense of running a boring business together. That goes too far from legend and too much into the doldrums of history. We need a bit of both in our love. We need some grandeur and ecstasy (the good; or, OK, the really good), but we also need some everyday care and concern (the enough). And we also need to appreciate that we are not everything for our partners, and nor are they for us.[15] We need to be good enough for each other, and accepting of each other's good-enoughness. It is only this that allows us moments of wonder while still enabling the meaningfulness of our own strivings to flourish.

A Circular Journey

The philosopher Todd May, who was one of the key philosophical inspirations of *The Good Place*, has argued that being ethical requires this recognition that both we and other people have meaningful lives to lead. Following this code leads to what he calls a "decent life," which is not too dissimilar from what I am describing in this book.[16] Good-enough relationships work hard to balance the needs generated by what makes life meaningful for each individual involved. Greatness-oriented parents, focusing on something supposedly much better than a decent life, sometimes forget this.

About a decade ago, the difficulty of learning this balance was the subject of Amy Chua's controversial memoir, *The Battle Hymn of the Tiger Mother* (2011). In the book, Chua detailed her experiences as a parent between two cultures: what she loosely calls the "Chinese" and "Western" models. (She acknowledges the limitations of the cultural stereotypes to some extent.) According to Chua, in the Chinese model, academic excellence and virtuoso musical performance are the sole goals of childhood, and daily hours of practice, insults, and harsh punishments are necessary means to these fabulous ends. In the Western model, the child's enjoyment and emotional well-being are prioritized; if they come out great at something, that's wonderful, but if not, well, no biggie. Chua further clarifies that even the more greatness-oriented Western models don't meet Chinese standards. If you want your kid to be the best at tennis or even just generally "self-optimized," you're missing the point. Chinese parents are not interested in how the child thinks about their optimization. They're interested in what they know are the best things for their children to be, and they will stop at nothing to override the laziness of their children and propel them to meet the parents' academic standards. (The only areas in which it is OK not to be the best in class are "gym and drama."[17]) This is parenting greatness on steroids: not only does the child have to be the best and the parents be endlessly dedicated to their child's perfection, but all children must meet a singular metric for greatness.

When Chua's book came out, it was first released as a selection in *The Wall Street Journal* that, in order to garner publicity, focused on the most unpleasant aspects of her parenting—things that many readers considered abusive. Nevertheless, her memoir was not a celebration of all the things she did; it was a "battle hymn," and it was a battle that she had lost. She had gone to war with her daughters over how to make them the kind of people who sit atop the social pyramid, and she had found that her attempts hit a furious wall of rebellion in her younger daughter, Lulu. In the book's climactic scene, the family is on vacation in Russia and Chua insists her daughter try the caviar. Her refusal to do so leads to an explosion of anger in which all the pressures of the childhood are exposed. Lulu says that she hates her mother and all that she has done. She shatters a glass in the fancy restaurant, embarrassing Chua and leading her to run out of the restaurant. But she returns after having an epiphany that there is a limit to "Chinese" parenting, one that, ironically, she comes to admit was the lesson of her own father, who had moved to the United States to get away from his own parents. She did not want to repeat this exile with her own daughters. It was her eventual realization that led many readers to defend Chua. They understood that she didn't come to praise her own parenting, but to bury it.

This shift in tone, however, only reflects a transformation of Chua's method, not what she takes to be the goals of her parenting. She tells us at the end of her story that she still wants her daughters to be wildly successful; she just doesn't want them to hate her in the process. And as should be obvious from the fact that many people don't have relentlessly pushy parents, there is no real correlation between method and end. It is true that some children, like Sophia, the older daughter, will excel because they were pushed, while others will rebel in furious anger, like Lulu. And some children will excel precisely because their parents did not push them, and they, in the context of a culture that only rewards greatness, rebel against their parents' own acceptance of an "ordinary" life.

The question we should ask about Chua's parenting or any other parenting is not just what kinds of rewards and punishments it uses (although these of course really matter), but what exactly its goals are. The unfortunate assumption is often that there is no option between pushing children to maximal success and being completely absent. We have not yet culturally embraced Winnicott's insight about the good-enough parent: that although it reduces the burdens of perfection, it is still a difficult and demanding mode of raising children. It requires us to practice a kind of discipline that is as foreign to Chua as it is to an absentee parent: to be able to both give enough *and* withhold enough from our children. In this complicated balancing act, our children learn an ethics other than the single-minded pursuit of their own success. They learn that ordinary pleasures matter, that cooperation is difficult and fundamental, that joy and tragedy are copartners in existence, that we need to be creative and adaptable because the path is not always set out for us, that we need to learn to appreciate people who have different gifts and virtues, that success at math or writing or piano-playing is but one metric of human accomplishment, that we should not pursue our own goals at the expense of others, that the privileges we have bind us to a social contract to help others achieve them, that the unnecessary pains we suffer bind us to a social contract to ensure that no one else has to suffer them.

I am very glad that Chua opened up to her daughter's needs and helped teach other parents to do the same. But the point of giving and receiving counsel from stories is that we can only properly hear it if our own story is in the right place. Since Chua's story is still framed by the opposition between success and failure, the counsel she receives and the counsel she offers readers gets stuck at the level of method. The choice is not between being a Chinese parent or a Western parent. It's between teaching your children that the narrative of life is a story of winners and losers, or that it is about the struggle to ensure decency and sufficiency for all.

A Theory of Laughter

While the path to perfection is strewn with fights and tears, the good-enough life sometimes offers a more humorous route to decency. I have said that the good-enough life requires us to appreciate some degree of tragedy and difficulty in our relationships, and that it understands that good enough is all that life can offer. But it would be a mistake and a profound misunderstanding to overlook the comedic and joyous aspects that this other way of living makes possible. I would even say that the realization of the good enough may be one of the reasons we laugh.

One common theory of laughter, often traced to a 1709 essay by Lord Shaftesbury, is what is called the "relief theory." According to humor theorist John Morreall, "The Relief Theory is an hydraulic explanation in which laughter does in the nervous system what a pressure-relief valve does in a steam boiler."[18] Laughter allows us to release psychic energy that is otherwise burdensome on our minds. Perhaps the foremost exponent of this idea of humor was Sigmund Freud. According to Freud, humor allows for a release of psychic energy. In one example, he tells a story from Mark Twain about his brother. Twain's brother, according to the story, was working on a railroad project and got blown into the sky in an explosion. The punchline: when he came back down, he was docked half a day's pay. According to Freud, we laugh at this because the first part of the story sets up an emotional debt—to pity Twain's brother—that we are immediately released from when it proves to be a humorous story. Laughter is the expression of the release of this psychic debt.[19] This is how Freud, perhaps not surprisingly, understands the relation between sexual repression and jokes. Sexual humor creates a situation in which we no longer have to feel inhibited to repress our sexuality. It is not so much that the joke releases our sexual impulses as that it releases the energy we have been spending repressing them. Not part of Freud's theory, though I think it fits rather well, is that laughter may also express the feeling when we are released from the psychic energy that we have bound up with ascending to greatness.

Will Ferrell and Adam McKay's Hollywood film *Talladega Nights: The Ballad of Ricky Bobby* (2006) offers a good example of this lesson. *Talladega Nights* is the story of a racecar driver, played by Ferrell, who becomes one of the greatest Nascar drivers in the sport's history. Ricky's story is almost the opposite of Chua's daughters. His father, Reese, is completely absent from his life. He only returns briefly and somewhat randomly for his son's "career day" at school when Ricky is about ten years old. He comes in full of bravado and gives a rousing speech to the class about being cool. He insults the teacher, however, and gets thrown out. Before he abandons his son yet again, he turns around and gives Ricky the mantra that will guide his life: "If you ain't first, you're last." (Not too dissimilar from Chua's rule that her daughters always "be the #1 student in every subject except gym and drama.")

Ricky's lifelong quest is fueled (pardon the pun) by this logic. In every race he either finishes first, or finishes last by crashing while trying. (Ricky's dad's attitude is almost the opposite of Chua's, but he ironically has the same effect on his child.) Eventually a new driver comes along to defeat Ricky—a French racer played at a high pitch by Sacha Baron Cohen, who drinks macchiatos and reads Camus's *The Stranger* while he speeds away from the pack. Jean's victory and the spiral of doom produced by being second leads Ricky to lose his wife, his job, and his best friend. Ricky moves back home, where his mother recruits his father to come back into his life to help him recover his tenacity. Ricky confronts his dad about his mantra of being first or last and how it ruined his life. His dad responds with perfect comedic timing: "Aw hell, Ricky, I was high when I said that. That doesn't make any sense at all. . . . You could be second, you could be third, you could be fourth. Hell, you could even be fifth!"

This moment is not immediately so funny for Ricky, who is momentarily even more traumatized by the revelation that he's lived his life based on a nonsensical thing his dad said while high. But there is humor here for the viewer, whose energy has been bound up with the idea that Ricky's redemption means his becoming number one again. Eventually he, too, will realize the folly of this. Part of what's funny in this scene is simply the mistake of taking seriously a ridiculous thing that someone said on drugs. But there is also the moment of release from the demand of greatness: Ricky can now be redeemed not by winning, but by learning how to live without being number one. Laughing at the folly of greatness is one of the great joys of the good-enough life. That's why, as the comedian Larry David might say, the life we are seeking is "pretty, pretty, pretty . . . good."

The Paradoxes of Kindness to Strangers

In the poem "Famous," Naomi Shibab Nye writes: "I want to be famous to shuffling men / who smile while crossing streets, sticky children in grocery lines, / famous as the one who smiled back."[20] I can imagine Nye, or the person she is writing about, standing in line. She has had a harried day, teaching in the gig economy, raising her children, trying to find time to write. She has a few strands of patience left, and she is in a rush to get home and eat at last. She is in a slow-moving line with an underpaid and undervalued clerk, who, if she were writing during an event like the COVID-19 pandemic, would be putting herself at great risk simply to make everyone else's necessary shopping possible. A child has ripped open the candy they have been told not to touch. Perhaps they are spreading the virus. The lollipop sticks to their face. They do not understand the insane pressures and fears of the moment. They look up at Nye. Her psychic tension can break in one of two ways. She can explode: she can funnel her anger over her own condition at the child or the mother or the clerk. Or she can laugh: she can release the energy she has been holding in as she pushes herself to strive, to write, to be famous. Somehow, by some remarkable power of turning her life toward ordinary decency and care, by seeing that *yes*, this is actually funny, she manages the strength to smile back.

It is unfortunate to have to think of smiling back at a child as some kind of extraordinary achievement. But such small acts of interpersonal care become increasingly difficult in a greatness-oriented culture. This has a powerful impact on our general sociability. If we are all striving to be great and ignoring the ordinary interactions that constitute the bulk of our lives, we are going to be less friendly to others—both to our most intimate acquaintances and to those we do not know but with whom we share the world.

In 1973, two psychologists at Princeton University, John Darley and Daniel Batson, published the results of an oft-cited experiment with students at Princeton Theological Seminary. Darley and Batson wanted to test the "Good Samaritan" parable in the Gospel of Luke, in which a man is left on the side of the road by a priest and a Levite but helped by a Samaritan—a member of a group of religious outsiders. Darley and Batson theorize that the priest and the Levite may have been too preoccupied with religious matters to help, whereas the Samaritan was, according to them, probably not thinking about such things because "Samaritans were religious outcasts."[21] We should probably be somewhat suspicious of our authors, because there is no logical connection between being an outcast and not thinking about religion. But Darley and Batson, at any rate, offer another explanation: that the Samaritan, as less important in the community's life, probably had more time. This is also a somewhat dubious claim, but, in any case, it leads them to two possible hypotheses for why someone might be a good Samaritan or not: the content of their thought, and how much of a hurry they are in.

To test which explanation might be the prevailing factor, Darley and Batson gave some students from the Seminary an assignment: to go give a lecture across campus on the parable of the Good Samaritan. On the route, they placed a man in some visible distress (bent over, coughing, etc.) to see if the lecturers would stop to help him. And they added the key variable: some of the students were told they were late for their lecture, some of them were told they had a bit of leeway, and others were told that they had plenty of time. The results are staggering: 63 percent of the low-hurry theologians stopped to help, whereas 45 percent of the intermediate and only 10 percent of the running-late ones did.[22] It appeared to make little difference what the content of their thoughts were. Even those who said they had gone to the seminary to help others tended to speed past when they were told they were late.

But Darley and Batson do not tell us anything about those 10 percent who *do* stop. What leads one out of every ten to break the pattern of rushing over helping? Here Darley and Batson's original interpretation of the story may be of some interest: the priest and the Levite are of a different social class than the Samaritan. Studies over the past half-century have consistently shown that people living in poverty are more likely to engage in acts of direct mutual aid than those with wealth.[23] Is it possible that the nine in ten were simply not acculturated into mutual aid, while the one student was? Darley and Batson didn't ask, so we'll never know.

But this explanation does not seem entirely satisfactory either. Around the same time that Darley and Batson were performing their study, a set of social economists that included Roy Harrod, Staffan Linder, and Fred Hirsch were puzzling over a curious fact: growing affluence was decreasing available leisure time.[24] This was puzzling, because the assumption had been that as economies grew and people became wealthier, they would have more time for leisure. What the economists found instead was that people were working harder than ever. They offered two mutually reinforcing mechanisms as explanations. First, increased opportunities for consumption meant increased pressure on maximizing consumption. If there is so much to potentially enjoy, how do we know what to enjoy? One might think today of trying to decide what to watch on a streaming service such as Netflix (or which streaming service to subscribe to in the first place). There are so many choices, and because of our limited free time we feel pressure to maximize our choices by watching the best material available. This is what the psychologist Barry Schwartz calls the "paradox of choice": choice makes us freer up to the point at which it paralyzes us.[25] This first tendency is further compounded by the second development: as economies increasingly tend toward winner-take-all models in which there is ever greater pressure to make it to the top or fall to the bottom, leisure time is forced to compete with labor time. Even as someone might be struggling to decide what to watch on Netflix, they are also having half-thoughts about stocks they should have bought if they could afford them

(Netflix, obviously), or jobs they wish they had. And that's even if they make it to the couch at all. People at the top of the economy are working ever longer hours to maintain their social status, while those at the bottom are working ever more jobs in ever more hazardous conditions. The two factors keep pressuring each other: we work harder to get more leisure time, which is self-negating, and so we have less leisure time, which we put more pressure on to be as enjoyable as possible. In the language of this book: the quest for economic greatness and the quest for maximal leisure may make some wealthy, but it makes most people miserable.

What does all this have to do with Darley and Batson's study? Hirsch explains that unlike the general give and take of friendship, the benefits of coming to a stranger's aid are less immediate for the individual. Caring social actions—such as giving to the homeless on the street—have small piecemeal costs, but few immediate and obvious returns to the giver (which may be part of why those with fewer means are more likely to give— they are more likely to expect to be in a position of needing aid). But, Hirsch points out, this need for immediate return misses the point: "all individuals gain more from the minority of transactions in which they benefit than from the majority in which they lose on a piecemeal basis, [thus] there is a failure in organization."[26] In other words, even if we only benefit once in our lives from the kindness of a stranger, it will likely be worth more to us than what we lost giving out a dollar (or whatever we could afford to do) every time we were asked. What is meant to solve this error of organization is morality: "The Good Samaritan remedies a market failure."[27]

But there's the rub. A paradox of tragic proportions emerges: winner-take-all societies produce more and more losers, who, in turn, need more mutual aid, but, because everyone is caught up in the winner-take-all racket, no one is there or willing to help. So around the same time as the Princeton Theological Seminary experiment that asked no questions about class or economic pressure and its accompanying pursuit of positional goods (being at the top pulpit in the country, for example), there was developing a powerful socioeconomic logic to explain the very phenomenon they were trying to unravel. It is not just that being in a hurry as such has a transhistorical effect on our willingness to help. It is that in certain social conditions—such as the very unequal conditions against which Jesus inveighed, or the very unequal conditions that have been growing for the past few decades—interpersonal kindness diminishes within a sector of the population (and perhaps the class sector of the population that is most likely to attend a place like Princeton Theological Seminary). As we will see in the next chapter, this is a paradox that bedevils much modern conservative thought: even as it enjoins us to practice Good Samaritan ethics, it is trapped by an economic logic that rips the possibility of embodying such an ethical stance out from under our feet.[28]

To Heaven or A-fishing

The economy is not, however, the only site of the trouble with greatness that concerns us here. If we move from strangers to friends, we can see that other forms of greatness-pressure complicate our ability to engage meaningfully with each other. As a writer, I know all too well that perfecting one's craft can be such a pressure. When I am writing intensely, I am not a particularly good friend or partner. I am irritable when distracted and often lost in thought. Perhaps, you might say, this is the cost of doing something well.

A writing teacher who was encouraging me to be even more diligent about my language told me the following story about a writer. (I remember it being Flaubert, but I haven't been able to find the story anywhere.) The writer is asked by an interviewer what he did that day. He says: "In the morning I put a hyphen in a word. And in the afternoon I took it out." While the story was told to me as being about the pursuit of perfection, I see it now as an allegory of the futility of greatness. This writer literally spends a day attempting to perfect their writing so much that they effectively do nothing.

But this is not the only problem in this story, or in my own fixations on writing. In being so fixated on a hyphen, what has our great writer missed? What other insights have passed them by? What joys or moments with friends? What kinds of anxieties and absurdities have been created in their pursuit of perfection? And what are *we* as readers passing up—what noncanonical writers and stories have gotten lost? How can we hear of the meaningful lives of those who didn't perfect their use of hyphens, but did tell us a story that we could learn from immensely? Might *these* stories and experiences have been the things that would have improved the writer's book, rather than twiddling with their hyphens?

In a poignant scene in *Walden* (1854), Henry David Thoreau offers a critique of his own fixation on perfection along these lines. Sitting alone in his hut, Thoreau is reading some new translations of the works of Confucius, and they appear to be inspiring him to new heights of insight. He records that he feels himself "as near being resolved into the essence of things as ever I was in my life." If only he can think a little longer, he is sure, he will arrive at this resolution, at which point, supposedly, the anxious tumult of his mental life will subside, and he will be welcomed onto the other side of sublime experience. But suddenly his friend the poet appears to ask if Thoreau wants to go fishing. He is thrown from his reverie and never recovers it.

Dismayed, he asks: "Shall I go to heaven or a-fishing?"[29] The interruption has made the decision for him. Thoreau has been condemned to a quotidian outing.

Or so it would seem. Later in the book, Thoreau returns to his reading of Confucius, and records a few of the lines that he was meditating on. One of them is: "Confucius says truly, 'Virtue does not remain as an abandoned orphan; it must of necessity have neighbors.'"[30] To feel oneself resolved into the essence of things is, I imagine, about the greatest insight one can have. But even if one achieves it, what does one do next? How does a person who has had such an insight proceed to live in a world in which they have to eat and drink and defecate and be interrupted all the time? Unless one can find the essence of things *in* these daily encounters, it is bound to be a fleeting resolution. Indeed, these daily encounters, full of such minor annoyances, cannot produce that mystic feeling of transcendence. But they can produce something else: a genuine appreciation for the good-enough world that, in all its limits and sufferings and difficulties, is still as radiant as heaven itself. Perhaps Thoreau did, indeed, arrive at his resolution, just not the one he was looking for. Thus he also records this thought from Confucius about where to find insights: "They are every where, above us, on our left, on our right; they environ us on all sides."[31] They are even in our mettlesome friends. We can never be fully resolved on our own, because who we are is bound up in our relationships.

As Zhuangzi and Huizi Were

I'm not sure if my two best friends, however, are pleased that I am writing this book at all. They are too polite to say so, but they give tell-tale signs. Although they ply me with questions about all sorts of small occurrences in my life, they rarely ask about this book. When I do something they consider great, they remark on the "irony" that I am the one writing a book about being good enough. (They are not good for my humility.) Whenever anything goes wrong, they say I can't blame anybody because my life is still "good enough." And sometimes they bring up their understandable doubts about a White, able-bodied, cis-hetero, middle-class US-American man going around and telling everyone else to be good enough, even if I'm trying to redefine the meaning of the phrase. More fundamentally still, they believe that life should be about excess, grandeur, exquisite beauty. They live their lives in the pursuit of these goals, and, with their generosity, they try to enable others to live lives of intense splendor as well. What are they doing hanging out with this good-enough lifer?

Zhuangzi might help to answer this question. He was a Taoist philosopher who lived around the fourth century BCE in China. His thoughts and stories are compiled in an eponymous book that is rich with parables of a frequently humorous and skeptical nature. It speaks of "free and easy wandering," of rejecting social norms and mores and finding a more genuine and joyous way of living together. One of my favorite stories is a brief scene where Zhuangzi is taking a stroll with his perpetual antagonistic interlocutor Huizi. Zhuangzi remarks that the fish look happy. Huizi responds that since he's not a fish, he can't know if the fish are happy. Zhuangzi replies: you're not me, so how do you know if I know that fish are happy?[32] In another conversation, Huizi complains that he has a useless tree that he feels burdened by, and Zhuangzi responds by praising the useless tree as a model for the good life: "loaf and wander there, doing lots of nothing there at its side, and take yourself a nap, far-flung and unfettered, there beneath it."[33]

When I first read the book, I thought of Zhuangzi as the undisputed victor of these disagreements. But when I began research for this book, I couldn't find my old copy and so bought a new translation by the scholar Brook Ziporyn. In Ziporyn's introduction, he makes a simple point that turned my reading of the book on its head: Zhuangzi and Huizi are best friends! Ziporyn even goes so far as to suggest that the whole book may be part of a secret, ongoing dialogue with Huizi.[34] What might this dialogue be about? Huizi's teaching is summed up in *Zhuangzi* as pointing to a single conclusion, which echoes what Thoreau learned from Confucius: "Love all things without exception, for Heaven and earth are one body."[35] This seems like the right teaching, so what does Zhuangzi disagree with here?

Ziporyn suggests that Zhuangzi disagrees with Huizi's insistence on his ability to prove, once and for all, that this is *the* ethical truth. Ziporyn comments: "In doing so, he [Huizi] implicitly asserts the unique ascendancy of his own position and practices, as the one who can victoriously demonstrate and proclaim this [truth]. It is to this, it would seem, that Zhuangzi lovingly and laughingly objects. . . . Zhuangzi seems to adopt everything from Huizi except his answers—and his concomitant status as 'the one with the answers.'"[36] What Zhuangzi objects to, in other words, is Huizi's claim to having reached the top of the hierarchy of knowing. He wants Huizi to experience not just the perfection of insight, but also the joyful humility of doubt.

What bonded them in friendship was not homology, but proximity with difference. What makes friendships work, at some level, is this balance, this closeness that also has an edge. Because there is no completion available to us in life, no single shared understanding. Because part of the fun of friendship is seeing how someone so close to you can still disagree. And I think this is beautiful to us because it reveals the truth of good-enoughness: there are no perfect friends with whom you would have a stasis of agreement. There is the dynamic joy of discovering, again and again, that your friend is good to you, your friend helps you sustain and maintain, but your friend is only ever good enough for you, can only ever offer you some combination of sympathy and disagreement.

And this is also what secures the value of friendship, no matter the economic conditions. Because no matter how pressed for time we are, no matter how much we may think that our pursuit of being atop the hierarchy of wealth or knowledge may overwhelm the need to go fishing, the truth is that our success cannot resolve us into the essence of things, because any such insights eventually dissolve into the chaos of our shared world. Our great material value will not provide us the meaning we think it will, because only the values of neighborliness can secure our joy. Having to disagree with our friends or spend time away from our consuming pursuits may feel like a diminution of our power, but the opposite is true. Our strength comes from tarrying with the difficulty of shared needs and differences. Some of de Botton's words on loving relationships are relevant to friendship here: "The person [or people] who is best suited to us is not the person who shares our every taste (he or she doesn't exist), but the person who can negotiate differences in taste intelligently—the person who is good at disagreement. Rather than some notional idea of perfect complementarity, it is the capacity to tolerate differences with generosity that is the true marker of the 'not overly wrong' person."[37] Even I might be friends with people who believe in greatness, or they with me, as Zhuangzi and Huizi were.

We'll See

I talk to my mother on the phone about once a week. Given the peripatetic life I've been living for the past few years due to circumstances somewhat outside of my control, we talk a lot about whatever various new plans I've come up with for increased stability. The plans usually unwind for whatever reason, but in the midst of the COVID-19 pandemic, my attempts at stability became a joke. Each time I have some new foundation, my mother finds herself repeating to me a bit of old country wisdom: If you want to make God laugh, make plans.

There is a story closer to Zhuangzi's time that illustrates this aphorism. It appears in the Taoist-affiliated work, *Huainanzi* (around 139 BCE). It is a famous parable that has many variations, and I prefer the oral version I've heard on various occasions slightly more than the one in the original text.[38] It goes something like this: There is a family on the frontier whose horse runs away. The neighbors come by and say how unfortunate this is. The father says, "We'll see." Soon the horse returns and brings with it several wild stallions. The neighbors say how lucky the family is. The father says, "We'll see." One day, while the son is trying to tame one of the stallions, he falls and breaks his leg. The neighbors exclaim the misfortune. The father says, "We'll see." Soon after, the king's soldiers come to conscript young men for war. The neighbors say now how lucky the broken leg is. The father says, "We'll see."

I read the story as yet another indication of the value of being open to imperfection. The neighbors are certainly right to say that what happens, in the moment, is fortunate or unfortunate, but the nature of life is that things that appear one way at one time will often morph into other meanings. That Amy Chua had a terrible and embarrassing fight with her daughter was bad, but it led to her realization about the limits of her parenting (and not to mention some fame as an author). That my early relationships kept falling apart was painful, but it taught me something about self-analysis, expectations, and the hard work of opening oneself up to counsel. Failed relationships or thwarted expectations are not necessarily bad things.

In a moving TED talk, "Good and Bad are Incomplete Stories We Tell Ourselves," the writer Heather Lanier brings this essential lesson into another domain. Not surprisingly given her title, she begins with the story of the man and son and their constant reversals of fortune in the *Huainanzi*. But this is not for her an abstract lesson; it is the story of her first child. She tells the audience that she had initially hoped for a flawless "superbaby" and had done everything in her power—supplements, organic everything, exercise to the max—to ensure having "not just a good baby, but the best baby possible." When her child was born at 2.15 kilos with the ultra-rare Wolf-Hirschhorn syndrome, her doctor told her that the child was the product of either "bad seed or bad soil," and she, herself, saw the situation as "unequivocally bad." But this imposition of cultural logics around what constitutes proper development, she quickly realized, had blinded her to the joys of being with her child, who loved reggae, gazed intently at everyone, and was performing constant small miracles of her own unique formation. As Lanier came to understand this, she began to resist the normalizing trends of her child's physical therapists, who kept trying to make her daughter work against her own body in order to be more like other kids. She realized that her daughter could have her own form of the good life, with its own limitations and strengths, and it was her job to help her achieve that, not some imagined perfect way of being.

But then perfection crept in in a second way. People began to assume that her daughter was "one of God's special children," some magical being there to teach them something wonderful. She had to learn to resist these kinds of romanticizations of her daughter being "angelic." The problem here was that these well-meaning friends were simply placing new undue burdens on her daughter, creating of her the image of the perfect child in a new way. This threatened to take away from her daughter the kind of messy complexity that all of our good-enough lives can offer. "My kid is human, that's all," she concludes, "And that is a lot."[39]

If This Is Good Enough

It is because of stories like Lanier's that I believe that the good-enough vision of the world is not reserved for those who live comfortable and relatively easy lives. But there are reasons to ask about its applicability in all circumstances. In the previous chapter, I raised the question of whether it makes sense for a privileged person like me to be writing about the need to aspire to good-enoughness. I did my best to admit that there are strict limits on what I can say, and that there are reasons to concede that some degree of excessive effort may be needed to overcome the depredations of the past, but only if that pursuit remains constantly subordinated to the broader need for creating a good-enough life for all. The pandemic that began in 2019 has thrown into stark relief the reality that through *much* of history *most* of humanity has not had decency and sufficiency. Does it make any sense to speak of good-enough relationships in the midst of such conditions?

We have some profound documents attesting to the difficulty of answering this question. In 1958, the Italian chemist Primo Levi, a survivor of Auschwitz, published *Si questo è un uomo* (literally *If This Is a Man*; translated into English as

Survival in Auschwitz). The book begins with these remarkable words: "It was my good fortune to be deported to Auschwitz only in 1944." Levi means that because of the war's demands for more laborers, such late-arriving prisoners were kept alive a little longer in order to perform hard labor. This is the source of his "good fortune." But to encounter these words is purposefully jarring: can there really be good fortune to be had even in how one is put in a concentration camp? Levi, on my reading, wants this to remain as a question. "If this is a man" is a genuine conditional statement about the degrading conditions of Auschwitz, not a plea begging for affirmation.

Much of what Levi documents is how the "ordinary moral world" crumbles within Auschwitz.[40] The debate between whether to be a "moral saint" or a basic decent person is meaningless when stealing a piece of a neighbor's bread may be the only thing that can keep you alive. In light of this, Levi pauses to consider why he is even writing his book: "we can perhaps ask ourselves if it is necessary or good to retain any memory of this exceptional human state." He responds that "no human experience is without meaning or unworthy of analysis, and that fundamental values, even if they are not positive, can be deduced from this particular world which we are describing."[41] He rejects out of hand the idea that what has happened in the camp is an exposure of the fact that humanity is "fundamentally brutal, egoistic, and stupid" without civilization. Rather, it reveals something peculiar about civilization itself. In a decent civilization, according to Levi, people should ensure that the weak do not become too weak nor the powerful too powerful. But in certain historical moments such as the one in which he finds himself, a "ferocious law . . . is openly in force." To explain what this law is, he cites the Gospel of Matthew: "To he that has, will be given; from he that has not, will be taken away."[42] This is the way in which the concentration camp functions: a few "saved" individuals are the ones who, by no real logic, just keep surviving. They cannot help their compatriots, the "drowned," who, by an equally absurd logic, just keep falling. In the camp, one is no longer a socially connected human, but a record of contingent fortune.

What this means for Levi is that *if* one can be human in Auschwitz, it would only be because somehow, by some grace, one manages to continue acting (or at least believing) that this ferocious law is not fully operative. For Levi this is embodied by his friend Lorenzo, who arrives after Levi has been in the camp for some time already. "By his natural and plain manner of being good," Lorenzo keeps alive for Levi the remote possibility of goodness more generally.[43] There is something undefined that keeps Lorenzo outside of the reduction to suffering and need that otherwise overwhelms the camp. "The personages in these pages are not men. Their humanity is buried, or they themselves have buried it, under an offence received or inflicted on someone else. . . . But Lorenzo was a man. . . . [And] thanks to Lorenzo, I managed not to forget that I myself was a man."[44] It is genuinely not clear if the basic, decent, ordinary goodness that makes life valuable can be sustained in the twisted starkness of Auschwitz. But if it can, one path to it is found through something that happens in the decency of friendship.

We might push Levi's claim further in other contexts. There are, I think, grounds for saying that although it is obviously not good enough for there be situations of such horror in our world, that does not render it impossible to live some elements of a good-enough life under oppression. Indeed, the assumption of impossibility may lead to the denial of decency and meaning attainable by people who live in such conditions. This was part of the point made by Ojibwe writer David Treuer in his book

The Heartbeat of Wounded Knee (2019). He begins as follows: "[This book] is adamantly, unashamedly, about Indian life rather than Indian death. That we even *have* lives—that Indians have been living in, have been shaped by, and in turn have shaped the modern world—is news to most people. The usual story told about us—or rather, about 'the Indian'—is one of diminution and death, beginning in untrammeled freedom and communion with the earth and ending on reservations, which are seen as nothing more than basins of perpetual suffering."[45] Across some four hundred pages, Treuer shows the reader why every part of this view of Indigenous life is wrong. The past is more complex, and the present more vibrant. There is tragedy, yes, but also creativity, cunning, and success. On a personal scale, that includes the realization of the vitality of his own family—his mother, the lawyer who fights for Ojibwe rights, and his father, the Holocaust survivor, who finally found where he belonged while living on the reservation: "I was a refugee . . . an outsider. I was told throughout my life I wasn't enough, I wasn't good enough, I didn't belong. When I came here I felt at home. I felt like people understood me."[46] And on a national scale, it includes nations like Tulalip, bordered within Washington State, which since its founding in 1855 has suffered as many social problems as any other Indigenous polity. But today, through creative communal practices and decisions, there is a thriving social democratic, autonomous government that provides free healthcare, education, childcare, retirement options, and a universal basic income. Treuer sees in Tulalip not "just what a tribe could be . . . but what America might be."[47]

There is a real risk that outsiders will fail to see the power and vitality of peoples if they assume that oppression means that there is no possibility for them to live a good-enough life. This is a tricky balance that writers like Levi and Treuer labor to express: how to clearly acknowledge the terror of the situations without erasing the power of the people who live through them. Historians of slavery in the Americas have also worked through this difficult terrain for many years. Especially since the 1970s, and building on research by W.E.B. Du Bois and others, historians have written to refute the general assumption of Black passivity during captivity, as well as to show how complex cultures and ways of life both endured from the past and developed at the time.[48] According to historian Vincent Brown, this repositioning allows historians to "at least tell richer stories about how the endeavors of the weakest and most abject have at times reshaped the world."[49] Such work questions the tendency to so steadfastly declaim the horrors of slavery that we forget that people—*generations*—lived entire lives in these conditions.[50] Brown and others want us to see that, without in any way excusing these conditions, we can still speak meaningfully about the lives that people led and the values they tried to carry with them and pass on. Ella Baker—the civil rights organizer I discussed in the previous chapter—identified with the importance of these stories for shaping her own worldview. Her maternal grandmother had given up certain limited privileges she enjoyed on the plantation as someone who worked in the owner's house when she refused to accept an arranged marriage. She was sent back to the fields and possibly subjected to greater violence, but she and the man she chose to marry became exemplary community members after Emancipation. They worked hard to ensure that as many people as they could afford to help had food and housing. Baker's democratic ethos, insisting on the dignity and right to sufficiency for all, was grounded in such stories.[51]

And in the post-slavery world of African American culture, the literary critic and historian Saidiya Hartman has similarly questioned the way we normally understand the lives of poor, young, Black women in the early twentieth century.[52] They are viewed as objects of pity, but Hartman believes we should recognize them as "social visionaries and innovators."[53] In one example from her archival research, she comes across an unbearable-to-look-at photograph of a young girl, naked, posed for some viewer's pleasure on a horsehair sofa. Unflinchingly, Hartman writes: "I envisioned her not as tragic or ruined, but as an ordinary black girl, and as such her life was shaped by sexual violence or the threat of it; the challenge was to figure out how to survive it, how to live in the context of enormous brutality, and thrive in deprivation and poverty."[54] Hartman then suggests what this might look like: "the beauty of the black ordinary, the beauty that resides in and animates the determination to live free, the beauty that propels the experiments in living otherwise ... Beauty is not a luxury; rather it is a way of creating possibility in the space of the enclosure, a radical art of subsistence, an embrace of our terribleness, a transfiguration of the given."[55] To *not* see this is to victimize these women all over again, to refuse to appreciate the beauty they created from within conditions that put most of our daily complaints to shame.

In her concluding thoughts, Hartman links this loss of sympathetic appreciation to the constant focus on the heroic figure—the Martin Delany, the MLK—who somehow managed to rise above the morass and become a great man. But in only recognizing the great man, we fail to see the wonderful words and worlds of these visionary women. Hartman returns to a phrase she used in reference to the young girl in the photograph—"possibility in the space of the enclosure." She tells us that one source of this thinking for her is the etymology of "chorus" in the Greek language: "*to dance within an enclosure.*"[56] The chorus in Attic tragedy often contrasts positively with the great hero onstage who will inevitably fall in the course of the drama. Of course, it is the names of the heroes that we remember; it is their stories we tell. But "The chorus is the vehicle for another kind of story, not of the great man or the tragic hero, but one in which all modalities play a part, where the headless group incites change, where mutual aid provides the resource for collective action."[57] Developing the abilities to relate to each other and to find what is meaningful and glorious in each other requires a shift in perspective away from greatness and towards our various possibilities—maligned though they have been, oppressed though they are. Aspects of a good-enough life are possible in the midst of a terrible world, and we have an ethical injunction to bear witness to their existence.

A Good-Enough President?

To say this is not in the least to excuse the tragedies of our past and present, to say, well, anything can be excused because anyone can live well enough even in terrible times. A good-enough worldview appreciates such a possibility, but it still keeps up its normative horizon: a world that is decent and emotionally and materially sufficient for everyone. While there are things that we can do in our individual philosophies or in our relationships to move us in this direction, there are limits to what we can achieve without the political will to reform our institutions.

There was perhaps no leader in US history who espoused good-enough relational values better than Barack Obama. In his memoir *Dreams from My Father* (1995), Obama expresses a keen skepticism regarding the pursuit of excess. Upon arriving in New York, he remarks on his disappointment at the infinity of desire for more: "a more expensive restaurant, a finer suit of clothes, a more exclusive nightspot."[58] And this disappointment, he tells us, is not just about the moral issues. It is political: "Beneath the hum, the motion, I was seeing the steady fracturing of the world taking place. . . . It was as if all the middle ground had collapsed, utterly."[59]

To find meaning in this fractured world, Obama turns to our good-enough moments of relation. Once, while lonely and disillusioned as a tourist in Barcelona, he is approached by a kindly man from Senegal, with whom he shares little language, but who offers to buy him a cup of coffee. He wonders about the meaning of this encounter, and the wandering yearnings of his soul, "Until I settled on the fact that this man from Senegal had bought me coffee and offered me water, and that was real, and maybe that was all any of us had a right to expect: the chance encounter, a shared story, the act of small kindness."[60] This belief in the value of small acts of decency carried into his political career. In his defining speech from the 2004 Democratic National Convention, Obama said that "the true genius of America" was not to be found in skyscrapers, military might, or material wealth, but "a faith in simple dreams, an insistence on small miracles; that we can tuck in our children at night and know that they are fed and clothed and safe from harm."[61]

And yet, Obama seems to assume that the pursuit of greatness is what ensures the possibility of this good-enough life. In his DNC speech, he prefaced the above comment by remarking: "Tonight, we gather to affirm the greatness of our nation."[62] And his inaugural address, four years later, followed a similar line: "In reaffirming the greatness of our nation we understand that greatness is never a given. It must be earned."[63] Obama certainly believes that America has not always earned the right to call itself great, but he still believes that the greatness of the nation is the goal. The problem is that a nation set on greatness will inevitably produce exclusions, misrecognitions, and brutal

repressions of those not deemed to be building this "greatness"—
or simply those who are not citizens of the "greatest" nation. If
the nation's pursuit of greatness is the very thing that creates the
"steady fracturing of the world" that he wants to overcome, then
why does Obama slip back into greatness rhetoric? There are
certainly contextual reasons, especially the fact that Obama had
to battle against intense and unforgivable racism. This manifested especially in the claim that he was not American, or was
even un-American, and this put especial and undue pressure on
him to affirm mainstream values.[64] But I do think he had his
own reasons as well.

My concern here, of course, is not that Obama used the word
"greatness." It's about how the ideology of greatness appeared
in his administration. In *The Tyranny of Merit*, Sandel offers an
excellent overview of the research on this topic by popular political writers like Jonathan Alter, Thomas Frank, and Neil
Barofsky.[65] They all note how Obama's administration was
staffed through a belief in the meritocratic process, with a heavy
dose of both Ivy-educated professionals and leaders from the
corporate world. As Sandel points out, while there is nothing
in theory wrong with such people, the historical experience of
US politics had before shown the folly of a reliance on "the best
and the brightest." That phrase, after all, was the famous title of
David Halberstam's book on how a similar crop of elite thinkers
had blundered their way into the United States-Vietnam War.
In this case, the result was not quite as catastrophic, but it was
still a serious blunder.

Obama's first major act as president was to deal with the ongoing damage of the Great Recession. During his transition to
the White House, he faced a choice. He could either focus on
shoring up the basic structure of the direly unequal economy
he inherited from Reagan, Clinton, and the Bushes, or he could

alter course and redirect the economic might of the country toward a more egalitarian formation such as FDR had done in a previous moment of economic crisis, and as Joe Biden is somewhat attempting to do in his presidency as I write these words. Obama chose the path of inequality.[66] There are many competing theories as to why, including his basic acceptance of neoliberal economics, his desire to win over Republican support, and, most generously, the possibility that restoration of the old economy was the best path to stabilization for everybody.[67] All of these are likely causes. But it is also the case that Obama's fundamental orientation toward greatness was central to his choices. As Frank put it, "Obama deferred to Wall Street in so many ways because investment banking signifies professional status like almost nothing else." And in Berofsky's words: "The Wall Street fiction that certain financial executives were preternaturally gifted supermen who deserved every penny of their staggering paychecks and bonuses was firmly ingrained in [Obama's] Treasury's psyche." Indeed, Berofsky continues, it was so firmly ingrained that not even the fact that these were the same people who had just caused the economy to crash could sink in.[68] Over the next eight years, these executives would repeatedly fail to help those left out in the recovery, leading to continued electoral losses for Obama's party and helping to pave the way for the rise of Trump. But when Obama began to plan his post-presidency, he returned to Silicon Valley executives and the McKinsey consulting group to figure out what he should do next.[69]

Greatness may appear as the best path to the good-enough life for ourselves and our relationships, but, as we have seen, it in fact subverts these very aims. This is no less true in our political and economic lives. The political-economic mantra of the modern United States has been that governments should enable as much unfettered growth as possible, because such growth will inevitably help everyone in society. Even if inequality grows, that is OK, because those at the bottom will still be in a better position relative to where they would have been without such growth. The problem with this argument, as I will discuss in the next chapter, is that it is entirely factually wrong. Inequality impedes growth and destabilizes society. Like all forms of greatness-orientation, its claims to produce a better world are belied by our experience. In his analysis of Obama's economic recovery plan, the economist Paul Krugman concluded that Obama's work had been good—it did help stabilize the economy—but in terms of actually making a better economic life for the nation and the world, it was "not good enough."[70] What might such a good-enough vision of our economic life look like?

4

For Our World

Let's say you began this book a skeptic, but now that you've read the first few chapters, you've decided to reorient your life around the idea of being good enough. (I know that I'm not that convincing, but let's say so for the sake of argument.) You've stopped aspiring to be the best, and, beyond that, you've seen through the absurdity of even thinking there is such a thing as the best. You've come to appreciate the inevitable suffering and limitations of existence without always trying to turn them into positive lessons. You appreciate that you are part of an interdependent world where your own actions find their deepest resonance in how they complement the activities of others. And to that end, you're trying to focus on promoting and participating in a world that is decent and sufficient for everyone. You've learned to gain strength from the profundity of the everyday and the meaningfulness of simple decency. You've recalibrated your sense of the purpose of parenting, love, and friendship, moving away from a desire to be among the greats and toward an understanding of the values of dissonance as much as communion.

But now you encounter a problem. Everyone around you is still striving for greatness. They really appreciate your new laid-back attitude and sophisticated philosophy of life, and they'd really like to hear about it sometime. But seeing as they have to write ten books in six years to have a shot at tenure, master the cello so they can teach their kid, or work three jobs to scrape out a living, that "sometime" looks like it will be about a decade from now. And, with everyone else so busy, you don't find a good-enough world to be a part of, and so what else do you have to do but fall back on all your old habits of strife, anxiety, and dismay?

The logic of the good-enough life is predicated on the fact of our fundamental interdependence. This means that living a good-enough life in the midst of a society that is oriented toward greatness is extremely difficult (even if, as I noted in the previous chapter, people manage to find paths to elements of it in the direst of circumstances). I see the general difficulty every year when I welcome a new crop of first-year students to my classes. I hear them talk about how they're passionate about sculpture but will be studying "financial engineering," or how they really care deeply about inequality and so plan to make as much money as they can to help fight it. This drive for economic success is hard to derail. After all, in a winner-take-all economy with vast inequality, if you do not strive to be at the top of the economic pyramid, you run the risk of facing ongoing economic precarity. And yet, as I mentioned earlier, when I describe my book research to my students, they all look much more excited and joyous than when they talk about macroeconomics problems sets, or the competitive pressures of an internship on Wall Street. Many of us intuitively recognize that living in a good-enough society would benefit all of us, but how do we get there from here?

In industrialized, capitalist societies, the most common answer has been, ironically, that we arrive at good-enoughness for all through the pursuit of greatness for the few. This is, as I will discuss below, the basic claim of the liberal tradition (in the sense of free-market economics, not political sensibility) from Adam Smith to Friedrich Hayek, and even, as we saw at the end of the last chapter, Barack Obama. The basic argument can be boiled down to the claim that though the pursuit of great fortunes creates vast inequalities, it nevertheless raises the general standard of living across the board. In the United States, this claim was backed up by the famous "Kuznets curve" (1955), which predicted that capitalist growth would force inequality to rise up to a certain point, and then begin to level off before declining, even as growth continued. In the pithy phrase associated with John F. Kennedy, "A rising tide lifts all boats." The trouble was that once there was sufficient data, it entirely disproved the claim.[1] Rising tides actually do exactly what we would expect them to: lift the yachts and the warships and drown the small family rafts and personal canoes.

Of course, for many on the political left, no such extensive data was necessary to prove what Karl Marx and others had long argued. According to this argument, although it is true that capitalism is better than most previous economic systems, it is nevertheless a ruthless, exploitative, and alienating system in which those with access to capital are able to make their profit off the toil of others. Since the primary aim of the capitalist is economic gain at any cost, owners of capital take part in a competitive downward cycle. They constantly seek out the lowest wages possible, the cheapest equipment possible, and the least liability possible. One does not have to be a rapacious and greedy owner to see that if you pay good wages to your employees while the owner down the block does not, the other owner can have cheaper prices and may drive you out of business. (It's also possible, though, that you will incur higher costs because of constant turnover, and the store down the block will have healthier and happier employees who are more productive.)

There are many other issues with using the capitalist system to pursue growth, including the way it can encourage and legitimize inequalities, environmental despoliation, baseless speculation, and deadly habits (think Exxon, Bear Stearns, and Purdue Pharma).[2] In theory, capitalism has ways of dealing with this through proper regulation, organized labor, and legal constraints. The trouble is, however, that when you have so much wealth concentrated into the hands of so few, the levers of government are easily controlled by wealthy interests. Economic plutocracy inevitably subverts political democracy. Political scientists have demonstrated that the agendas of the wealthy are carried out with alarming frequency over the policy desires of everyone else, with some even claiming that the United States is better considered an oligarchy or plutocracy than a democracy.[3] This does not mean that capitalism (a too-general term to describe different possible forms of market-driven economies) necessarily produces all of these problems, but its current relentless drive for competition and profit for some means that capitalism as we know it is bound up with greatness for the few and difficulty for the many. So, at the very least, our current capitalist system is nowhere near good enough.[4]

Unfortunately for those who have sought to overcome this system, the first major modern attempt to implement a more egalitarian society, in twentieth-century Russia, was a catastrophic failure. There are many contentious debates about the cause of this failure.[5] And it is important to remember that writers in favor of more egalitarian economies were among the earliest critics of what was happening in Russia. The revolutionary socialist Rosa Luxemburg, for example, was highly enthusiastic about the revolution in principle, but she was also highly critical of the legitimatization of dictatorship by Lenin and Trotsky. Already in 1918 she condemned the fact that freedom was being restricted to those who supported the new regime: "Freedom only for the supporters of the government, only for the members of one party—however numerous they may be—is no freedom at all. Freedom is always and exclusively freedom for the one who thinks differently."[6] Meanwhile, liberal socialist Bertrand Russell, after vising the Soviet Union shortly after the revolution, similarly believed in the world-historical potential of the event but expressed dismay at its trajectory. He predicted that the Soviet Union would become an imperial power, be part of a "prolonged world-war," and ultimately succumb to the forces of capitalism. All three came to pass.[7] Russell and Luxemburg thus saw clearly that the problem in the Soviet Union was a dictatorship, not the promise of a more egalitarian economy.[8]

There are many reasons for why this move to dictatorship came to pass, but it seems plausible that a form of greatness is again one of the issues. One thing that stands out is that countries like the Soviet Union greatly diminished *material* inequalities but exacerbated what Hirsch called *positional* inequalities. So far as the data is available, it is clear that economic inequality was significantly reduced between 1917 and 1989. Nevertheless, access to power was deeply concentrated in a few leading figures, and access to perks like certain goods, vacation places, and freedom of movement was limited to elites. Many bad decisions were made because too few people with too little input were making them.[9] Soviet communism, in other words, never fully dealt with the problem of greatness in a social order.[10] To understand why our current world is so full of these greatness-fueled inequalities and destructive behaviors, we will need to overcome such social issues as much as economic ones. Indeed, we'll have to overcome the social vision—the idea of building a society around greatness—that lies at the heart of modern economic thinking.

Of course, a lot of greatness thinking in society is not just about the economy, but also about social orders. We live in a world that retains ideologies of greater genders, greater races, and greater abilities, all of which must also be overcome. You may rightly wonder why this chapter focuses on the general economy at all, rather than the ongoing inequalities that have to do with race, gender, ability, and other aspects of identity. First of all, it is important to note that none of these are disconnected issues. Here again the COVID-19 pandemic has functioned like an X-ray of society's failures to ensure a good-enough life for all. Data from within the first few months of the pandemic quickly showed that in the United States, disease prevalence, fatality rate, and economic hardship were all disproportionately concentrated among Black, Latinx, and Indigenous peoples.[11] Similar racial disparities were seen in many European countries.[12] In Singapore and several countries in the Middle East, virus incidence and economic hardship also landed heavily on migrant workers from poorer nations like Bangladesh.[13] Globally, the economic toll also fell disproportionately on women, in part because they are frequently assumed to give up their jobs to care for children and family members, and in part because they are overly represented in professions hit by the pandemic, like domestic labor and aged care.[14]

These trends are exposed by crises, not created by them. The economic system that we live within is predicated on the idea that some kinds of activities (like high finance) are more valuable than others (like delivering food and caring for the sick and elderly). In countries with long-standing histories of racism, it is not an accident that the more highly valued activities have been the province of primarily able-bodied White men or other powerful racial or ethnic groups. The system came into being with racial, gendered, and ableist assumptions baked in.

Political scientist Cedric Robinson has argued, for example, that modern capitalism emerged out of the racial history internal to Europe. The Irish, Tartars, and Slavs (from whom the word "slave" originates) were considered inferior and thus available as unpaid and enslavable laborers.[15] This early racism created the basic structure that would deepen and expand into New World slavery, focused especially of course on Africans, but also including Indigenous peoples and these earlier European ethnic groups (now raised up to the status of "indentured servant" in the racial hierarchy, along with later-arriving Asian immigrants).[16] Whether our current economic system *requires* racial divisions or not is debatable.[17] At the very least, it requires an underclass of menial laborers who are underpaid and undervalued, and who, in order to justify their position, are often racialized. And it is relatively clear that the modern capitalist system was forged through its racial divisions. As historian Walter Johnson puts it, "There was no such thing as capitalism without slavery: the history of Manchester never happened without the history of Mississippi."[18]

Nor did much economic growth happen without the unpaid labor of women. Feminist scholars associated with the Wages for Housework Movement in the 1970s, including Mariarosa Dalla Costa, Selma James, and Silvia Federici, argued that modern capitalist accumulation is predicated on a mystification of the role of women's labor. While non-enslaved manual laborers are at least paid for their production, women's labor of *re*production—of producing and sustaining the very humans who would go work in the factories—was never compensated. As Federici puts it, capitalism mystifies women's labor as a "natural resource or personal service, while profiting from the wageless condition of the labor involved."[19] This is a problem of recognition, of what kinds of labors are seen and valued, and what kinds are simply expected and naturalized. More recently, economist Nina Banks has argued that Black women's labor over the past century has added unrecognized nonmarket value to the economy by providing services left unoffered by a neglectful state. She suggests that an intersectional analysis of gender, race, and the economy would lead to a recognition not just of housework, but of this community activism as well.[20]

Disability rights activists have further raised the question of how our current economic order can handle those who are not productive in the same ways as other people. While feudal societies have many disturbing elements, historians believe that they may have incorporated people with disabilities better. Since maximum productivity was not the goal, it is likely that there were ways for people to engage in community production and reproduction at different paces and with different capacities. With the rise of labor standards in industrial capitalism, people who had found grooves in community life were suddenly excluded. This period saw the beginnings of institutionalization and exclusion.[21] As disability activists and scholars Marta Russell and Ravi Malhotra have argued, this was not just about exclusion, but also commodification. Institutions eventually became profitable businesses—often by providing inadequate care at the taxpayer's expense.[22] As a result of these shifts and policies, people with disabilities in the United States are three times more likely to live in poverty than others, not to mention having to face social exclusion and stigma.[23] This situation is not just endemic to capitalism, but to any productivist mindset that equates human value with economic production.[24] As such, Russell and Malhotra argue, people with disabilities offer a powerful criticism of our economic system as reductive of all human value to particular forms of labor. They write: "Employability, aptitude for earning money and even work chosen during one's free time are not, a priori, the measure of what it means to live, to be part of the human race."[25]

These scholars and activists challenge the common response to a recognition of these problems: that the best way forward is to simply include more people in the current economic system—to ensure that everyone, no matter their race or gender or ability, can have access to the same opportunity to be a winner in society. Indeed, this argument faces a lot of headwinds if we follow these writers and really think through the problems. The challenge of racial capitalism is not just racism, it's whether or not the current economic order can function without some kind of underclass, and if it cannot, whether some kind of racial formation will tend to emerge to explain who deserves to be part of that underclass. The challenge of feminism is not just about including women in the workplace; it is about asking whether we currently have economic models that can properly value the labors of raising children, maintaining a home, and caring for family and community, regardless of the gender of the person who does it. The challenge of disability studies is not just about overcoming negative assumptions about someone's capacities, but about whether the social order can promote a meaningful understanding of everyone's values if the economic system is designed to pay for only particular kinds of labor.

Combatting these and other challenges is another area where we can see the value of promoting a good-enough life for all, regardless of one's current identity or class position. Based on the normative values of good-enoughness generated so far in this book, we can say that a good-enough approach to our socioeconomic order would be predicated on principles including: (1) recognizing the value of different kinds of labor as connected parts of a meaningful society, none of which is possible without the others (no presidents without janitors); (2) allowing people to strive more for the sake of the task (excellence of the craft it-self) than for wealth or mere survival; (3) ensuring respect and decency and quality of life for people not able to engage in tra-ditional forms of labor; (4) taking concrete steps to redress past exploitation, not by vengeance, but by careful attention to inte-gration into the good-enough, which may require consideration for those of any background who haven't had previous advan-tages, or who remain subjects of stigma even when they have achieved equality in class status; (5) relying on everyone's abili-ties to cooperatively participate in ways not commanded by a punitive state or corporate monopolies; (6) by bringing in more people and more technology, allowing each of us to do less, so that there is both more abundance and leisure; and (7) under-standing and appreciating that the results of this system will still be imperfect, that some inequalities will remain and some fail-ures will occur, but those inequalities will be limited and those failures will be shared by everyone, as will any success made during a recovery.

Such solutions will likely require a pluralist approach that makes room for cooperative enterprises, government-run insti-tutions, and private initiative. We already have all of these things; we just have to improve and restructure them. And any doubt that we can make a fair and just world should be laid aside by the remarkable technological revolutions we have created. If we can innovate our way to outer space, surely, if we apply the same energy and imagination, we can create a good-enough life for all. Across the board there will need to be regulation ensuring that there is a decent floor below which people do not fall, and a low ceiling above which people do not ascend and amass too much power over others. We may not all be in the same room, but we should at least all share in the same good-enough house. And though this may seem like a far-fetched dream, I believe we are in fact closer to achieving it than we realize. Still, there are major obstacles standing in our way.

The Path of Pinheads

The idea that greatness-oriented economies benefit all has a significant origin in the writings of Adam Smith. According to the opening pages of his *Wealth of Nations* (1776): "It is the great multiplication of the productions of all the divisions of labour, which occasions, in a well-governed society, that universal opulence which extends itself to the lowest ranks of the people."[26] Although Smith and contemporary capitalists are much farther apart than the latter tend to claim (note that "well-governed society" part), the basic justification is the same: if we grow the general pie, it will swell "universal opulence" and benefit the "lowest ranks" as much as everyone else. According to Smith, to properly grow the pie, we need a proper division of labor, which is to say, a logical parceling out of an industry. Smith's famous example is pinheads. Whereas one pinmaker could only do all the various operations (straightening, cutting, and grinding the wire; making the head; attaching the head to the wire; painting the head, etc.) to make a full pinhead a few times in a given day, by splitting up the tasks companies are said to be able to make nearly fifty thousand a day.

Setting up this division of labor also requires a division between types of laborers, and between labor and capital. For example, there is the inventor (or inventors) who came up with the idea of a pinhead in the first place. And there are the manufacturers of the machines that help cut and grind the wires. And there are the landowners who guide the construction of the building where the pins are made. And there are the investors who put up the money to buy the machines and pay the workers before the first pins are sold.

This process of the division of labor, however, only explains a small part of modern economic growth. It especially ignores women's unpaid labor, the colonial extraction of resources, and the slave trade. The general logic of growth is highly contested, but one plausible explanation also includes an increasing use of "natural capital"—extraction and energy usage. Some economists even argue that the unseen labor of coal and oil is a better explanation of today's wealth than any feature of modern capitalism.[27]

These limitations in Smith's causal argument aside, he is not unaware of the fact that the divisions of labor create tensions. He worries about the tendency of owners to overwork and thus burn out their employees.[28] And he is critical of laws in his day that forbid the equivalent of worker unions and do not set minimum wages, but allow managers to conspire to keep wages down.[29] "No society," he tells us, can be "flourishing and happy, of which the far greater part of the members are poor and miserable."[30] If Smith were alive today he would as likely be a social democrat as the type of neoliberal economist who claims to follow his teachings. But his top-down logic still supplies much of what is behind today's economic world. By this logic, the system requiring the drudgery and difficulty of cutting pin wires at subsistence wages for one's whole life is still better than any other economic structure because it grows the general pot. Yes, some may live great lives of opulence and leisure while others toil away, but the opulence of the few ultimately benefits all the rest of us.

The famous image that Smith gives for how this works is the invisible hand. In *The Wealth of Nations*, he explains the concept in the context of a discussion of domestic versus foreign trade. Smith suggests that, with some significant exceptions, people with capital will tend to prefer to invest in domestic rather than foreign industries because such investments take less time and are more trustworthy, and one has better recourse to the law in one's own country.[31] When a capitalist thus invests domestically, they do so not in order to help the local economy, but to help themselves. Smith draws from this his famous conclusion: "By directing that industry in such a manner as its produce may be of the greatest value, he intends only his own gain, and he is in this, as in many other cases, led by an invisible hand to promote an end which was no part of his intention."[32] Individuals attempting to do good, or the state regulating for the public good, Smith suggests, would only diminish the general growth of capital. And, recall, it is the growth of capital that is said to improve everyone's lot.

This is not, however, the only place where Smith mentions the idea of the invisible hand. It plays a more articulated role in his earlier work, *The Theory of Moral Sentiments* (1759; Smith revised the book in 1790 and stood by its conclusions). It might surprise readers who are only familiar with *The Wealth of Nations* to open *Moral Sentiments* and find that it begins as follows: "How selfish soever man may be supposed, there are evidently some principles in his nature, which interest him in the fortune of others, and render their happiness necessary to him, though he derives nothing from it except the pleasure of seeing it."[33] Smith doubles down on this point a few pages later: "To restrain our selfish, and to indulge our benevolent affections, constitutes the perfection of human nature; and can alone produce among mankind the harmony of sentiments and passions in which consists their whole grace and propriety."[34] Come again? Adam Smith, who is most famous for telling us that our selfish pursuits will make everyone better off, is saying here the complete opposite. How are we to make sense of this?

The seeming contradiction is at the heart of Smith's complex theory of human nature. According to Smith, our fundamental desire in life, as I noted in chapter 1, is to be loved.[35] And so we spend much of our mental labor trying to figure out how to receive love. We watch the world around us and see who is loved, and who we spontaneously love or hate. And our normal conclusion from this process is unfortunate for the development of benevolence: "the respectful attentions of the world [are] more strongly directed towards the rich and the great, than towards the wise and the virtuous."[36] Smith does *not* think this is a good thing. "The disposition to admire, and almost to worship, the rich and the powerful . . . [is] the great and most universal cause of the corruption of our moral sentiments."[37] But he does think that this is just the way humans are.

So Smith has a problem to solve. Human beings want love and respect above all else, and they see that there are two paths to that: wisdom and virtue, or wealth and greatness of rank. The ideal path is through the former, but the most recognizable path is through the latter. This is doubly problematic, because not only does the latter path take us away from our goal of virtuous life in civic harmony, but it actually undercuts that goal by "corrupting" the very sentiments that should hold society together. (Smith, it seems, would agree with some of what Fred Hirsch had to say about how economic greatness destroys the very Good Samaritans it puts us in need of, as I discussed in the previous chapter.) Smith does not think this is the special insight of philosophers. He believes that we all know at some level that greatness (of rank and wealth) is a corrupting force both for society and for those who pursue it. Nevertheless, we tend to forget this and focus on the mundane pleasures that wealth and power afford, and thus approve of and desire to be like the great.[38] In these crosshairs of circumstance, what is to be done?

This is the moment where Smith conjures the idea of the invisible hand. Although the pursuit of greatness corrupts social morals and produces endless anxiety for the individual, in so doing it "rouses and keeps in continual motion the industry of mankind."[39] This is the key to understanding what will happen in *The Wealth of Nations*. Society as a whole needs general wealth to grow in order to bring us to a state of comfortable and quality living. But, according to Smith's (inaccurate[40]) history, if we actually consider what it takes to grow that wealth, to carry the burdens of greatness in our social formations, then we would never do it. It will corrupt our souls and divide our social fabric, but we need it to raise the general quality of life. Smith's solution is to say that while the visible hand of greatness performs these terrifying acts, the invisible hand gives us progress for all, because even as the rich act like fools and drown out common decency, even as they greedily hoard land and riches, they can only do so by returning some amount of their bounty to the rest of us. After all, Smith says, they can own endless fields, but they cannot eat all the produce that grows on them. And, besides, in the "economy of greatness," it is more enjoyable to use excess goods and resources to buy "baubles and trinkets" to show off your success than to hide it. The rich and the great are thus "led by an invisible hand to make nearly the same distribution of the necessaries of life, which would have been made, had the earth been divided into equal portions among all its inhabitants."[41] And for doing so, they get more of the non-necessary pleasures.

Smith justifies this material inequality for the great with a spiritual inequality in favor of the lowly. In this scheme, everyone will have what they need, those who have an excess of goods will also have an excess of anxiety and labor, and those who have fewer goods will have more of "what constitutes the real happiness of human life."[42] There is a famous story of Alexander the Great approaching Diogenes the Cynic and asking if there was anything the general could do for the philosopher. Diogenes asked him to get out of his sun. Smith alludes to this passage: "The beggar, who suns himself by the side of the highway, possesses that security which kings are fighting for."[43] Smith does not want the world to be how it is. He wants wisdom and virtue and the "benevolent affections" to reign. But he sees that the world is not made to enable this. And so he seeks another path. If we cannot stop people from trying to become great, at least we can design social institutions like markets and the division of labor that will help ensure that this pursuit does in fact aid all of us. Smith would like to overcome greatness, but instead he makes a Faustian bargain with it. Thus does greatness make cynics of us all.

One final point about Smith's invisible hand of greatness is worth pausing over. I noted above that the section in *The Wealth of Nations* where he defends the idea is about why capital prefers domestic markets. But Smith did predict that someday international trade might prove more lucrative for capital. This would inevitably mean that jobs that were once stable in the home country would move to others. Smith considered that this might cause considerable unrest, but his theory predicted that, in fact, there was nothing to worry about. "The capital of the country remaining the same, the demand for labour will likewise be the same, or very nearly the same, though it may be exerted in different places and for different occupations."[44] It was this basic idea that allowed a number of contemporary politicians and economists not to worry about the effects of globalization, or to claim that those who were resentful of losing their jobs to poorer-paying countries were simply not seeing the big picture.[45] It is why free-market conservatives who are anti-Trump refuse to see the connection between the policies they support and his election, even though the data clearly shows that counties where jobs were lost to NAFTA or permanent-trade status with China voted disproportionately for Trump.[46]

But if anyone was surprised by this outcome in 2016, it was only because they had not read their history. Karl Polanyi, one of the most astute observers of the political economy that led to the ravages of Nazism and fascism, had long ago seen that the same dynamic was then at play.[47] In 1944, he wrote: "To expect that a community would remain indifferent to the scourge of unemployment, the shifting of industries and occupations and to the moral and psychological torture accompanying them, merely because economic effects, in the long run, might be negligible, was to assume an absurdity."[48] That absurd assumption was at the heart of the rise of interwar authoritarianism. Since then, empirical and historical studies have consistently affirmed Polanyi's finding that market-driven inequalities produce civilizational-level crises.[49] The solution was equally known: in material and positional equality lies the salvation of democracy. People who have a say in their lives, who find that their efforts are meaningfully rewarded, that their failures are adequately understood, and that they can have basic trust in the decency of both neighbors and strangers—such people are not easily corrupted by demagogues. And since democracies thrive when they can work cooperatively with others and without fear of attack, that equality itself works best when it is shared *across* nations, not just within their borders. To embrace this basic truth is to abandon the pursuit of economic and national greatness and appreciate that nothing less than global solidarity based on decency and sufficiency for all is the best path for peace and security.

The Road to Serfdom

After the Second World War, it seemed for a time that progressive economics had won the battle of ideas. In 1974, the newly elected head of the British Conservative Party, Margaret Thatcher, found that even her Conservative colleagues were enthralled with the left-leaning prescriptions of thinkers like Polanyi and especially John Maynard Keynes. In a meeting with the party's research department, she famously grabbed out of her bag a copy of Friedrich Hayek's *The Constitution of Liberty* (1960) and slammed it on the table: "This is what we believe!" she reportedly yelled.[50] A decade earlier, US Senator Barry Goldwater had made a quixotic, far-right bid for the presidency. His small-government, low-tax, economics-first platform was "much influenced" by an earlier book of Hayek's: *The Road to Serfdom* (1944).[51] Although Goldwater was trounced in the '64 election, his California campaign cochair, the former Hollywood star Ronald Reagan, would become president in 1980. Reagan, like Thatcher, was deeply influenced by Hayek.

That Hayek's ideas would come to have such a far-ranging influence was by no means assured. When *The Road to Serfdom* was first published, its central thesis—that any government intervention into an economic sphere that could otherwise be controlled by the private market would *necessarily* lead to tyranny—was attacked on both the left and the right. While Keynes approvingly wrote to Hayek about his moral vision of freedom, he thought his argument about government intervention was dangerous and unprovable folly. And even colleagues on the right, like the University of Chicago's Frank Knight, thought Hayek's arguments were vastly oversimplified and inconclusive.[52] Nevertheless, the book received major press at the time, including a mixed review by George Orwell and a celebratory statement in *The New York*

Times Book Review.[53] Then in 1945, luck struck when the book was condensed and circulated to the nearly 9 million subscribers of *Reader's Digest.*[54]

But though it became a popular hit and made Hayek something of a star, the book did little to further his academic reputation. Even the conservative University of Chicago economics department did not want him, though he wound up with a post in their Committee on Social Thought. In need of a pension (Hayek was reputed to be not so good with his own finances), he moved to universities in Freiburg and then Salzburg, and was little known in some academic circles. When he won the Nobel Prize in Economics in 1974, it was said that many major economists had never even heard of him.[55] This was perhaps not surprising, since, as Avner Offer and Gabriel Söderberg have recently detailed, the Nobel Prize in Economics was invented in 1969 by neoliberals at Sweden's central bank as part of their assault against social democracy.[56] Although the prize did in the early years go to some social democrats, it was often awarded to thinkers attacking this then widely held economic model. Most Nobel economics prize winners, at least, were at the height of their fame at the time they won. Hayek was the first to see his reputation salvaged, and his citations increase dramatically, because of the award.[57]

Hayek's key argument, like Smith's, is in part an unwilling concession to greatness. His main aim, he tells us, is to stop the accumulation of power in the hands of the few. His target in *The Road to Serfdom* is the rise of totalitarian states. And his argument is that the best way to keep totalitarian states from rising is to stop them from assuming control over the direction of the economy. Hayek, I should be clear, appreciated the impulse behind central planning to break up the power of corporations. He sympathetically cites the liberal socialism of Bertrand Russell, for example, and he maintained something of a friendship with Keynes throughout his life. But he claims that Russell's argument is based on "the tragic illusion" that one can "extinguish power" by locating it in a central government.[58] To the contrary, doing this places more power in the hands of a single entity—the central planning committee—than is available even to the most powerful corporations. Avoiding central planning, in theory, should reduce the general power of anyone over anyone else. "To split or decentralize power," Hayek continues, "is necessarily to reduce the absolute amount of power, and the competitive system is the only system designed to minimize by decentralization the power exercised by man over man."[59] Hayek makes a lot of claims about necessity, and that his system is the "only" one that can stave off fascism. But the logical chains almost always falter under scrutiny. Even fellow economic liberals (in the traditional sense of the word) like Jacob Viner and Lionel Robbins, who advocated strongly for capitalist markets, pointed out that, no, totalitarianism does not follow from social welfare projects, and, no, giving power to businesses does not make society freer.[60]

Just as much as *The Road to Serfdom* is a screed against socialism, it is also dead set against the "wooden insistence" of some liberals on "the principle of laissez-faire."[61] Hayek was not a laissez-faire capitalist. Indeed, he did not think that business should operate without government intervention. Rather, he argued that the government should set up the conditions in which businesses can compete with each other. There should be planning, but it should be "planning for competition," not "planning against competition."[62] It is this competition alone that, again in theory, should ensure the possibility that no single actor assumes too much power. Remarkably and perhaps inconsistently, Hayek was thus not opposed to breaking up monopolies, prohibiting the use of certain poisonous substances, placing maximums on working hours, putting in safety regulations, having an "extensive system of social services," regulating patents, or having strong standards about preserving the environment, limiting pollution, and reducing noise.[63]

But where consistency against non-market actors returns, and where most of his importance for modern life lies, is with his arguments for vouchsafing a system for the pursuit of greatness. Hayek's concern ultimately is not the freedom of the system; it's the preservation of an elite.[64] We can see this if we look at some of his arguments in *The Constitution of Liberty* (1960). He argues, rightly on this starting point in my opinion, that human beings can never know the totality of information. It follows for him that, because we cannot know, we have no choice but to design a society in which individuals are at "liberty" to pursue whatever projects they see fit—within basic legal constraints that are equally applied to everyone. Only by so doing can we ensure the kind of progress and growth that benefits all members of society. Here Hayek follows Smith quite closely.

He continues by arguing that an attempt to limit or curtail reward, or the attempt to suggest that everyone in society deserves a certain equality of living standard, will undo the very possibility of such progress. If we determine today, for example, that everyone should have universal broadband access, that would mean diverting to this aim individual creative powers that might otherwise be working to create something even better than broadband. For a society to say that we need to make sure everyone has something before we make the next big advance is, according to Hayek, to effectively ensure that such advances will never occur.

This is the basis of his defense of inequality as a good thing for everyone. By allowing some people to have better things before others, we guarantee that those better things will eventually be held by everyone: "The rapid economic advance that we have come to expect seems in a large measure to be the result of this inequality and to be impossible without it. Progress at such a fast rate cannot proceed on a uniform front but must take place in echelon fashion, with some far ahead of the rest."[65] Even if this were true—I'll say more in a moment about why it's not[66]— what should give us pause here are the purposes to which Hayek will put the claim. Perhaps most gallingly, he uses it as a justification for massive inherited wealth. According to his argument, wealthier parents will, on the whole, be able to produce better children, who will in turn make greater advances, which will in turn benefit the rest of society.[67] Somehow, by Hayek's logic, the pursuit of greatness for the few is meant to produce a better world for the rest of us, even if it is appallingly unfair and even unconcerned with the actual abilities of those deemed great. At least Hayek, who, unlike his followers, never claimed his economics could create "equality of opportunity," is honest about what this economic system means.

Like Smith, Hayek is not arguing that any of this is a *good* thing. He simply maintains that "men being what they are," there is no better path available for our social world.[68] He repeatedly expresses sympathy with the socialist viewpoint, and he seems earnest here. In an interview, he even suggested that in his youth he "would be described as a Fabian socialist."[69] So if he indeed thinks that greater equality is the correct impulse, but that any attempt to actually create it would undo progress and growth, the obvious question to ask is if there is any evidence for this being correct. According to an increasing majority of contemporary economists, ranging from Thomas Piketty to number crunchers at the Organization for Economic Co-operation and Development (OECD), historical experience has shown Hayek to be the Ptolemy of economics.

He simply has got everything backwards. Indeed, according to the currently available economic data, the *reverse* of his claim is true: inequality is what impedes growth.[70] The numbers are straightforward. As Thomas Piketty has shown, for example, in the United States, from 1950 to 1990 the GDP growth rate was an average 2.2%. From 1990 to 2020, it was 1.1%. The inflection point is in the 1980s, during which time Reagan (and to an extent Bush and Clinton after him) let top income tax rates fall from 72 to 35%. In turn, from 1990 to 2020, the top 1 percent's share of national income rose from 12 to 18%.[71] As the rich got richer, the economy grew more slowly. Meanwhile, researchers have shown that growth in highly unequal societies tends to lead to recessions and depressions.[72]

Why? Heather Boushey, an economist currently working in the Biden administration, lists a few key points. First, inequality is an "obstruction," because it inhibits a majority of people from contributing their talents and abilities to the economy. Second, inequality "subverts" the public processes that can enable everyone to participate by creating too much power in the hands of the wealthy. Finally, it "distorts" the economy by making it appear as if everyone is benefitting, when only in fact rewarding the few. In a commonly cited statistic, for example, although worker productivity has been steadily rising for the last four decades in the United States, wages are stagnant.[73] In general, better paid workers are more motivated workers, have more capital for consumption, and also are less likely to become politically disenfranchised and thus support regressive policies that threaten the stability on which growth depends.[74] (And this does not even factor in whether GDP growth rate is a good measure of economic or social progress, given that it says nothing directly about the well-being of individuals, or the environment on which their lives depend.[75]) This suggests that we need a Copernican revolution in how we think about the economy: away from top-heavy to bottom-up. This is not only morally better; it is also logically so.

And it is not only growth that is at stake here. It also applies to the very innovative progress that Hayek claims for the competitive enterprise system. To see why, simply return to the example of putting more social resources into expanding broadband access. We know from autobiographical accounts that most of Silicon Valley's advances were developed precisely because its early founders had—through their privileges—extensive early access to computers.[76] Hayek would say that this shows the logic of his claim: the privileged had early access and thus were able to develop hardware and software that the rest of us now benefit from. But imagine a different scenario. Computers and the internet—having been developed largely through the US government and military—were considered a public resource from the beginning.[77] Instead of having a lucky few get early access, any interested student could have computer time. You might have had thousands—if not more—of very highly qualified people early on. With their combined abilities, who knows what more wondrous progress they might have made, and, equally if not more important, what disasters of concentrated power in the tech world might have been avoided? And, moreover, since the resources would have been *understood* as being public, the profits could have been kept public, and these could then have been plowed back into ever more research and development, instead of payments to stockholders to hide in overseas untaxed accounts.[78] The motto of the tech industry has been, "We'll climb up ahead of the rest of you and then throw you back down a ladder. Good luck lifting yourselves up to it." Perhaps the motto should be that of the National Association of Colored Women (founded in 1896): we need to be "lifting as we climb."[79]

And there is other evidence against Hayek's fundamental assumption of the relationship between competitive enterprise and progress. Or perhaps better put: there is insufficient evidence that competition is the best way to create progress.[80] Developments happen more quickly when everyone works together for a common goal. After all, competition slows the pace of discovery by dispersing knowledge, creating perverse incentives (trying to make money rather than trying to solve the problem), and fragmenting the potential collective energy. Cooperation enables knowledge sharing, the ability to focus on the project rather than the profit, and the collective dynamics that propel knowledge. As scientists who worked collectively on developing synthetic rubber to aid the US military during World War II reported, the solution was "the result of a thousand little discoveries made by a small army of well-funded industrial chemists. Those scientists remembered it as a golden age, when men who had formerly labored as rivals in different companies could collaborate with a shared sense of purpose."[81]

At the beginning of the COVID-19 pandemic, it seemed like many understood this historical lesson. There was a sense of global cooperation around topics like the global economy and how to develop a safe vaccine as quickly as possible.[82] Scientists and governments appeared to be spurred on by the possibility that we might even have been able to entirely avert this catastrophe if there had been global cooperation ahead of time. As pandemic-prevention expert Peter Daszak related to science journalist Jennifer Kahn: "'The problem isn't that prevention was impossible. . . . It was very possible. But we didn't do it. Governments thought it was too expensive. Pharmaceutical companies operate for profit.'" Kahn added: "And the W.H.O., for the most part, had neither the funding nor the power to enforce the large-scale global collaboration necessary to combat [this lack of motivation]."[83] New cooperation was promised in light of this failure.

Very quickly, however, competitive feelings resurfaced, with countries struggling to get the first vaccine to prioritize the well-being of their own citizens, and companies focusing on reaping the financial rewards of selling doses. Scientifically this makes little sense because it impedes the sharing of information. Practically it makes little sense because it ignores global interdependence, both in the sense that variants of the virus have developed and spread, and because economic recovery in a globally connected world requires a global recovery. Morally this race to be first makes little sense because it makes it less likely that vulnerable populations, rather than simply those in wealthy countries, will receive the vaccine first. Politically it might make sense in that the winner of the vaccine race could be a national hero, but it may not even work there, especially if the rush creates a dangerous product.[84]

The competitive spirit did not wholly overtake the vaccine planning, and the World Health Organization managed to engage 150 countries to help ensure that vaccines would be globally available, although for many in poorer nations, those vaccines did not arrive soon enough.[85] And why did the vaccine have to be an issue of national wealth in the first place? Researchers at the Universities of Helsinki and Oxford in fact had vaccines ready to deploy cheaply very early on in the pandemic, but decisions to partner with private companies (in Oxford's case, reportedly due to pressure from the Gates Foundation) meant that profit considerations overtook public health concerns.[86] Meanwhile, the United States has largely allowed pharmaceutical companies to reap the profits of what the public paid for, and patent laws prevented more rapid diffusion of the vaccines, which risked allowing continued global economic damage alongside the proliferation of potentially dangerous variants.[87] And none of this is even scraping the surface of how the focus on private economic growth has led to decades of deterioration of the public sphere, which in turn has helped create a misinformation nightmare inhibiting vaccination even in countries that have sufficient supply.

Here again, then, is an example of how plans designed around economic greatness undercut the very values they promise to deliver. They promise progress but in fact impede it. They promise the best possible life for all but only deliver for the few. They promise a social order that promotes peace and prosperity but in fact leads to authoritarianism and war. And what remains unfortunate is that, in spite of repeated claims otherwise, we in fact have excellent models for other ways to design our lives and societies. In this particular case, we had that model given a forceful articulation in the very same year that Hayek published his greatness-affirming blockbuster: Polanyi's *The Great Transformation*. In spite of the title's invocation of greatness, the book is in fact a paean to the good-enough life.

The Good-Enough Transformation

Polanyi saw the essential lie at the heart of the liberal argument going back to Smith. This argument, again, is that if we set up a system that enables the pursuit of wealth for the few via the competitive market, it will create both prosperity and inequality. They in turn justify this inequality by claiming that everyone's lives will improve through the prosperity, even if some lives improve more than others. What Polanyi saw quite clearly was that no social order could actually be maintained when top-heavy markets were being put into effect. The resulting inequalities and environmental destruction would simply create too much tension, leading to social upheaval. In Polanyi's words: "Such an institution [of market-based society] could not exist for any length of time without annihilating the human and natural substance of society." For Polanyi, the key is to correctly understand the relationship between the economy and society. Whereas liberals want to put society and even morality on a market basis, Polanyi wants us to understand the economy as "embedded" within society.

To understand what this means, it is important to be clear about what Polanyi means by market-driven economies. He does not have any opposition to markets for commodities, which are as ancient as culture itself. What concerns him is that liberal capitalism makes almost everything into a commodity. He is especially concerned about what he calls the "fictious commodities" of land, labor, and money. According to Polanyi, for most of human history, land, labor, and money were not subject to markets, but to community standards and norms—hence, they were embedded in society. This may have certain disadvantages depending on what those norms are. But markets, too, have norms, and those norms tend to reward some and disenfranchise others. By making the necessities of life into commodities, into things sold in a market, we hamper society's ability to deal with problems that may result in the market's maldistribution of basic necessities. Hence there is perpetual homelessness, poverty, and food insecurity, even in economic boom times.

This is part of why self-regulating market economics almost always goes out the window in a national crisis. While some economists and politicians continue to call for the business cycle to do its work and the weakest businesses to simply fold, reasonable people will mostly come to abandon their "economic principles" to save us from the annihilation that Polanyi predicted.

During the 2008 financial crash, even the ostensibly libertarian Koch brothers backed the TARP bailout when they saw their stocks crashing.[88] And in response to the coronavirus pandemic, ideas like governments printing money to pay idle workers were implemented by conservative governments in places like the United States, Australia, and the UK.[89]

This simple act of putting the needs of society over those of the market is what Polanyi famously defined as socialism: "Socialism is, essentially, the tendency inherent in an industrial civilization to transcend the self-regulating market by consciously subordinating it to a democratic society."[90] In this sense, there is no society that exists without socialism. And all economies in the world today maintain a balancing act between their socialist and market-driven sectors. What has largely been lost since the ascendancy of neoliberal economics is this balance. The result has been that the socialist tendencies that work to ensure democratic control over our societies are increasingly drowned out by the demands of profit.

If Polanyi's definition of socialism is correct, then much of what passes for understanding it today is simply wrong. Some writers insist that the only correct definition of socialism is "government ownership of the means of production,"[91] but socialism has many meanings, and for Polanyi it means democratic, *social* ownership of the means of production. (Otherwise, he would have called it governmentalism!) As economist Richard Wolff puts it, "When workers collectively and democratically produce, receive and distribute the profits their labor generates, the enterprise becomes socialist."[92] Not government, not private corporations, not powerful individuals, but everyone having their share of the wealth and well-being they help create—that's socialism according to Polanyi and Woolf. Wolff notes that there is no single path forward from this basic principle, and Polanyi does not give us a clear outline either. There are still many complicated questions about the role of government, individuals, markets, and cooperatives, and how they relate to each other. The point is that democratic socialism is not (or at least not for Polanyi) about government ownership (although it may involve the same kind of mixed economy we see today around natural resources, utilities, and essential services). Socialism for him is more fundamentally about how to ensure that society as a whole has a more equal and democratic stake in global wealth.[93]

This social ownership, Polanyi also makes clear, does not mean social *control*. One of the terrible losses in our vision of society today has been the idea of "freedom versus equality"— that is, the claim that we can either have individual freedoms subordinated to the demands of social justice, or individual liberty at the expense of social justice.[94] As many contemporary critics of this position have pointed out, the very framing of this choice is problematic.[95] To think of freedom versus equality reduces freedom to personal whim and perverts equality into collective nightmare. Equality and freedom are in fact inseparable from each other. A society that ensures decency and sufficiency for all, and drastically limits the concentration of power and wealth, ensures that no one has too much power over anyone else.

This is why, in concluding his book, Polanyi speaks of a "right to nonconformity" and the creation of ever new "spheres of arbitrary freedom."[96] He appears to mean that we should not be constrained by the dictates of efficiency or forced into permanent, terrible labor just to survive. Contemporary advocates of a more equal economy follow this line. Political theorist Albena Azmanova, for example, has argued for policies that both provide secure employment *and* encourage people not to stay in it too long. She advocates for both stability and leisure as goods that should be shared, and argues that industrial society could, if it were well organized, provide these. After all, because of the current shape of our economy, there are many people dedicating more than the hours necessary to maintain the general welfare. People have to do what the anthropologist David Graeber bluntly called "bullshit jobs"—jobs with no purpose other than to have a job and its attendant social standing. Graeber estimated that about half the work done in the world today is such labor. And he argued, like Azmanova and Polanyi, that providing both standardized income and standardized leisure could create more freedom to pursue our interests and values.[97]

In a more entrepreneurial mindset, Thomas Piketty has argued that, even within the constraints of the current economy, there would be much greater freedom if everyone were actually endowed with the economic capacity to pursue their ideas. He suggests very progressive taxes coupled with strong public services and an automatic inheritance of 125,000 euros for everyone at age 25. This would allow "everyone to participate fully in economic and social life," while also keeping inequality from driving both the material and positional economies to extremes. Maintaining the tax system on a permanent basis would ensure that everyone in every generation really did have something close to the same opportunities.[98] Whatever one makes of these different proposals, the point is that what they all provide is *more* freedom *because of* more equality.

There will undoubtedly still be issues here about time and resources and interpersonal struggles. Some proposals might still fail. We are not talking about utopia, remember. We are talking about a vision of a society that provides a good-enough life for all. And this is what Polanyi promises is possible when we limit the influence of the market to dictate everything. Society is difficult. Working with others and persuading and convincing them, or making oneself open enough to be convinced by them, is a difficult task. Polanyi concludes: "Uncomplaining acceptance of the reality of society gives [us] indomitable courage and strength to remove all removable injustice and unfreedom."[99] Not all injustice and unfreedom is removable. There is no utopia either of the market or of society for the simple reason that human beings interacting with each other in social life with their different desires and dissonant beliefs will have to live with solutions that do not please everyone. One can respond to this fact with Hayek's abandoning any concept of justice in the name of allowing the great to prosper. We have seen what kind of world that creates. Or one can respond with Polanyi's invocation to embrace the complexity, difficulty, and beauty of working toward common social goals without relinquishing personal whims. We have had glimpses of that world, and there are many new ideas to help it come into being. But before we can get to them, we have to climb over one more hurdle of greatness.

Why Philanthropy Is Not the Answer

Up the hill from where I teach the first-year students, the philosopher Peter Singer offers his legendary ethics class, which is, by many accounts, a remarkable, open-minded course. But in his own writings, he has increasingly subscribed to the greatness worldview. In *The Most Good You Can Do* (2015), Singer urges his readers to give away as much of their wealth as possible, which seems like a fine idea. However, he relates that one day he was asked about whether there is an ethics to how one makes one's money. In a word, Singer says no. Any wealth earned by someone who will give it away is better than wealth earned by someone who won't. If you didn't make that money, someone else would, so committing to making money and giving it away is the most good you can do.

Although Singer identifies with the political left, his position here is remarkably similar to Andrew Carnegie's. It was Carnegie, after all, whose canonical defense of capitalism and philanthropy held that capitalists should be allowed to make as much as they want in whatever rapacious manner that they want so long as they then leave very little to their children. Instead, he suggested it should be taxed away, or, preferably, given away by the great men (always men) themselves for public works and educational institutes.[100] What gives the lie to this type of argument is that it is nothing more than a vicious cycle. Businessmen make vast sums by brutally treating their workers—Carnegie does not shy away from admitting this. They then use the money to fund universities. Those universities fund a new generation of businessmen who, in the pursuit of profits to give away, act like Carnegie by mistreating *their* workers. This is the endless cycle of greatness justifying itself as helping others, but then only managing to reproduce all of its misery.[101]

And "justify" is the key word. Piketty has shown at great length that capitalism is just the latest of a number of unequal regimes that have found ways to make themselves appear not only natural but beneficial.[102] John Kenneth Galbraith wrote pointedly of these justifications: "The grounds have been many and varied and have been principally noted for the rigorous exclusion of the most important reason, which is the simple unwillingness to give up the enjoyment of what they have."[103] But Carnegie of course will not admit this. He claims his work is "not only beneficial, but essential for the future progress of the race."[104] This is the language of kings and clerics, the logic invented to suit those who are doing the inventing. Marx and

Engels may have overstated the case, but they were not entirely wrong when they said that the ideas of a given era are the ideas of the ruling class.[105] Philanthropy is a very clever justificatory idea—so clever that we sometimes forget that it is only a justification and not, in fact, necessarily a benefit to the rest of us, nor essential for our progress.

Indeed, it is remarkable the prestige that philanthropy enjoys today, given that it was once considered deeply problematic in countries like the United States. There were frequent criticisms that philanthropy was just a public relations cover to hide the origins of ill-gotten gains. In the spirit of the times, President Theodore Roosevelt declaimed: "No amount of charities in spending such fortunes can compensate in any way for the misconduct in acquiring them."[106] Consider the case today of George Soros, whose initiatives have been an important force for democratic causes over the past two decades, and whose criticism of "market fundamentalism" (that is a belief system more than an empirical science) was an important blow to neoliberalism's prestige.[107] All the same, Soros's money came from finance capitalism, and his famous bets against the British pound and the Thai baht made him a fortune while destabilizing both of those countries. Some have even drawn a direct line between Soros's actions and Brexit. As a generally approving *New York Times* profile noted, "The industry that made him a billionaire contributed significantly to the circumstances that now imperil what Soros the philanthropist has tried to achieve."[108]

But although the giving may not compensate for the damage, it can cover over it. Today Bill Gates is, undoubtedly, a significant philanthropist whose giving to education and scientific causes is truly important. This reputation, however, is in marked contrast to how Gates was thought of before his giving. As one

New York Times report noted: "Twenty years ago, people associated the name Gates with 'ruthless, predatory' monopolistic conduct that gave him 'the reputation of a modern-day robber baron,' said Charles Lowenhaupt, a wealth adviser in St. Louis. . . . His philanthropy has helped 'rebrand' his name, Mr. Lowenhaupt added."[109]

As a result, and in spite of some the conspiracy theories that he is trying to control us with vaccines, the causes Gates champions have a fair amount of traction. Through his wealth, he can not only guide research at a scale only plausibly matched by governments, but he can also help affect government policy.[110] Gates's stature as a man who is using his wealth to help others means he can decide *how* others get helped. Sometimes he is certainly in the right—it's hard to imagine a good-enough life today without vaccines. But his profit-minded pursuit of these things has also been roundly criticized for slowing down vaccine production and distribution during the COVID-19 pandemic.[111] And it's also important that some of the opposition to even his good policies may come from the very fact that he is one of the world's wealthiest humans. According to the historian of philanthropy Rob Reich, this was the fundamental reason for early opposition to the practice of philanthropy in the United States. Philanthropic foundations "were considered a deeply and fundamentally *antidemocratic* institution, an entity that would undermine political equality, convert private wealth into the donor's preferred public policies, could exist in perpetuity, and be unaccountable except to a handpicked assemblage of trustees."[112] Perhaps one of the best examples of this process is that such foundations are not only accepted, but beloved today. None of this would have happened, according to Reich, without John D. Rockefeller wanting to start a *tax-deductible* foundation and having the money, connections, and political clout to force an unpopular bill through Congress.[113] If I have to choose between David Koch trying to fill our atmosphere with toxins and Bill Gates trying to make us healthier, I'll choose Bill Gates, but I'd rather have a democratic voice in the process myself.[114]

However, by Singer's logic, Gates versus Koch really is the best available option. "Those who think the entire modern capitalist economy should be overthrown have conspicuously failed to demonstrate that there are ways of structuring an economy that have better outcomes. Neither have they indicated how, in the twenty-first century, a transition to an alternative economic system might occur."[115] It is not clear why Singer believes that we can have only unfettered make-as-much-as-you-possibly-can capitalism. Indeed, most people who oppose the current system *have* sketched viable alternatives and *have* shown how to transition to them. Supporters of progressive capitalism like Joseph Stiglitz and Mariana Mazzucato have proposed relatively straightforward changes that build on the current system and embody elements of practices that have worked in the recent past.[116] What stands in our way is not the lack of an alternative, but the active labor of those today who, like Carnegie in his era, benefit from the current system to keep things as they are. One of the best ways to fight back is to continually remind ourselves of the other models out there. Progressive capitalism is a popular option, but other available economic systems can bring us even closer to a good-enough life for all.

Some Plans for a Good-Enough World

If you've agreed with me so far in this book, you appreciate the goal of a life with less burnout, anxiety, strife, and anger, and with more ordinary joys, mutual recognition, and cooperation, while still understanding that some degree of dissonance, failure, and suffering is inevitable. What I've tried to argue thus far in this chapter is that our current social and economic systems work against this kind of life. Along the way we have seen glimmers of other ways of organizing society that can support the good-enough life. I now want to bring these glimmers more clearly into view.

The nature of markets is, as we have seen, to be a powerful force in the growth of economies, but to distribute the money and power they generate terribly unequally across a society.[117] Thus the simplest way to move from a greatness-oriented society to a good-enough society is to reduce the power of markets. This was the essential lesson of what is most generally called "social democracy," and it was the basic mixed-economy framework that guided post–World War II Europe, North America, Oceania, and Japan, and later parts of Southeast Asia, South America, Africa, and elsewhere. According to the historian of politics Sheri Berman, this was effectively "the end of history," when we had everything figured out. There were markets for most things and some degree of inequality, but the basic necessities of life were taken care of through welfare. Public housing and job assistance also took some forms of labor and land out of the market system. Profits were taxed heavily to reinvest in education, infrastructure, and public goods. Extensive union membership ensured good wages and fair working conditions. Universal healthcare was provided (except in the United States), and robust systems of unemployment insurance, early childhood care, and social security for old age took care of people at moments when it was not possible for them to take care of themselves.[118]

But, of course, history never does end. Social democracy had deep flaws, and it tolerated still extensive levels of material and positional inequality.[119] Often this inequality was racialized. In the United States, for example, parts of the progressive economic policy unleashed by the New Deal excluded some African Americans, immigrants, and Indigenous people from its bounty, and, most treacherously, coincided with putting Japanese Americans in internment camps.[120] Early social security and unemployment laws, for example, excluded farm and domestic workers, who worked in industries that employed nearly half the Black population.[121] There was also well-documented discrimination in access to affordable housing. Such early exclusions multiplied over the years and have helped perpetuate the racialized economic inequality we see today.[122]

Moreover, wealthy social democracies never managed to extend their bounty beyond national borders, and they did little for postcolonial states. Indeed, they often fought back development in those countries in the name of growing their own wealth. When states in Latin America, South Asia, and Africa began to push forward a "developmentalist" agenda and attempt to replicate the Keynesian growth models of the West, they threatened the extensive profits that Western states extracted from neocolonial ownership of land and resources.[123] In order to maintain power, Western nations backed military dictatorships, which resulted in what journalist Vincent Bevins calls "the mass murder campaign that shaped our world." In Indonesia alone, the toll is estimated at over one million lives.[124] This has also created ongoing economic problems, as these dictatorships borrowed and wasted money for which many nations are now still on the hook.[125] These interventions were often done in the name of fighting totalitarian communism, but many of them took place against social democratic and democratic socialist governments who were simply trying to even the international economic playing field.[126] The United States was often the primary mover, and stories of the military or CIA intervening to protect business interests in Guatemala, Iran, and elsewhere are relatively well known.[127] But I have to admit to being shocked recently watching documentary footage of a Swedish company's unionized workforce calling in the Liberian military in order to break up a unionization effort of local workers at a mining site.[128] Although Scandinavian countries and citizens were often more supportive of global egalitarian action, many of their companies were not.[129] Actions like this helped create global instabilities and enable (but of course do not justify) the immigration politics that today are putting pressure on social democracy in countries like Sweden.

Indeed, at the same time that social democracies grew their wealth through unequal global power, they also let inequality grow at home, slowly loosening their progressive systems in the face of international competition and fluctuations in commodity prices, especially oil. This eventually meant blowback for their global failures. They never fully developed a responsible way to ensure that fiscal justice would exist across borders, and thus they lost jobs and tax revenue.[130] It is certainly true that this provided jobs that were otherwise absent in developing countries, but it is also true that these jobs were often terribly paid, dangerous, insecure, and environmentally hazardous.[131] Social democracy was ultimately defeated less by its own flaws than by the assault of wealthy elites who wanted to increase their power, but the global faults certainly left an opening. A good-enough world must be a good-enough *world*.

In response to the Great Recession of 2007–9, there was something of a "Keynesian resurgence" as many policy makers realized that only government intervention and deficit spending could hold back another great depression.[132] A decade later, while there remained holdouts during the economic downturn created by COVID-19, some of the strongest bulwarks of neoliberal thought began to fall. Even the editorial board of the *Financial Times* called for a return to the Keynes-inspired New Deal. Indeed, they even went further: "Radical reforms—reversing the prevailing policy direction of the last four decades [i.e., since 1980, the beginning of the neoliberal era]—will need to be put on the table. Governments will have to accept a more active role in the economy. They must see public services as investments rather than liabilities, and look for ways to make labour markets less insecure. Redistribution will again be on the agenda; the privileges of the elderly and wealthy in question. Policies until recently considered eccentric, such as basic income and wealth taxes, will have to be in the mix."[133]

Given that there is this movement occurring even in neoliberal corners, it is not surprising that the upheavals of the early twenty-first century have also created a growing interest in democratic socialism. There are important overlaps here. Keynes himself had warned against viewing socialists as the enemies of his economics. The split was not between social democrats and democratic socialists, but between those seeking to make peace and improve the general welfare in the world as a whole, and those who sought "power, prestige, national or personal glory, the imposition of a culture, and hereditary or racial prejudice."[134] Both social democracy and democratic socialism oppose this greatness-oriented worldview, and thus the rational economic debate in terms of a good-enough life is not these two against each other, but these two against greatness.

Still, social democracy and democratic socialism are quite different. Social democracy shares its roots with democratic socialism (and somewhat ironically, the Social Democratic Party was originally the more radical, as it was the official organ of Marxist politics in Germany). Both were born out of the frustration of socialists with the orthodox Marxism that reigned in Europe at the time.[135] Democratic socialists, with Eduard Bernstein being perhaps their foremost theorist, saw that capitalism was not leading to the expected contradictions and revolution.[136] Indeed, as Smith predicted, general opulence was growing. Nevertheless, that opulence continued to accrue unevenly and unjustly. Bernstein argued that these trends could not be reversed without establishing a less revolutionary and more democratic platform, less predicated on class antagonism and more dedicated to cross-class work for the common good. Marxists warned that any such collaborations would inevitably water down their message, but Bernstein argued that this was a risk worth taking. He may have been right: according to historians like Berman, in the interwar period, the early implementation of social democratic policies helped stem the rising fascist tides in places like the United States, the UK, and Sweden. But the Marxists also had a good point: entering democratic politics inevitably meant compromise. These were the compromises that led to the social democratic welfare state we know today.[137] So while democratic socialists and social democrats (now the name for the moderates) share this fundamental origin, they also depart on the key question of ownership. Social democrats tend to work with taxes and regulations to redistribute wealth and guarantee services. Democratic socialists tend to work on changing ownership structures to "predistribute" wealth in more egalitarian ways.

According to Gary Dorrien, a specialist on the history and theory of democratic socialism, its aim is "a fully democratized society in which the people control the economy and government, no group dominates any other, and every citizen is free, equal, and included."[138] To this end, democratic socialists work to create the world as a cooperative community that reverses the essential logic of competitive capitalism. In the latter, private gains are maximized and then distributed—if ever—to the public. In the former, all work together to directly grow the shared wealth. If general opulence is indeed the key to general well-being, democratic socialists and other egalitarians ask, then why go through the bizarre practice of enriching the few first? Why not directly aim at increasing general well-being? This practice today goes by many names—industrial democracy, economic democracy, the pluralist commonwealth, participatory socialism, worker self-directed enterprises—but the basic idea is the same: if we are to actually live in a democratic society, then that democracy must exist as much in the workplace as in the country.[139] (And, at least in the context of the United States, a term like "economic democracy" may be more politically viable than other names for a fairer economy.)

Furthermore, the fact that democracy does not function that way in the workplace is the *cause* of its not working that way in the country: uneven economic power inevitably means uneven democratic power. This was part of why Franklin Delano Roosevelt proposed an "Economic Bill of Rights" in 1944 as a supplement to the political Bill of Rights that currently exists in the United States. This second bill included, among other rights, guarantees for a job, food, clothing, housing, and education—and not just at subsistence levels, but with "a decent home . . . good health . . . a good education."[140] The logic of adding the second bill is that things like freedom of expression will be perverted through dominance by the few in a society that is too economically uneven.

There are many models and debates for how to go about achieving this more democratic society—whether it is more social democratic or democratic socialist or not captured by these names at all.[141] And many of these models, though we may not hear about them while reading the daily business news or watching the Dow Industrials Index, are already in existence. Since World War II, large German and Swedish firms have had "codetermination" between shareholders, managers, and laborers. In this system, a certain amount of board seats and voting power are set aside for workers.[142] The plans are somewhat limited (shareholders retain the most power), but more expansive versions have been proposed in those countries, as well as by Labour in the UK under Jeremy Corbyn and in the US presidential campaign platforms of Bernie Sanders and Elizabeth Warren.[143] Perhaps the most famous version was the "Meidner Plan" in Sweden, which offered a transitional model for ownership of large corporations. In this plan, 20 percent of all profit from a given year would be reinvested in a company's stock and held by the workers. Over time, as the workers' share of the general stock grew, they would come to assume ownership of the company. The plan was ultimately defeated as the Swedish Social Democrats fell out of power, but it has had important legacies—such as the current proposals.[144]

There are also a great number of companies that were founded to be worker-owned, perhaps most famously the multi-billion-dollar-revenue-generating Mondragon Corporation, a federation of cooperative enterprises in the Basque country. There are also smaller-scale enterprises springing up every year. One promising path has been the "Cleveland model" (or the "Preston model" in the UK), in which coops work in an integrated manner with "anchor institutions" in the community, such as hospitals and universities.[145] In Cleveland, the Evergreen coops have grown up around these institutions, and include an industrial-scale laundry, solar energy production, and hydroponic vegetable growers.[146] Their sustainable practices produce sustainable wages for their employee-owners.

Economic power can also be democratized at a more general level, such as in sovereign wealth funds. These are publicly held funds that are to be used for the sole benefit of the public. One of the most famous examples is the "Norwegian model," in which a combination of funds and state-owned enterprises hold about 60 percent of the wealth in the country. The funds are used for public spending projects, or to cover losses during economic downturns. Although it may seem a far-fetched Scandinavian model that is difficult to implement in other countries, it is in fact relatively common elsewhere.[147] Gar Alperovitz points out that there are enough versions in the United States to speak of "everyday socialism, all the time, American style."[148] And, more often than not, these projects are in conservative "red states," including the Alaska Permanent Fund, the Texas Permanent School Fund and Permanent University Fund, and The Permanent Wyoming Mineral Trust Fund. Not to mention that 25 percent of the electricity in the United States is supplied by locally owned utilities or energy cooperatives.[149] While those permanent funds are largely based on oil extraction, there are also collective ways to create a greener economy, more focused on regeneration of resources than their degeneration through consumption.[150]

These different social systems also foster different types of social interactions. Research has shown that cooperative systems tend to produce better communication, friendliness, helpfulness, coordination of effort, orientation to task achievement, orderliness, higher productivity, feelings of agreement, ability to see other's points of view, self-esteem, and hope about future interactions.[151] And as Riane Eisler, adrienne maree brown, and others have pointed out, the values of egalitarian, partnership-focused systems also promote greater gender, racial, and ability equity.[152] (This was perhaps part of why, throughout the twentieth century, African Americans have been at the forefront of developing cooperatives, and there are promising programs today with Latina domestic workers in cities like New York.[153]) In these systems, after all, the aim is for each to contribute what they can to an overall goal in which they will all share the benefit. And "benefit" itself is redefined from a purely economic logic to the social values of working well together and to the various forms of value that all of us can provide. Time and again it has been shown that workplaces that foster participation both positionally (less top-down and more equal power) and materially (shared rewards) increase productivity, happiness, and a sense of purpose.[154]

As just one example, consider Gravity Payments, an online credit card transaction company headquartered in Seattle, Washington, run by Dan Price. One day in 2011, an employee named Jason Haley told Price that he was cheating his workers by paying them only $35,000 a year while his salary was over $1 million. Price was initially shocked and offended, but after speaking to friends trying to live on amounts similar to the salaries he paid in quickly gentrifying Seattle, he eventually heeded Haley's message. Price realized that although he had founded the company through his risk and entrepreneurship, he was entirely dependent on his workers, and could not justify living his comfortable life while they scraped by. His initial step was tentative: he implemented 20 percent raises, thinking it would be a one-time thing. But over the course of a year, he found that the raise more than paid for itself with increases in productivity and decreases in turnover. In 2015, based on academic research suggesting that earnings of around $70,000 a year would help create a happy and stable life for employees, Price instituted that figure as the company's new minimum wage, and slashed his own salary to the same amount to pay for it.[155] In 2020 he reported the results on Twitter: "*Our business tripled *Staff who own homes grew 10x *401(k) contributions doubled *70% of employees paid off debt *Staff having kids soared 10x *Turnover dropped in half *76% of staff are engaged at work, 2x the national average."[156]

Price's model is in stark contrast to a more famed company headquartered in Seattle: Amazon. In 2019, Amazon initiated a search for "HQ2," a second headquarters outside of Seattle. Although people in Seattle warned of the growing inequality and gentrification that the presence of Amazon could cause, there was still widespread excitement across North America for the potential jobs and tax revenues the headquarters could bring.[157] Cities offered billions of dollars of subsidies to one of the world's richest companies. In the end Amazon chose two cities: Alexandria, Virginia, just outside Washington, DC, and Long Island City, Queens, a neighborhood in New York City. According to journalist Alec MacGillis, who has extensively chronicled Amazon's role in the modern world, these choices were the "ultimate example of the winner-take-all, rich-get-richer dynamic of today's economy, in which growth and prosperity flow to the handful of cities that are home to the tech giants that control ever more of daily commerce." At least, he noted, Amazon was up front about its aims, writing in a company-issued statement: "Nowhere did Amazon say HQ2 was a project designed to help communities in need."[158]

This quickly became painfully clear to poor communities in New York. As soon as the announcement was made, a fight ensued over whether the company should be allowed into Queens, and under what conditions. There was particular concern over whether Amazon would be "neutral" on unionization (that is to say, would not oppose unions), which they refused to do. Rather than engaging the fight, Amazon pulled out of the plan.[159] Amazon's not coming prevented increases in the kinds of problems that Seattle had experienced and that are already rampant in New York: ever-increasing property prices and growing income inequality between the well-paid managerial staff and the low-paid workers. (Long Island City is near Elmhurst, one of the poorest areas in the city and one of the hardest hit by COVID-19, in large part because it has so many workers in low-paid but essential jobs.) Still, Amazon's not coming did take away the possibility of jobs and tax revenue.

From the good-enough life perspective, what is missing from the Amazon-Queens story is another way of bringing work to an area like Queens that does not rely on an anti-union, inequality-driven company. One solution would be to replace Amazon with something like Mondragon or the Cleveland model—a single large cooperatively owned businesses, or a collection of smaller such businesses. It could even have been Amazon itself, had Jeff Bezos taken advice from his neighbor Dan Price. But because our collective social mindset is so premised on great founders and entrepreneurs, the idea that Amazon would have an egalitarian mindset or that it could be replaced by cooperatives never really entered the public discussion.[160] This is why it matters so much that our leading ethicists like Peter Singer cease claiming that winner-take-all capitalism is the only viable system. Claims like this cloud out our imaginative power to actually transition to the many available forms of economic democracy.

The combination of public ownership, collective ownership, and private ownership is what Alperovitz calls the "pluralist commonwealth."[161] The point is not to create the perfect economic system that will resolve all of our social issues. It is to create one that will enable decency and sufficiency for everyone. What the experience of the last few centuries has taught us is that the winner-take-all capitalist system of Hayek and others is simply incapable of delivering this. It distributes rewards unevenly, and its promises of eventual smooth distribution are simply never realized. While it has taught us a lot about markets and the growth of wealth, its logical premise for distribution is, ultimately, completely illogical. Imagine an analogical situation in which we create an irrigation system that floods one field at the top of the hill in the hope that the rest of the water would eventually make it to the bottom. Or in the more pungent analogy from businessman and shared wealth advocate Djaffar Shalchi: "Wealth is like manure: spread it, and it makes everything grow; pile it up, and it stinks."[162]

A more logical irrigation or manure system, like a more logical economic system, would simply distribute the resources as evenly as possible to the fields. And it would ensure that it does so without spoiling the environment itself in the process. But even in such a regenerative economy, some days there would be leaks; some days the sun would shine too brightly; some days there would be scarcities of water. This cannot be stressed enough: *economic democracy is not easy.* Those who look to democratic socialism or other more egalitarian forms of the economy as some kind of panacea are, I think, sorely mistaken.[163] There is simply no system that can fully deal with all the issues that might arise in the endlessly complex emotional and social lives of interdependent human beings. In a cooperative system, many questions arise: Does everyone deserve an equal share even if they don't put as much energy into their work? How will interpersonal conflicts be handled without strict hierarchy? Will collective decisions be made by a simple majority, or consensus, or modified consensus? If arriving at consensus takes many long meetings, is it fair to exclude people who cannot stay because of family care needs? What space will be allowed for people who would prefer to work less and make less money, or work more and make more money? When times get tough, will economic democrats continue to insist on equality, or will they create new systems of division?[164]

Morton Deutsch, one of the leading theorists of human cooperative behavior, has argued that there are three social factors that make cooperation work: substitutability (the possibility for one worker to swap labor with another), cathexis (personal rapport), and inducibility (the power of group attraction). However, these are also the very things that overwhelm it: substitutability eventually leads to each member finding work they prefer, cathexis leads to cliques, and inducibility leads to a deadening conformity.[165] Deutsch still believes strongly in cooperation, but only a cooperative system that is prepared to acknowledge and work through the development of these problems.

The point of shifting toward increased economic democracy is not, therefore, because it will solve all our problems, but because it will give us good-enough problems, instead of the great ones we currently face. A global society that followed Polanyi and abolished markets for labor, land, and money could not then expect all the problems in these areas to then simply disappear. There are very interesting, if presently difficult-to-imagine, suggestions here—such as the idea espoused by Martin Luther King and others of a guaranteed income—but all of them would have to begin from the premise that they will be no more and no less than good enough.[166] Any new economy would be no less than good enough because our aim would be to design a society, step by step, in such a way as to *aim* at decency and sufficiency for everyone. In this economy we would not work to live off the opulent excess of the great, but to build up the tremendous energies of the many. But the new system would also be no more than good enough because it would have to be prepared to deal with complexities, difficulties, and inevitable failures. Only the assumption of failure allows us to prepare for the troubles to come.[167]

Limiting the Positional Economy

I've spent most of this chapter discussing the macro social dynamics of developing a connected world that provides a good-enough life for all. To this end, I've largely focused on economic theory. But as I've noted here and in previous chapters, economic inequality is not the only cause of our greatness-oriented society. It is also the product of what Fred Hirsch called "the positional economy." As I use the term, it refers to a variety of things ranging from awards, leadership positions, and beach-front properties, to the attention one receives from a friend or mentor or lover versus what they give another person. The positional economy can also be an intense site of ableism, racism, and sexism, as, even among people with similar material wealth, conscious or unconscious prejudices can influence who wins jobs, awards, attention, or respect.[168] Creating an economic democracy must be coincident with continued work for equal rights across these spheres of identity.

The existence of a positional economy is one of the arguments that libertarians like philosopher Robert Nozick have used to discredit the idea of material equality. Even if we get rid of vast differences in wealth, Nozick says, we will simply find other ways to compare ourselves and create new centers of power.[169] Sigmund Freud similarly doubted that overcoming the problem of material inequality would do much to stem the problems of aggression and social discord, which he traced more to sexual than economic competition.[170] In a sense, this is the corollary of the problem with which I started this chapter:

just as human relationships find their limits in social systems, so can social systems be upended by the tragedies of human relationships.

Several science fiction writers have considered this problem, including Cory Doctorow in *Down and Out in the Magic Kingdom* (2003) and Ursula Le Guin in *The Dispossessed* (1974). In Doctorow's novel, automation has cured scarcity and death, and people can live forever going through different adventures without concern for food or health. But because there is still a positional economy, they trade on "whuffie," a kind of currency of esteem. (Doctorow doesn't investigate the potential problems of inherited prejudices in his esteem economy.) The more whuffie one collects, the more one can do, including, in the main plot of the novel, taking control of Disneyland. In Le Guin's *The Dispossessed*, a radical anarchist colony is established on a nearby moon. "Propertarianism" is abolished, and everyone lives for the collective. "Don't egoize" is the colony's parenting version of saying "Say please and thank you." While inequality is largely annulled materially, it excels positionally. Expertise—or a reputation for expertise—becomes particularly meaningful. While no material benefits accrue, the appointed experts still feel the satisfaction of having the power to make major decisions.

In a brief, astute reading of Doctorow's novel, Peter Frase notes that the book correctly perceives that even material abundance cannot overcome the problem of power. Nevertheless, he suggests that it is a fallacy to assume that the new positional economy is merely a replication of the old material one. While in the material economy, the risk is that one kind of value— money—overwhelms all the others, in the world of whuffie, one can get esteem for a great many actions. Somewhat like the societies envisioned by Walzer and other virtue ethicists (discussed in chapter 2), this "is not a world of no hierarchies but one of *many* hierarchies, no one of which is superior to all the others."[171] Le Guin's novel, although critical of the ossification of the once radical anarchist society, concludes even more strongly on the side of equality, with the vindication of the society's core democratic and decentralized values, once reignited by the actions of the novel's hero.

These alternative visions make some sense of why the positional economy is different from the material one. With all due respect to Freud, sexual competition simply doesn't have the same overarching power that the economy does, largely because while wealth begets wealth, having one lover does not beget having many, nor does it pass down through the generations. Economic inequality, furthermore, translates more easily into other kinds of power. As Shakespeare famously put it in *Timon of Athens*, gold "will make black white, foul fair, / Wrong right, base noble, old young, coward valiant . . . / This yellow slave / Will knit and break religions, bless the accursed, / Make the hoar leprosy adored, place thieves / And give them title, knee and approbation / With senators on the bench. . . ."[172] Certainly fame can have a similar effect, as when it helped Ronald Reagan and Arnold Schwarzenegger become the governors of California, or Al Franken a senator. But while one comedian made it into the US Senate, about half of its members are millionaires.[173]

Nevertheless, the question still arises: if wealth meant less in society, would we just wind up with fifty percent former actors in the US Senate? This poses real dilemmas for the good-enough life, because, again, the life we are looking for here is not just about everyone having materially enough. It is also about fulfilling our social and psychic needs. And being disenfranchised while other people make decisions that upend your life is a damaging experience for individuals and communities.

Since rectifying such imbalances in the positional economy has received much less attention than economic matters, I find the potential solutions more provisional, but still bountiful.

One area to begin our consideration starts in a terrible place: what Primo Levi called the "ferocious law" of Auschwitz that I discussed in the previous chapter. According to Levi, again, this law was best explained by a line from the Gospel of Matthew: "To he that has, will be given; from he that has not, will be taken away." Levi believed that civilized life kept this law at bay, ensuring that no one had too much and no one too little.

Two decades after Levi's account, however, the sociologist Robert K. Merton returned to this line from Matthew (although he seems to have been unaware of Levi's citation) to coin what he called "the Matthew effect." For Merton, this was not a law confined to situations of unfathomable injustice, but a generally functioning rule for how benefits accrued in society. Studying interviews of scientists who had received Nobel prizes and comparing their accomplishments with people who had not, he noticed a pattern: "eminent scientists get disproportionately great credit for their contributions to science while relatively unknown scientists tend to get disproportionately little credit for comparable contributions."[174] To be sure, Merton's point was not that the eminence of these scientists was undue, but only that once they received their initial credit, the prestige snowballed, often to the point of obscuring the valuable contributions of others. You might think, well, that's not so bad: it's a very different "Matthew effect" than what Levi described. And that is undoubtedly true, and there is no analogy here besides the citation to Matthew. I recall Levi only to mark that all Matthew effects—all systems that reward some repeatedly and take away from others repeatedly—are harmful, even if in drastically different ways.

Consider in this more everyday context a situation in which there is one top prize given to all the graduating environmental scientists in the country, which offers them millions in seed money for research. Although hundreds of well-qualified people apply, only one can be chosen. As with most applications, no idea really stands out, but there are fifteen to twenty that seem to deserve the award. At an impasse, the committee chooses one of the ideas because it most closely aligns with their own research interests (which they of course think are the most important). As it turns out, this idea wasn't actually very good for reasons that simply could not be clear at the time (no fault of the applicant or the committee; the experiments simply had to be done to find out). Meanwhile, some of the ideas that did not get funding would have been major breakthroughs, but they never get realized. Indeed, the scientists who had those ideas, perhaps because their scientific abilities far exceed their writing abilities, never get recognized. At the same time, our winner, even though completely unsuccessful, now has the prestige of having won the top award. And so when another round of grant funding comes up, the committee thinks, "Well, this person was considered the best, so they probably are," and they just keep winning rewards. Some of their ideas are good, some are bad, but the prestige accrues nevertheless, while those who lost just keep losing. In a competitive job environment where only the winners prosper, this not only means careers can be ruined, but that some of the best ideas get lost.

There are some clear ways to counteract this process. One is anonymous review, in which previous accomplishments are not listed. This means no letters of recommendation and no CVs. This process, aside from the case of journal articles, is extremely rare, in part because track records can matter, and in part because it only cuts out bias about the person, not about the project itself. Another option that is gaining traction, especially in the sciences, is the idea of doing lotteries for grant rewards.[175] These lotteries are not just for anyone who applies: there is a weeding out to assure general quality. There may also be weighted factors to ensure diversity in the identities of the winners, which can help offset other advantages, such as access to mentorship. The lottery process ensures decent quality, cuts down on Matthew effects, and also opens up applications to ideas outside of the mainstream.[176] It can thus be a key component in reducing the power of the positional economy of prestige.

A more radical option, even more attuned with the good-enough life, is to decrease the positional power of the Matthew effect for awards by simply granting equal funding. This idea is also gaining traction in the sciences, which seem to be far ahead of the arts and humanities in thinking through the dilemmas of grant funding.[177] Perhaps that is because of the better documented discontent among scientists. For example, a recent study of scientists found that an eye-popping 97 percent said that they spent more time working on proposals than on their actual work. An almost equal number—95 percent—wanted to see changes to the system.[178] And researchers have found that if simply *everyone* who qualified (a relatively low bar) were given equal funding, there would still be more than enough money to go around to fund major research initiatives (not to mention more collaborative projects).[179] Not only would more projects be pursued, but people would not have to spend all their time applying.

One can imagine these practices being useful in other spheres of achievement. Athenian democracy, for example, used a lottery system to determine who would be a representative in the administration of the city. The aim of the system was not only to ensure that no one held power for too long, but also that everyone would be capable of governing effectively. A modified system like this could work in modern democracies, with free training for anyone interested, a rigorous application process, and a "good-enough" cutoff, ensuring ethics, integrity, and knowledge of current issues. This would be one way, at least, of making elected office a triumph of who made the cutoff, rather than who was the best campaigner, fundraiser, or demagogue. This has also recently been suggested as a way of removing the partisan rancor from choosing Supreme Court justices in the United States.[180]

Others have argued for more extensive use of lotteries. Alexander Guerrero, a philosopher of law and politics, has proposed what he calls a "lottocracy."[181] In Guerrero's system, rather than power concentrated in a single, elected legislative body of those deemed most worthy (meritocrats), there would be a number of legislative bodies of randomly chosen—lottocratic—citizens who would be given time and resources to deliberate together on each issue. Part of the logic of this, as Hélène Landemore, another theorist of lottocracies, has pointed out, is that elections tend to favor the powerful, the wealthy, the well connected, the tall, the charismatic, and the eloquent. Obviously, none of these identities help make better policy.[182] Rather than hiding the luck of being born wealthy, tall, or charismatic, this system makes a more egalitarian luck the *basis* of who gets chosen. It's no longer a question of individual success but of ensuring the general quality of the citizenry such that anyone, at any time, can fulfill the requirements of representation.

Landemore's argument goes beyond simply making a case for greater participation because it is a morally good thing to do. Building on work the world over—from the *gram sabhas* of India to the National Public Policy conferences of Brazil to one-off events like the Great National Debate on climate in

France—Landemore argues that there are genuine improvements from these processes. This research builds on millennia of work by communities both powerful and disenfranchised who have worked out cooperative ways to ensure that everyone has a say in their lives. The academic theory that backs it up for Landemore comes from the work of organizational researchers Lu Hong and Scott Page. They argued that cognitively diverse teams outperform teams with higher but homogenous metrics. To explain this, Landemore uses a mapping metaphor: a homogenous team may reach the highest point of a given peak, but they might not realize that they missed genuine resources in a part of the terrain that they overlooked.[183] Landemore argues that we should understand democratic processes of diverse groups, chosen randomly, as both normatively and practically superior to groups of even those deemed the best and the brightest. As a case in point, she mentions the Yellow Vest movement in France, which erupted after the French administrative elite imposed a gas tax in order to curb emissions. The goal of curbing emissions is right, but the method has to meet the needs of the many, not just those who can afford to live near where they work.

There are also lottery-based models for other applications. In the eighteenth century, at the University of Basel, academic appointments were picked by lot after the best three candidates had been chosen.[184] More recently, Barry Schwartz proposed what he calls a "good-enough" system for admission to selective colleges.[185] Michael Sandel has strongly advocated for this as well.[186] Under this system, applicants would have to meet certain basic criteria for academic and extracurricular achievement. Those criteria could be designed to factor in variations based on systemic inequalities or even personal histories. And they should, in my opinion, prize civic and intellectual engagement over test scores.

Once those criteria are designed, all applications that meet the criteria would be put into a lottery for admission. Given that top colleges, by their own admission, reject many more good applicants than they can accommodate, this makes the presently arbitrary system more honestly random.[187]

The real advantages of the lottery system are not just that they help us find more good-enough applicants, but also that they contribute substantially to the good-enough life. If there are basic cutoff criteria for college admission that you have to meet and everything else beyond that doesn't matter, then you can have your childhood back. You do not need to pursue every last possible thing to do (unless you really want to) and can instead spend more time connecting with friends and family. For parents, it's also a good way to make the whole "to be or not to be a Chua-inspired tiger mom so my kid gets into Harvard" moot. The system also erodes the positional power of these schools or rewards, because if it's just down to a lottery, then the snobbish allure of having been admitted for no particularly better reason is annulled.

There are also things that individuals can do in the absence of systemic changes. Currently the most famous and elite in any field tend to crowd out others by soaking up opportunities and platforms. Rather than crowd out, they could focus more on crowding in. A famous professor, for example, might insist on having an adjunct share the stage with them for their keynote. A famous artist might insist on having a show with an overlooked colleague. We may also give more social esteem to such activities. Rather than being impressed that someone wrote one more book or made one more painting, we might marvel at their humility in not doing so, but instead writing a foreword or a book review for others. This could trickle up into the prestige economy. Perhaps there could be more shared awards rather than singular winners. (Who ever thinks the Oscar goes to the right film or person anyway?) And there might be more awards directed to otherwise unrecognized people.

Open contests also help. I myself got to write this book because I won a "philosophical op-ed" contest. Contests are good because they open up outside of networks and names. But a different judge might not have picked me, and someone else, probably equally worthy, would have gotten the platform to write *their book.* Theirs might have made the world a better place than mine. Or perhaps worse. We'll never know, and, because there is always more talent than attention, and always more kinds of talents than those that get valued, the point cannot be just to reward winners. Here systemic change is needed.

As Fred Hirsch argued long ago, perhaps the most important way to cut into the positional economy is by simply having fewer perks for the winners.[188] The easiest way to do this is to have things be more publicly available. If there are better public schools, the advantage of private schools diminishes. High-quality universal healthcare limits the privilege of paying more for care. Beachfront properties that can be used for a few weeks a year by everyone on a rotating basis reduces the pressure on everyone to try to make enough to buy a vacation home. First-class tickets could be given out by lottery, or, even better, every seat on a plane could just be comfortable enough with none particularly better. (And if someone thinks that this goes against any reasonable business model, I'd like to know how they think it's possible for humans to achieve the remarkable feat of *flying* but fail to be able to make a plane that's nice for everyone on it.) These measures, again, are better for almost everyone in a society: of course I'd like my own beachfront property, but I'd rather everyone be able to have access to one of the state- or community- or cooperatively run facilities on a rotational basis than let massive estates go to waste for most of the year. Socializing goods, contrary to what some people say, doesn't eliminate individual preference. Rather, it finally enables billions of individuals whose lack of wealth currently deprives them of individual preference to express and sometimes realize their desires.

In her book *The Sum of Us*, Heather McGhee makes an important argument about how another aspect of social position—racism—has negative effects in all of these domains. As I noted in chapter 2, McGhee shows how, in issue after issue, a belief that one race should be ahead of another continually leads to policies that undo progress for both. Building on the work of political economists Woojin Lee and John Roemer, McGhee argues that the positional economy of racial hierarchy was a major contributing factor in upending the material economy of social democracy in the United States.[189] She argues that moving beyond racism would have a "solidarity dividend" for everyone's benefit. She concludes poetically with the homonym (some/sum) in her title: "We are so much more when the 'We' in 'We the People' is not some of us, but all of us. We are greater than, and greater for, the sum of us."[190] I would only add that the sum of us is more than the United States—the whole world is better off when it works not to ensure that some are great, but that all are included.

All that said, none of these are perfect solutions. There are obvious flaws in these systems and obvious risks, and we'll have to be vigilant for those. We are reminded of this by writers like Nozick, Freud, Doctorow, and Le Guin, as well as daily facts like the persistence of racism and sexism regardless of class equality. And that is, again, the point of thinking of our goal as being good enough: it reminds us that our solutions will, in turn, need their own fixes. It's also true that there is nothing that the good-enough life can do for a parent who does not give their children equal attention, or people who experience the bitterness of unrequited love. There is no social or interpersonal or even individual measure that can solve this. But that's the whole point of becoming good enough in the first place: to learn to appreciate failure for its own sake, to gain skills for dealing with the inevitable suffering of existence, to learn to think of your life as a point in a nexus of meaning, sufficiency, and limitation.

A Thought Experiment

Perhaps I've lost some of you at this point. Perhaps you nodded in agreement with me about individual and familial values but think now I've just gone too far. Perhaps you are imagining an unpleasant world of mediocrity, where there is little incentive to strive and create. Perhaps you think these plans will rob us of the strange wonder of human exuberance. I do not think that is the case, and I do not intend to argue for it. I believe strongly that greatness-oriented societies have done much more damage to human potential by limiting the number of people who can explore it. I believe that the good-enough life will continue the liberations of the presently bounded energies of so many underappreciated humans. I believe that a reasonable reckoning with the facts will draw us all to this conclusion.

But perhaps the good-enough life still does not appeal to you. Perhaps you prefer our current lottery system to the one I am describing. Our current world is, indeed, a lottery. By some combination of luck and talent and industry, you may get the winner-take-all prize. In the good-enough world, although you will never win it all, you are promised to win a fair share. So let's try a thought experiment, borrowed from the philosopher John Rawls.[191] Imagine that you have to choose between the greatness-oriented world and the good-enough-oriented world, and that you do not know where you would wind up in the social hierarchy of either society. Knowing full well that no matter what you do, contingency may push you to the top or the bottom of either, where would you really want to live?

Let's make it less hypothetical. Imagine that you are, in fact, the lucky winner who sits atop the present social hierarchy. You have access to the best in housing, food, education, healthcare, entertainment, and leisure. And you decide to go on a hiking trip. You go camping and have a wonderful guide and food and rest. And then one day you have a terrible heart attack. Because all the best hospitals are in the cities and suburbs, and there have been severe funding cuts where you are, there is no adequate care available for you in the rural area. Do you still want a world in which you have, when you don't need it, access to the best medical care, and no access to it when you do need it? Or would you rather live in a world that ensures good-enough healthcare for everyone, everywhere? And if it's not you hiking, now imagine that it is your child, or friend, or distant cousin, or someone you've never met, someone whose life you may very well have had if luck had broken differently for you, and as it may yet do tomorrow. Are you still sure you want to risk it all for a chance at having the best of everything?

You might respond, as Hayek would, that this is not a question of choice; it's a question of human nature. People will naturally seek out their position on the top of the social pyramid, and we cannot constrain them without falling into tyranny. I cannot deny that some hierarchical striving is part of our human nature. But there are other parts, too, and our aim should not be to capitulate to what destroys us, but rather to embrace what lifts us up. And doing so, I will argue in the next chapter, may just be necessary for saving the very planet on which any life—great, neglected, or good-enough—can take place.

5

For Our Planet

I have so far tried to make the case that the pursuit of greatness in our individual, interpersonal, and social lives is self-defeating. Not only is the end goal never achieved, but along the way we damage or destroy the many meaningful, everyday experiences we could have created. I have argued for refocusing on these other experiences and learning to build a world together that aims to be decent and sufficient for all, if still inevitably imperfect. Each step along the way has been related to the next: we strengthen our capacity to create a good-enough life for all by embodying what that would mean as individuals, in relationships, and in our social formations. All of these steps matter a great deal. But perhaps the most significant reason to embrace the good-enough life today resides in our relationship to nature, where the attitude of greatness is threatening to damage our life-sustaining environment beyond repair.

Before we can deal with this largest issue, however, we will have to come to terms with how we think about human nature. After all, one of the commonest responses to the critique of greatness is that there's nothing we can do about it. It's in our DNA; we are driven by the processes of evolution to seek being at the top of the pyramid no matter what. It is often said that even if this is not the case for everybody, it is at least the case for some humans—the leaders, the alphas, the heroes. And from a racist angle, it is sometimes said that greatness is the destiny of certain cultures or races. Because I assume most readers of this book do not share this last point of view, I will not say too much about it. But I will spend some time making the case for why we are not hardwired for greatness. It matters that we move beyond our neuroscientific assumptions about greatness because we may otherwise be tempted into thinking that, yes, a life that focuses on preserving the decent and sufficient natural world that makes life possible is the right thing to do, but, humans being humans, they will almost necessarily exploit, overpopulate, and decimate.

You might also doubt the value of good-enough responses to the catastrophic problems of climate change. On this point you are right, if we take "good enough" in the colloquial sense of just doing the bare minimum. I wish there were simple changes available to evade climate catastrophe. I wish that switching from plastic to reusable bottles, flying less, driving a hybrid car, building solar panels on our homes, and planting more trees would be enough to stave off these effects. But while all of these are good things to do, they are not sufficient. Indeed, they are already too late. As David Wallace-Wells, author of *The Uninhabitable Earth*, tells us in stark terms, "We have already exited the state of environmental conditions that allowed the human animal to evolve in the first place."[1] We will certainly be able to keep living on this earth, but, according to the 2019 World Meteorological Organization report on climate change, "We are currently way off track to meeting either the 1.5°C or 2°C targets that the Paris Agreement calls for."[2] At the 1.1°C rise we have already seen, the result has been millions of climate refugees, mass extinctions in the natural world, endless unpredictable weather events, and billions of dollars in damage to property and livelihood.[3]

Here again the histories of racism, classism, and colonialism ensure that the distribution of this pain is severely unequal. According to a 2020 summary of research on the effects of affluence on climate change, "the world's top 10% of income earners are responsible for between 25 and 43% of environmental impact. In contrast, the world's bottom 10% income earners exert only around 3–5% of environmental impact."[4] And yet, in part because of geography, it is the world's poor who are likely to bear the brunt of climate change's destruction. Not only will this lead to loss of home, sustenance, and life, but it will also compound the ongoing problem of foreign debt. Even as wealthy countries continue to extract value from these poorer countries, and even as that extraction leads to environmental degradation, they still continue to demand interest payments on loans whose principle has already been paid.[5] This current crisis builds on decades (at least) of what Reverend Benjamin Chavis Jr. in the 1980s called "environmental racism"—the institutional process of exploiting inequalities in order to systemically dump environmental problems onto marginalized communities.[6] Responding to these crises has meant—in spite of frequent media representations otherwise—that people of color and those living in poverty are often at the forefront of movements for environmental progress.[7] One study in the United States found, for example, that while 25 percent of White people were worried about climate change, that number more than doubled for Black people and nearly tripled for Latinx people.[8]

In response to the unprecedented situation of climate catastrophe, it comes to feel logical to hope for greatness to overcome it. Some believe that if we give enough money to the smartest people and then let them reap maximal rewards, it will benefit all of us through new, green energy solutions. Others believe that if we find and enable the greatest leaders, the rest of us won't have to do much. This is understandable—given the inertia of our present response to climate catastrophe and the need to quickly transform our world, we may have to rely a little bit on great actors. But the trouble with relying on the great few is, as always, that it robs us of the tremendous energies and capacities of the good-enough many. It makes us dependent on systems outside of our control, leaving most of us to feel increasingly anxious and adrift, alienated from our power to be a positive force in our world. Equally, it sets up a battle of the elites, in which the greedy and power-hungry cynics have so far been winning out over those who are diligently pursuing adequate policy solutions.

And even if the "good elites" win, the result may be new clean technologies, but ones whose economic benefit creates further divisions in our world. Indeed, a major global model for how to decarbonize the economy, from a team of more than twenty authors, suggests that we may not even need many new technologies. The team argues that focusing on technological change distracts us from the fact that what's really needed is the political will to decrease wasteful consumption and transition to the already-existing green technologies that can solve this problem in the short term.[9] And promoting the idea that a green economy will lead to good-enough lives for all, rather than make some tech entrepreneurs fabulously wealthy, may help convince more people to join the cause.

Focusing on great leaders and innovators to save us also ignores how the ideology of greatness has been part of how we got here in the first place. Philosophers and intellectual historians have considered this possibility for some time. For example, in *Dialectic of Enlightenment*, a densely written treatise from 1944, Theodor Adorno and Max Horkheimer argued that a belief in mastery over nature helps enable humans to believe that they should have mastery over each other.[10] In 1967, historian Lynn White argued that the biblical idea that humans have dominance over nature had led to contemporary ecological crises.[11] In more recent years, researchers working at the intersection of psychology, sociology, and ecology have found remarkable parallels between inaction on climate change and what is called "social dominance orientation," a metric of how much someone believes that there should be hierarchies and inequalities in society. The more someone believes in human hierarchy, the more likely they are to believe that humans do not need to worry about climate change.

One interpretation of this phenomenon is that there is a correlation between the idea of hierarchy and the idea of mastery over nature. People who express a sense that some people should dominate or rule over others tend to also believe that they can control and subdue nature. Heather McGhee and Kirsti M. Jylhä suggest another possible interpretation. They argue that this isn't just about a sense of domination, but also a belief that those who "deserve" to be protected—those who have made their way to the top of the hierarchy—will be saved from the effects of climate change.[12] In some ways they are right: those at the top will be able to afford certain protections that others cannot. But, as McGhee argues, there are still limits: we all "live under the same sky."[13] As floods and wildfires over the past few years have shown, no one is safe from the ravages of a rapidly changing climate. This is thus another instance where good-enough for all is better than great for some.

Some readers might counter that we are simply at a low point in our mastery and control. We are great, the natural world is great, and the combination of our greatness will someday result in a great world. We just have to keep pushing. By this logic, we are like a mythic person who has been pushing a massive boulder up a steep hill for centuries, and if we give up now, the boulder will come crashing down and all our progress will be for naught.

We are not the first society to believe this. In the fifth century CE, explorers from Polynesia settled Rapa Nui, a small island abundant with plant and animal life, as well as solidified volcanic ash. The people flourished there for eight centuries or so, reaching a population of about 10,000 on a sixty-four-square-mile island. As they expanded, they began to build sculptures—*moai*—to honor their ancestors. They used the volcanic ash to build massive stone sculptures, as tall as thirty feet and as heavy as eighty tons. Exploiting the island's abundant forests, they constructed complex systems to transport these statues from the quarry in the center of the island to the hills on its outer edges. Year by year, they built more and more transportation systems, felling more and more trees. Aided by the rats they had introduced to the island who crippled the young saplings, they soon found themselves on barren land. When a Dutch ship arrived on Easter Day 1722—hence the European name, Easter Island—they found a desolate wasteland populated by the few hundred inhabitants who had survived.[14]

The anthropologist and novelist Ronald Wright, from whom I have taken this account, calls this kind of history a "progress trap." He writes, "Progress has an internal logic that can lead beyond reason to catastrophe. A seductive trail of successes may end in a trap."[15] What is remarkable about Rapa Nui, as Wright and others have pointed out, is that they might have known they were in a trap. Because of the small size of the island, they may have been able to see when the last trees were being felled. And yet they did it anyway. Perhaps they had a belief system that suggested that honoring the ancestors mattered more than the trees. Perhaps they didn't see how quickly the rats were getting at their saplings. Perhaps they didn't actually see the last tree fall, but rather the changes in the ecosystem led to a sudden "tipping point," such as threatens the Amazon today.[16] Perhaps everyone knew what was going on except for a powerful class that controlled the monopoly of violence on the island. We don't really know. But what we do know is the harrowing lesson they teach us: at the end of rolling this boulder up the mountain, we may very well look out from our tremendous achievement onto an earth that can barely sustain human life.

Wired for Whatever

Consider two contrasting descriptions of what life was like for early humans. According to one, it was "nasty, brutish, and short." There was constant violence, no law, and perpetual illness. According to the other, it was more of an idyll. People lived harmoniously together and with nature. Their lives may have been short, but they were peaceful and joyous. If you believe the former account, which comes from the seventeenth-century philosopher Thomas Hobbes, you probably think that the millennia since have been nothing but progress as we have established law, medicine, and civility. However unequal or unpleasant some features of the present may be, we have to concede that they are so much better than the past that we should respect whatever process got us here. (Steven Pinker is a prominent exponent of this worldview today.[17]) If you believe the latter, often associated with the eighteenth-century philosopher Jean-Jacques Rousseau, you probably think that progress is more superficial. Sure, we have better health and live longer, but we also have more war and anger, and we have betrayed our fundamentally decent human nature. (Rutger Bregman is a prominent exponent of this.[18])

Neither of these accounts is exactly right. There is plenty of evidence, as I noted in the first chapter, that early human life was actually rather pleasant and leisure-filled. But there was also probably a fair amount of war, violence, and insecurity. The trouble with the Hobbes-Rousseau debate is that it makes it seem as if humanity is either good or bad, when our experience tells us quite obviously that we have the capacity for both tremendous generosity and spirit-breaking cruelty. Perhaps the winner here was then in fact their successor, Immanuel Kant, who suggested that what defined our nature was neither evil nor goodness, but "the free power of choice" to act in one way or another. Kant did not mean that we were innately free, but that, if we worked on our constitutions (that is, both how we are individually constituted and our political constitutions), we could become the kinds of beings who acted justly more often than not.[19] I do not entirely agree with Kant, but I do think his basic idea here is correct: we are not determined to be either good or evil, but rather must work through our competing impulses. We are capable of remaking our world and ourselves in ways that make decency or terror more likely.[20] Our nature provides the resources for us to become better, but it also contains the seeds of our own destruction. We are, I might say, neither good nor evil, neither great nor base, but simply good enough.

The primatologist Frans de Waal gives further evidence that we have these multiple potentials in his book *Our Inner Ape* (2005). According to de Waal, part of what constitutes us as humans is our chimpanzee-derived genetic heritage. Chimpanzees, one of our closest genetic relatives, have a strong hierarchical structure built around androcentric power and status. While the Hobbesian account would end here, telling us that we will never escape our inner violence and quest for power, de Waal continues: "We have the fortune of having not one but two inner apes." It turns out that we share as much genetic material with

bonobos as chimpanzees, and bonobos are a matriarchal, cooperative, and friendly species. Having two inner apes, according
to de Waal, "allow[s] us to construct an image of ourselves that
is considerably more complex than what we have heard coming
out of biology for the past twenty-five years."[21] We have "a gamut
of tendencies from the basest to the noblest."[22] Who we are—as
individuals and a species—is not *determined* by nature, but
rather exists in the complex entanglement of who we've been,
who we can become, how we reflect on that process, and what
kinds of institutions we manage to build in response.

Recent work in cognitive science further underscores this
complex image of who we are and can be. While it is certainly
true that some of us may be born with stronger tendencies in
one direction or another (more ambitious or slothful, more
generous or miserly), it is equally true that who we became is
inseparable from what cognitive scientists call "cognitive ecology," or the ways in which our thinking is part of a wider sym-
bolic, cultural, and natural ecosystem.[23] The cognitive ecology
model breaks with the once standard "representational and
computational model" of the brain, in which the brain is something like a computer that can be studied to understand how it
processes and distributes information. The cognitive ecology
model sees the brain in line with "4E" cognitive science: as embodied, embedded, extended, and enacted. In this model, we
cannot understand the mind on its own (as something hardwired for greatness, for example), but only as part of an interactive relationship with our bodies and environments.[24] This
complexity of cognition does not make the achievement of a
good-enough life any easier—there are so many layers here!
But it does make it *possible*. Because we are not hardwired by
our DNA or our brains to be any particular thing, but rather are
ourselves indeterminate, dynamic, and ongoing processes, we

need not fear that somehow greatness and hierarchy are a necessary part of our condition. They are one part of our "gamut" of possibilities, not our destiny.

This also matters for the issues we discussed in the last chapter. Recall that part of why Smith and Hayek argue that we have to deal with greatness is because of "men being what they are."[25] According to their logic, we may very well want a world in which everyone has decency and sufficiency and no one has too much more than anyone else, but that's just not how we are built. The conservative political philosopher Thomas Sowell argued that this reckoning with how humans are was a clear ideological split between conservativism and more progressive traditions. Sowell called these the "constrained" and "unconstrained" visions. In this account, constrained thinkers like Smith and Hayek tend to try to work with our flaws by producing generally functioning systems. Unconstrained thinkers like Rousseau and Marx try to revolutionize who we are so that full justice can reign. The essential difference between the two, Sowell says, is "whether or not inherent limitations of man are among the key elements included in the vision."[26] This idea has a quite a bit of traction still today. Moderate conservatives like *New York Times* columnist David Brooks often use it to explain their policy proposals. Brooks writes: "In the unconstrained vision, you ask: What's the solution? In a constrained vision you ask: What's the best set of trade-offs and reforms we can actually achieve? The constrained vision is wiser."[27]

In many ways, the good-enough life is about having a constrained vision of reality. It does not imagine that there are perfect solutions to everything, and it believes in the wisdom of appreciating our limits. My concern, however, is that the definition of constrained versus unconstrained in this strand of conservative thought incorrectly poses the problem of human nature. It says there are certain ways that human beings are, and because of this we have to make policies adapted to how they are. This was the basic point that Smith and Hayek used to defend the very concentrations of power they claimed to be opposing. But because human nature is so flexible, the correct question is not constrained or unconstrained, but rather: what parts of ourselves do we want to put more or less constraint on? If we have "two inner apes," one that seeks hierarchy and status while another seeks cooperation and equality, then the greatness vision works to constrain the latter while the good-enough vision works to constrain the former. Neither vision, of course, is about complete constraint. In the greatness world, there is still cooperation and equality, only less than there might otherwise be, and in the good-enough world, there is still some hierarchy and status, only much less than we have today. As such, Sowell's idea that conservatives better respect human nature and our limitations is simply incorrect. He is making a choice about what to constrain, no more or less than what I advocate.

Surviving the Fittest

Some might respond that of the two apes within us, one remains dominant because there is always a competitive race for survival. This is one of modernity's essential claims for greatness: that it is baked into the logic of evolution. According to Charles Darwin, life is a "struggle for existence." Its major engine, natural selection, is "daily and hourly scrutinizing, throughout the world, the slightest variations; rejecting those that are bad, preserving and adding up all that are good; silently and insensibly working, *whenever and wherever opportunity offers*, at the improvement of each organic being in relation to its organic and inorganic conditions of life."[28] Such words make it sound as if the restless pursuit of improvement is not only natural, but the very means of survival.

Darwin inadvertently gave further credence to this view of evolution by approving of Herbert Spencer's phrase "survival of the fittest" as a synonym for natural selection.[29] Darwin opted for Spencer's term because he feared that "selection" implied too much conscious activity on the part of nature. His point was not that nature consciously chose the best adaptations, but that, in the struggle to survive, those attributes of an individual that were most conducive to success would be "selected" by virtue of their ability to help us reproduce. As Stephen Jay Gould puts it with the brevity of wit: "It got colder before the woolly mammoth evolved its shaggy coat."[30] In turn, nevertheless, those shaggy mammoths were overrun by humans, climate change, inbreeding, and possibly their own overuse of freshwater resources.[31] The fittest are not fittest forever.

This is one of the basic quirks of evolution and why "survival of the fittest" introduces as many linguistic problems as it solves. "Fittest" is not an absolute term in either Spencer or Darwin. It refers, quite narrowly, to the adaptation between an organism and its environment. Darwin reminds his readers: "Let it also be borne in mind how infinitely complex and close-fitting are the mutual relations of all organic beings to each other and to their physical conditions of life."[32] "Fittest" in this sense then is not like how some person is the fittest one at the gym. They are not the best-looking, strongest, most ethical, or most powerful. They are simply the most suited to survive in the complexity of an environment. In an environment where height provides a better view of predators to run away from, tall people might survive better. In another, where predators tend to attack the tall people that they can see above the bushes, short people might be better off. Sometimes being too "fit" in the colloquial sense can in fact be a problem. Consider, for example, that many of the young and healthy people who have died of COVID-19 did so because their immune systems were *too* strong and overzealously fought the virus, resulting in a "cytokine storm" that attacked healthy organs as well.[33] Adaptations that are advantageous in normal times often fail in extreme moments. In times of drought, for example, scientists have observed that the largest giraffes are the ones who die quickest, since they require the greatest caloric intake.[34]

Indeed, one consequence of evolution is that adapting to some aspects of one's environment often makes one maladapted in other respects. Evolutionary geneticist Jerry Coyne explains how this happens on multiple fronts. Human birth is an obvious example. Our brains kept growing and becoming larger, but our pelvis had to remain relatively narrow for us to be able to walk and run efficiently.[35] Hence the terrible pain of giving birth. Other adaptations that help us reproduce can have similar setbacks. It is possible, for example, that the same genes that give men virility enlarge their prostates later in life.[36] Indeed, because of advances in science, culture, and technology, humans present a particularly vexing picture for fitness. We evolved to love sweets and fats because their high caloric intake reduced the amount of food we needed. Now that same encoding produces some of our worst health problems. But we are unlikely to lose the desire for sweets and fats because (in terms of human evolution if not individual childhood well-being) their toll comes late enough in life that they rarely affect one's ability to reproduce.[37] Perhaps it is not surprising that "natural selection" and "survival of the fittest" are inexact terms: like evolution itself, they solve some linguistic problems while producing others. Evolution, properly understood, does not lead us to think that the greatest and most powerful are likely to survive. Rather, it offers a rather eloquent two-part summation of the good-enough philosophy: problems create solutions, and then solutions create problems. The complexity of life and environmental interactions means that no perfect adaptation can result.

To survive in this imperfect world, we need each other. Darwin may have recognized this when he insisted that he referred to the struggle for existence "in a large and metaphorical sense."[38] He writes, for example, "A plant on the edge of a desert is said to struggle for life against the drought, though more properly it should be said to be dependent on the moisture."[39] In this example, the "struggle for existence" is not *between* individuals, but a collective effort. There are, of course, plenty of examples where animals and plants do compete for scarce resources, but Darwin's brief suggestion here is that how we understand that competition is no more fated than our human nature. It is a choice. We can understand the struggle as a ruthless process against each other. Or we can understand it as a shared struggle to help as much of the planet as possible to survive and live well.

Even if evolution is as much or more about mutual aid than struggle, there are good reasons to doubt whether we should map our understanding of human life onto natural history.[40] Groups or nations wanting to increase their power are likely to use just about any justification of their efforts. No one needed Darwin to speak of the struggle for existence and the survival of the fittest for some groups to enslave, rape, pillage, and attempt genocide against other peoples. But the idea that there were "great races" that could, nevertheless, lose the genetic struggle for survival gave ideological fodder to some of the nineteenth and twentieth centuries' worst atrocities. Indeed, this double move is the key to much racist horror: it is not just about how great one group believes itself to be greater, but also about their illogical and hatred-based fear that some other group will dilute its gene pool and make it "less great."

This is the basic fear of "degeneration" and "miscegenation." It is an idea that connected American racism to Nazism. As Timothy Ryback, author of *Hitler's Private Library*, writes: "Hitler's most valued book on America was *The Passing of the Great Race* [1916], by . . . Madison Grant, who claimed that American greatness, built on the Nordic stock of its founding fathers, was being eroded by the allegedly inferior blood of immigrant races. Hitler quoted liberally from Grant in his speeches and is said to have sent him a letter describing [the book] as 'my bible.'"[41] And according to Roger Griffin, one of the foremost experts on the history of fascism, this fear of lost greatness is the essence of the fascist creed: "Extensive study of the primary sources of Fascism . . . convinced me that the core of its mentality was . . . devoting, and, if necessary sacrificing, individual existence to the struggle against the forces of degeneration which had seemingly brought the nation low, and of helping relaunch it towards greatness and glory."[42]

This is part of the underlying logic of the presidential campaigns of Donald Trump. I am sure that many people who chant "Make America Great Again" simply identify with the Republican Party or a general belief in the United States as a great country and do not intend to invoke this racist history with their words. But Trump himself decided to build his campaign on this slogan after a long history of racist remarks and actions. He then announced his campaign with a racist description of immigrants, made regularly racist remarks throughout his presidency, ignored the rise in hate crimes based on his rhetoric, doubled down in his last year as president by stoking anti-Asian-American sentiment during the pandemic, and generally governed by trying to eradicate every element of Barack Obama's legacy.[43] And as the data clearly show, even if many of Trump's supporters do not support racism, anti-immigrant and racist sentiments were part of his winning electoral strategy in 2016.[44] As such, his words and actions are part of the history of terrors undergirding "American greatness."[45]

We should not, nevertheless, assume that it requires explicit racism to echo this history, or that the problem is limited to the Republican Party. As scholars like Khalil Gibran Muhammad have shown, ideas about "greater races" infect many US institutions, perhaps most notably the criminal justice system. As Muhammad shows in great detail, the history of US criminal justice in the twentieth century is predicated on a two-pronged approach to dealing with crime: social services for Whites and incarceration for Blacks. How did this come to pass? Because of an assumption that poor European immigrants had the capacity to improve with the right help, whereas Africans were presumed inferior no matter what.[46] The history of institutional racism means that "great race" ideas need to be systemically rooted out.[47]

I am sympathetic to those who, like Obama himself, may want "American greatness" and "American exceptionalism" to refer to another history entirely—one in which the United States is unique among nations in its ability to create a good life for all its citizens. But I think we are better off avoiding this whole history of pitting nations against each other and trying to see which is best. We are better off without thinking of the world analogically with nature's struggle for existence. Because unlike many of nature's creations, we can choose what elements of our plural natures we want to cultivate and embody. And there is nothing about our world that benefits from some nations or cultures or races doing better than others. Such competitive desires create the poverty, wars, and failures to act effectively on global issues like climate change that we see today. If we manage to overcome these challenges, it will not be because the fittest survived, but because we managed to survive the very idea of there being some who are more fit to live than others.

Evolving to Be Good Enough

Although we should not design our societies based on our visions of nature, it is worth noting that Darwin's ideas about struggle have been challenged by contemporary evolutionary theory. Concerned about Darwin's tendency to express the processes of evolution as trends toward optimization, and, equally, the tendency to pervert this idea into social hierarchies, the philosopher of science Daniel Milo has argued that a particular idea of good-enoughness better explains evolution: being "good enough not to die off."[48] As he meticulously worked through the scientific literature on evolution, Milo found that the data suggests some important changes to Darwin's theory. He never disputes evolution as such. The basic idea of evolution—"descent with modification," the theory that all species derive from billions of years of changes to some primordial living form—has proven correct. Darwin's claimed process of evolution—natural selection, or survival of the fittest—is also true and has plenty of examples, but it doesn't explain the entirety of evolutionary processes. Milo suggests that three others—genetic drift (random mutations in genes), geographic isolation, and founder effects (genes of migratory groups that start new populations elsewhere)—account for much more change than they are given credit for. These are not particularly controversial ideas in evolutionary theory, but Milo suggests that they are underemphasized in how the general population understands evolution. Our vision of change is too much about natural selection's perfecting processes, whereas the record in fact shows things that are rather random, bizarre, or unfortunate (such as the examples of childbirth and aging I noted above). Further still, since the aim of evolution is reproduction, it prefers to stand still once it achieves this basic feat. After all, what better way to survive than by following the pattern of someone else who did?

Milo's concern is that overemphasizing natural selection's competitive processes enables a moral fable to design society on similar terms. Indeed, even viewing it as a competitive process imputes something onto nature because the point of evolution is to be good enough to survive and reproduce, not necessarily stop someone else from reproducing. Changing our understanding of evolution, he hopes, may help us move away from cutthroat competition and toward an appreciation of the fact that, quite frankly, we already won the evolutionary game. We have no difficulty producing enough food, shelter, clothing, and medicine for all of humanity. What we lack is a functional system of distribution, in some part, Milo suggests, because we keep thinking that we are competing with each other in order to survive.

Throughout his book, Milo offers philosophical explanations at places where the science runs out. This begins with an attempt to explain why the first group of human explorers left Africa in the first place. Milo dismisses the various available theories about natural conditions and suggests that they were the sufferers of a new "virus called 'elsewhereism.'"[49] This "virus," which he suggests may come from a particular gene mutation, enables one to imagine a future in which the things that are wrong in one place might be solved somewhere else, or in some other way of living. This ability to imagine a better future, Milo argues, helped us to realize that we were not entirely bound by nature's offerings and could transform it to our advantage. It is to this transformation in our brains that we owe our ability to create the societies of plenty that we have.

But like all things in evolution, the solutions produced by elsewhereism have created new problems. Milo singles out what he calls "the excellence conspiracy." This is a system "in which virtually everyone takes part and in which we collectively ensnare one another."[50] Milo blames our hyperactive elsewhere neurons, the very ones that enabled us to become who we are, because now that we no longer need them to resolve the basic issues of survival, they still cannot rest. "They are the cabal plotting the excellence conspiracy."[51] We pursue excellence not because it is "excellent" to do so, but because we're not smart enough to see that it is not in fact in our best interest anymore.

Or at least, according to Milo, not in most of our best interests. He does think that there should be a "few necessary elite" who "maintain the safety net and expand it as required."[52] But the rest of us should embrace our strangeness and imperfection, appreciate that we are good enough to survive, and not burden ourselves with running in a rat race or filling in a pyramid scheme that most of us will sink to the bottom of. I very much appreciate Milo and his advocacy of being good enough. But as his book concludes on this point, he does not take up an obvious question: who are these "necessary elite" and how are we to find them? As I have argued in previous chapters, if we have to train *some* to be elite, and those who are elite get to have all the advantages of power and position, then everyone who wants to enjoy these privileges will try to claw their way in, and we are very quickly going to get stuck in the excellence conspiracy all over again.

To avoid this, we need to focus our bored neurons on promoting and participating in the good-enough life for all. We certainly will never have a perfect society, but we can make it good enough in a more robust sense than just good enough not to die. We can be good enough in the complex way I have advocated throughout this book: decent, sufficient, appreciative of the ordinary, and creatively open to dealing with the inevitable limitations and setbacks. We have all the evolutionary tools to become this kind of world.

The Risk of Great Green Revolutions

Nothing makes the necessity of transitioning to the good-enough life more apparent than the threats of climate catastrophe and the collapse of earth's ecosystems. Our greatness-oriented model, especially in the economy, is simply incompatible with what some scientists call our "planetary boundaries," that is, "the environmental limits within which humanity can safely operate."[53] There are nine of these limits, including climate, freshwater and land use, nitrogen and phosphorous concentrations, and the maintenance of "biosphere integrity." The boundaries idea is not uncontroversial, and there are critics of different political persuasions who worry about how the idea might be used in too-powerful hands (creating population controls, austerity, and so forth).[54] The idea may also have scientific inaccuracies: the earth is a dynamic system, human technologies interface with it in sometimes surprising ways, and we do not have exact measurements for these things.[55] Nevertheless, we do know quite clearly some general guidelines, such as that above 2°C (or really even 1.5°C) of warming, our planet will undergo transformations that will make inhabiting this earth in a healthy and meaningful way much more difficult, if not impossible for many. I think it may be better to speak of "safe planetary conditions" rather than "boundaries," to signal that our concern is not an absolute knowledge of what the earth can do, but a relative knowledge of the fact that only under certain ecological conditions is the earth good enough to meaningfully sustain human life, however many billions of us there are.

According to this model, climate change and biosphere integrity are the two "core" features that regulate all the rest. Although the former gets more attention than the latter, they are related and equally important. Depleting our natural world has become a safe conditions problem.[56] It is no surprise that the two greatest challenges of the moment—climate catastrophes and zoonotic diseases (like COVID-19)—are related to these system-wide sustainability features. Our rapacious consumption and abuse of natural resources is coming back to haunt us, not only driving climate change and resource depletion, but also, by pushing into new terrains, bringing us into ever greater contact with other species and their viruses.[57] In places across the globe, catastrophic weather events such as fires, hurricanes, and typhoons, coupled with the damage wrought by the coronavirus, hammer home the truth of these destructive tendencies.[58]

It is a mistake to assume that modern conditions alone have brought us to the brink. In addition to the case of Rapa Nui, there are plenty of historical examples of human-caused planetary destruction that precede our current state of affairs. Forty-five thousand years ago, humans arriving to Australia at the same moment as a change in climate led to the extinction of the island's megafauna—giant wombats, kangaroos, koalas, and others. About 30,000 years later, the grisly feat was repeated on the American continent.[59] Humans are perfectly good at destroying their natural habitat no matter what their economic or symbolic-value system is.

Nevertheless, it is true that over time many peoples around the world learned how to live well within their natural habitats. They developed extensive knowledge of their land through experience and experiment, and that knowledge (sometimes called "traditional ecological knowledge") is a fundamental resource for learning to live better with our environment today.[60] But it is important to remember that these are *achievements* of learning to live with and understand the land, and not because Indigenous people are inherently more "natural." The idea that some peoples are automatically closer to nature than others plays on the old racist idea of the "noble savage," and it denies the agency and complexity of Indigenous peoples, including the many differences in how different peoples conceive of and relate to nature.[61]

Paying close attention to how big climate change plans affect local communities and interact with their knowledges and ways of life is fundamental. Although some world-transforming solutions for climate change problems (such as geoengineering) promise to reduce global warming, they also more or less guarantee wild swings in global weather patterns that will unevenly affect different populations.[62] Just as how in evolution every transformation of a species to better adapt to survive may create other problems for its well-being, so too does every technological intervention in nature produce risks and consequences.[63] Some of these are beyond our control, but some follow directly from the priorities and principles that frame our interventions.

The "Green Revolution" is the name given to a wholescale transformation of global food production led primarily by the United States that began in the 1940s and accelerated from the '60s through the '80s. It used collaborative research, public subsidies, chemical fertilizers, and genetic modifications to increase global food production, but it also led to greater carbon emissions from agriculture, soil erosion, increased diffusion of toxic chemicals, and other environmental degradations.[64] There were

also profoundly negative social consequences, as large agricul-
tural production was emphasized without any accompanying
focus on inequalities in land distribution or gendered labor.[65]
Overall food *in*stability as a result in fact *increased* in countries
where the Green Revolution took place, even as it decreased
globally.[66]

How did that happen? The food writer and historian Mark
Bittman notes that the massive decrease in global hunger in
these years happened almost exclusively in China, where there
was no Green Revolution. Instead, Chinese leaders focused on
state support for independent farmers, and the goal was to reduce poverty, not just increase crop yields. Having more crops
available does not mean they will be properly distributed, after
all. Much of the world's explosion of new corn products during
the Green Revolution in other countries, for example, went to
ethanol and high-fructose corn syrup. China's more direct if still
imperfect approach achieved more of what the Green Revolution promised: "Production tripled post-Mao, but, more important, the world's most dramatic decrease in poverty *ever* took
place."[67] That didn't happen because of technological change
alone, but because of the combination of technology, investment in ordinary people, and economic regulation.

There are risks that when it comes to climate change, we will
repeat or even exacerbate the problems of our current greatness-
oriented society, just as the Green Revolution did. We should
learn from this history to avoid just focusing on corporate-
driven, technological solutions that ignore social implications.
We don't yet seem to be learning this lesson at scale. Consider
the possibility, for example, that a group like Breakthrough Energy Ventures (BEV) helps develop important and viable processes to help clean up the planet and pursue sustainable
growth. BEV was founded by Bill Gates and is funded by a

who's who of the world billionaire elite: Jeff Bezos, Jack Ma, Richard Branson, Michael Bloomberg, and others. They invest in nuclear fusion, increasing battery storage capacity, replacing nitrogen fertilizers (one of the big problems exacerbated by the Green Revolution) with microbial ones, finding ways to sequester carbon, and other projects to promote "green growth" and reduce some of the terrible impacts that we have had on the planet—often ones, it should be noted, funded or produced by these very same people. Between their wealth and their star power, the members of BEV have the ability to fund and support these projects, as well as the capacity to influence governments to support them.[68] They also, of course, draw on technologies and systems that have been created using public money, such as the $22 billion International Thermonuclear Experimental Reactor.[69]

There is no doubt that the achievement of something as monumental as nuclear fusion would be a great boon to humanity. The question is how to ensure that we avoid the problems of something like the Green Revolution, creating deleterious side effects and exacerbating inequality. If BEV achieves a breakthrough, will we all benefit from it? Or will we all be forced to be thankful for being saved *by* billionaires *from* billionaires (by their technology against their own business practices), while many continue to live in conditions of squalor, told that on the horizon everything will be good if they just keep working hard?

Gates's 2021 book *How to Avoid a Climate Catastrophe* does not offer much hope that he has learned these lessons. He writes, for example, that rich countries will be the most likely to develop green technologies that they can then sell to the rest of the world. He acknowledges that rich countries have caused most of the global warming problem, but then does not seem to be particularly concerned that they take responsibility.

Rather, he seems to think, they should keep getting richer by helping the world get out of the crisis they themselves caused. His solution risks creating an ever-increasing spiral of global debt, in which wealthy nations use their advantage to careen ahead, rather than work collectively to lift everyone up.[70]

More with Less, or More from Less?

Such potential social problems associated with responding to climate change have created significant divisions within the environmental community. On one side is a group that draws inspiration from the idea of "degrowth" (in the word coined by the philosopher André Gorz in 1972), who argue that the current climate catastrophe shows once and for all that capitalism, endless growth, consumption, and inequality are simply incompatible with a safe and sustainable environment. According to this view, surviving the current climate situation forces us to create a world in which we—the affluent we—consume less and extract less. This vision does not mean some kind of ecological harmony or back-to-the-woods fantasies, as are sometimes imagined. Contemporary environmental activist and writer Naomi Klein, for example, is explicit about this: "Living nonextractively does not mean that extraction does not happen: all living things must take from nature in order to survive. But it does mean the end of the extractivist mindset—of taking without caretaking, of treating land and people as resources to deplete rather than as complex entities with rights to a dignified existence based on renewal and regeneration."[71] Nor does it mean that there will be no progress or development, or even "abundance," according to contemporary degrowth advocate Jason Hickel. His argument is that wealth today is generated by taking what is public (water, for example) and privatizing it for a fee (bottled water, say). If we reverse that process, and carefully manage the commons, we can have an abundance of resources that are collectively available. According to his argument, which directly attacks the theories of Smith that we saw in the previous chapter, we don't need private growth to create general opulence. Rather, we need general opulence *instead* of growth. We can, as it were, get more *with* less.[72]

These kinds of degrowth scenarios are unpopular with a cohort of thinkers who sometimes call themselves "ecomodernists."[73] Ecomodernists believe that the rhetoric of degrowth and economic equality is precisely the opposite of what is called for today. They argue that the best path beyond our climate impasse is through greater use of capitalist competition leading to technological breakthroughs. Degrowth, by their logic, is not only unnecessary (although they agree that overconsumption is a problem), but actually harmful. If we are going to have the kinds of big changes that we need to see in the world, we are simply going to have to rely on the existing structures of capitalist development to push through big solar, wind, and other projects. They are also big advocates of nuclear energy, which they claim has gotten a bad rap.[74] They oppose thinking of humans as "in harmony" with nature, and instead write of us as beings capable of developing our natural world to support ever greater prosperity from economic growth. One key to this belief is the possibility of "decoupling" growth from resource use, in large part through "dematerialization," in which technological efficiencies allow us to get more productivity from fewer resources. This is, in ecomodernist Andrew McAfee's phrase, the possibility of getting more *from* less.[75] The ecomodernist scenario is very appealing, perhaps more so than having to give up a lot of pleasures and privileges that affluent people now take for granted. So the question is: will it work? We can't predict the future, but we can raise some doubts.

One of the more engaging ecomodernist works is McAfee's book titled with that phrase: *More from Less* (2019). The book argues that we are all thinking incorrectly about natural resource use. Contrary to our expectations that we are using up our natural capital, McAfee argues, we are in fact getting increasingly more goods from increasingly less of the planet. McAfee is an eloquent cheerleader for this process of dematerialization. Part of what makes McAfee so convincing is that he presents dematerialization as a kind of new discovery to himself as well. Before he started research on the book, he tells us, he too was a fool like us who thought we were using up more and more. But then he came across research suggesting that efficiency gains in production and use were creating a new situation in which the economy was growing despite decreasing resource and energy use.[76] McAfee says he was shocked, and set out to understand how this was possible. He uses a stunningly odd metaphor to describe his conclusions. He calls them "the four horsemen of the optimist": capitalism, tech progress, responsive government, and public awareness.[77] McAfee concludes that if we keep on our path of tech progress and capitalism, and improve on responsive government and public awareness about environmental issues, we will be able to innovate our way out of climate catastrophe. I should be clear that he is not unaware of the challenges, and he rates our future as between "bad and catastrophically bad," but he thinks that a revised version of the current system is simply the best way to go because of the evidence he has unearthed.[78] In short, McAfee is saying, what we're doing is not good enough, but not because we are asking too much; in fact, it's because we're not being as great as we could be.

McAfee's claim hinges on dematerialization. He charts how general resource use in the United States and the United Kingdom has become decoupled from economic growth. Even as economies grow, in other words, the ratio of resource use is falling. McAfee calls this "the great reversal."[79] To show why this reversal occurs because of capitalism and technological progress, he gives several examples, including one that has accompanied me through the writing of these pages: the aluminum can. Beverage cans used to be made out of heavier steel, but companies switched to aluminum as a way to cut costs. This is the heart of McAfee's twin praise of tech and capitalism. As he said in an interview: "An important part of this capitalist component does involve really vicious competition. . . . If we only had one beer company in the world, that company wouldn't need to cut costs by saving money on aluminum cans. They could just pass those costs onto customers. So we actually need really nasty competition to provide the motive for saving money and reducing resource consumption through tech progress."[80] It's worth noting that how exactly this competition plays out, where these materials come from, what the conditions in the mines are, how the workers who do the extraction get paid, and other issues of social justice never factor into McAfee's account. Nor is there much of a discussion about how so many of the innovations we see rely heavily on technologies developed through public funding and scientific cooperation, not "vicious competition."

Further more, the example McAfee chose could not be a better illustration of why his competition-focused solution generates more environmental problems than it solves.[81] To see why, we only have to turn to his own source for this information about aluminum: Vaclav Smil, an encyclopedic chronicler of the world's energy uses and its history. McAfee correctly cites from

Smil's book, *Making the Modern World: Materials and Demate-rialization* (2014), which has data showing the ever-decreasing amount of aluminum used per can. McAfee does not mention, however, that Smil's eventual point is the opposite of McAfee's. In fact, Smil explicitly affirms the economic theory that "less means more," because as costs decrease, consumption rises.[82] This, in fact, is the case with those aluminum cans. As Smil relates, even though cans are lighter, greater consumption has erased that value. Between 1979 and 2011 (years for which data is available), "the weight of a can was reduced by 25%, but per capita consumption of aluminum cans doubled from 149 to 246 a year."[83] Moreover, aluminum takes four to ten times as much energy to produce as steel (depending on the quality of the steel in question). "Consequently, all weight reductions associated with replacing steel by aluminum result in a substantially higher overall energy cost of materials."[84] Smil, to be sure, is not against the very idea that using aluminum can help. He thinks it works much better than steel for lightweight, high-speed trains, for example. But he's just not convinced it's going to save the planet.

Another of Smil's examples can help us understand why the very cutthroat competition that McAfee relies on to reduce material use can eventually undo that progress. Consider cars and trucks. Smil looks at the evolution from the Ford Model T to the Ford Fusion, its current best-selling passenger car. Overall, he finds a whopping 93 percent increase in the mass/power ratio, showing the basic kind of dematerialization trend that McAfee registers. *However,* the Fusion is not Ford's bestselling vehicle; the massive F150 truck is. The F150, which is rarely used for its actual purpose of hauling cargo, is more often than not a status symbol, even a "plaything for the rich."[85] Factoring in the explosive growth of the SUV and truck market, on top of the general march of cars across the planet, Smil finds that the benefits of lighter materials have effectively been negated both by consumption and by the cutthroat competition to sell more fancy vehicles for greater profits.[86] Thus even where there is tech progress, it is undercut by the basic work of seeking profits.

Smil thus arrives at a different conclusion than McAfee. He accepts that decoupling is happening if we factor in resource use relative to GDP, but he doubts that this helps very much. After all, decreased use *relative* to GDP does not actually tell us much about how many resources are being used. As Smil said in a 2021 interview, "People always make a fundamental mistake between relative and absolute dematerialization. What matters is the absolute energy intensity and use of materials."[87] Even if we are making more efficient use of some materials, that does not mean that we are making efficient use of materials as such. From 1986 to 2006, for example, looking at as many material inputs into the economy as he could trace, Smil found that there was a 34 percent *increase* in overall usage.[88] We might be using less aluminum, but that's in part because we are using more plastic. According to Smil, we are dematerializing, but we are not doing so absolutely, and we are not doing so nearly quickly enough in relation to the currently existing planetary conditions. Furthermore, material use in the United States is only part of the story. As even McAfee admits, dematerialization is largely a story for affluent countries.[89] In part that is because they have access to better technologies and more efficient production methods, in part because there is some fudging of these numbers because they only record raw imports (your pre-made cellphone is not on the books), and in part because a large part of the major infrastructural development (requiring large amounts of steel and concrete) has already been accomplished. By all accounts, including McAfee's own, then, the global process is not dematerializing but accelerating. Still, McAfee's hope is that the combination of our greatness-oriented system of pursuing genius and profit means that we will manage a way out of our crises.

This hope is, I think, the crux of the matter. Even if McAfee's numbers were right, the normative values would still be wrong. The idea that we can just keep doing bad things until eventually we get everything right completely misunderstands that, even if it's theoretically true that we might someday get to the other end of the arc, we will have decimated the very basis of that achievement in the meantime. It is worth recalling Karl Polanyi's point about this, emphasizing now his remarks about nature: "Such an institution could not exist for any length of time without annihilating the human *and natural substance* of society."[90] I worry that what people like McAfee are basically saying is, OK, I know at this point we're not there and we are careening recklessly over the cliff. But don't worry: we are going to be able to turn this all back. Nature will wait for us to catch up to what we need to be doing. Society will buckle but it won't break. If we just keep with our greatness system of competing to be the best long enough, eventually everyone will see that we were right to do so. But here's where McAfee's four horsemen metaphor may be frighteningly and ironically correct. The techno-optimists are going to ride them over the cliff. And all the way down they will be telling themselves, in the words of that old joke: "so far, so good." It may be very good for the few, but it is not good enough for all. This is often the path that greatness-thinking takes.

Sharing in the Burden and the Bounty

Does this mean that a technological solution will never happen, and we must rely on degrowth? Some on the left, sometimes called "socialist modernists," have taken issue with what they view as this "austerity" mindset. The socialist modernists agree

with Hickel and other degrowth advocates that capitalism's ecological destructiveness needs to be overcome in any decent
future society. But they share the ecomodernists' vision of technological breakthroughs as the path to a better future. They
want technological abundance for all, and they think this is the
whole point of socialism.[91] Fredric Jameson, a leading Marxist
literary critic, puts the socialist modernist point clearly: "The
free-market right has captured the rhetoric of innovation and
'modernity' . . . [But] Marx alone sought to combine a politics
of revolt with the 'poetry of the future' and applied himself to
demonstrate that socialism was more modern than capitalism
and more productive."[92]

While such a vision may enable a less inegalitarian path to
technological transformation, it does not really address the material problems that Smil shows. It is in many ways still a vision
of endless growth and productivity and natural resource
availability—even if more evenly shared. And, as Klein and
Alperovitz note, the historical experience of authoritarian socialism has been highly incompatible with ecological sustainability.[93] Feeling bereft of political options, Smil arrives at a
rather pessimistic conclusion in a recent book, *Growth* (2019).
He sees human society so exploiting the conditions for safe living on this planet that, regardless of our economic system, we
will wind up with "degrowth not by choice but as a reaction to
cumulative (economic, extraction, consumption, environmental) excesses."[94] Does this mean we should pursue conscious
degrowth now? There are plenty of examples of already-
existing, conscious degrowth or nongrowth strategies, from
small communities resisting development to new national strategies to reduce energy consumption in places like Holland.[95]
But Smil thinks we are best to avoid putting all of our eggs in
one basket. We'll need a combination of political and technological changes, alongside decreased consumption.[96]

This aligns very well with the good-enough worldview's insistence on humility, which would suggest moving past the "degrowth *versus* technology breakthrough" debates and remind us that no one offers a perfect solution.[97] The affluent world certainly needs to consume less and be less wasteful. And we certainly need to develop new, regenerative technologies that are less harmful for the planet. The point is to ensure that a good-enough moral vision informs both of these paths. Degrowth practices must ensure that decency and sufficiency are achievable within their purview. And, if degrowth has any chance of being politically viable, it should be made clear that it is not about punitively taking things away, but about recognizing that a world that is good and sufficient for all is better for everyone. Indeed, as studies consistently show, wealth inequality and excessive affluence are main drivers of climate change, given that wealthy people use vastly more energy for leisure, housing, and other activities.[98] Although people may have to give up some of their material excess, they will gain the viability of a life-sustaining planet. Not a bad trade! A growing body of scientific literature indeed attests to the fact that we can both meet "decent living standards" and promote emotional and social well-being. But doing so will require technological advances, decreases in excessive and unequal consumption, and, perhaps most important of all, political transformation.[99]

This is equally true in terms of how we think about the technological changes we need. Greatness thinking responds to our current ecological quagmire by trying to find and reward the few who deserve more than others to live well and thrive. It defends this as the best path to save the rest of us. But historical experience should have taught us by now that this method does not help us achieve a world that enables flourishing for all. Good-enoughness responds to this situation by insisting that we find a way to ensure that we all share in both the burden and the bounty. McAfee is certainly right that we need responsible tech progress, but we don't need that to come from vicious competition. It should rather come from *vital collaboration*, even in the realm of finance capital. There is nothing inherent in entrepreneurial ventures that requires them to maximize profits. Indeed, Bill Gates and friends could perfectly well ensure that their investments are "for loss" to themselves and for gain to the public sphere. In this way they might focus on developing technologies that are ecologically necessary even if not maximally profit-creating.[100] And they could insist that the companies who receive their grants minimize economic inequality within their ranks. That they don't do this is not a fact of human or economic nature so much as a condition of our current economic thinking.

There are a wealth of plans for how to justly and safely transition the economy toward a sustainable model.[101] What we continue to lack is political will. During the 2020 presidential campaign in the United States, Senator Bernie Sanders offered a vision of the role world governments could play here. He would occasionally remark that his hope for climate change was that nations would stop spending trillions of dollars on their military and begin spending it on dealing with climate change. He often expressed skepticism at his own idea, couching it with conditionals: "But maybe, just maybe given the crisis of climate change, the world can understand that instead of spending $1.8 trillion a year collectively on weapons of destruction designed to kill each other, maybe we pool our resources and fight our common enemy, which is climate change."[102] It may sound impossible, although there were moments during the early days of the COVID-19 pandemic where international cooperation around sharing treatments and knowledge about how to fight the disease at least opened the possibility for such a monumental shift in our thinking about global relations. And it's also possible that nothing less than this shared global endeavor will be good enough to ensure that this planet can truly become a place that offers decency and sufficiency for all for generations to come.

A Good-Enough Relation to Nature

There are many people smarter and more informed than I am who can offer solutions to confront our ecological crises. While I have tried to sketch what appear to me as viable responses, the idea of being good enough can offer less any specific solution than a general ethical framework for thinking through our relation to nature. To begin with, no matter what type of solution enables humans to flourish on this planet, it must begin with the fact that the aim is for *all* humans to directly enjoy the benefits of this flourishing. The centuries of placing the few before the many, and telling the many that the benefits of the few were really being done for the many, should be over. If we are to truly inhabit a world that is good enough, it will have to directly create the kind of ecological well-being that sustains the planet equally. This means that any kind of geoengineering fantasy that would decrease heat in Europe but leave everything below the equator a savannah needs to be ruled out a priori. So should any solutions that do not compensate and uplift those already damaged by climate disasters—especially poorer nations who have had worse consequences in spite of making drastically fewer greenhouse gases. Whatever combination of solutions we rely on, they should all be compatible with the idea that everyone deserves decency and sufficiency, and that no one merits more than others. While some inequalities may persist—such is the inevitability of the good enough—they can and should be minimized.

Second, even if it turns out that we can innovate our way out of climate catastrophe, it does not follow that we can do so for our current ecological footprint. The declining stocks of biodiversity are a threat to the life-sustaining capacities of our one and only planet. Dematerialization, as we have seen, is very unlikely to happen quickly enough at scale to prevent the collapse of vast ecosystems if we keep up our current rates of consumption. We may have to seriously consider limitations on some of the privileges that the affluent world has come to expect and enjoy. But rather than think of this as a sacrifice, I have been trying throughout this book to encourage all of us to think of it as a tremendous gain. It means a world where there is less stress, anxiety, overwork, overuse, and injustice, and more joy, equality, respect, and an appreciation of the ordinary. I hope we don't have to limit too much, but I've tried to show why limiting the privileges of the few is better for everyone, even those who currently enjoy them.

Third, our view of nature itself should shift from great to good enough. The planet is imperfect. Just witness the fact that it produced a species that is threatening to destroy it! Even without humans, nature is no perfect harmony. It is a complex system that is full of both the wonder and the brutality that we see every day. Nature, like human nature, is not wired for anything in particular. It is many things, but one of them is not an endless resource to exploit. Nature is embedded in us and we in it. We are a part of the good-enough ecological system that has enabled life to flourish on this planet. We are a threat to that life, but we are also a potential savior of it. The dinosaurs could do nothing when the asteroid hit, and the climate turned against them. We can do something, even if we ourselves are that asteroid. The planet has been good enough to keep us alive; it is our turn to be good enough to it.

The Good-Enough Sublime

As I was researching this chapter, I often stayed out in the country with my aunt and uncle. They live right next to a small state park. Most days I would take breaks and walk around the park. In early spring, with mornings of perfect light and slight chill, I would stand near a few favorite trees on the bank of a pond. This year, as one of them began to shoot forth its spring buds, I had a wonderful and alarming feeling that I had never had before: I was shocked that the earth was still regenerating. All the dire predictions of climate collapse had made me finally appreciate the remarkable yet simple fact that day after day, year after year, this world persists. I could think of no other word for this feeling than "sublime."

Immanuel Kant might disagree with my word choice. According to Kant, nature produces a feeling of the sublime in us not because it grows, but because it may destroy us. When we are confronted with something that *could* kill us—overhanging rocks, lightning storms, volcanoes—but that does not do so, we are apprised of something unique in our humanity. This something is simply the ability to recognize the situation: we may have "physical powerlessness," but "at the same time," we realize "a capacity for judging ourselves as independent of [nature]."[103] What is sublime for Kant is not nature, but the realization that though nature may kill my physical body, "I" am something greater than this natural world.

I understand this feeling of the sublime, and how it toys with both the greatness of nature and the greatness of our human faculties. But when I was standing there watching those spring blossoms appear, what was sublime was not a question of magnitude, of whether I was greater or nature was greater. What was sublime was to realize as profoundly as I ever have that there are a whole range of exquisite emotions that become available to us when we stop thinking about greatness. What was sublime was simply the fact that the earth exists, and that I exist. More precisely, it was that our existences work together. What was sublime was that humanity and the earth are good enough for each other, that this utterly random universe has managed to become good enough to sustain life. In that moment I felt the joy and excitement of the possibility of living up to the tremendous gift of life that the earth has given us, returning the favor of its being good enough to us by our being good enough to each other, by finally creating the good-enough life both in our social and natural worlds.

I kept staring at the blossoming buds, but I suddenly lost the sublime feeling. I began wondering how many more years of them there would be. It is terrifying to think that if we continue our pursuit of greatness, we will, for the first and last time, no longer be good enough to survive on this planet. It does not have to be this way. I have argued throughout this book that humans across cultures and through the millennia have developed ways of living that promote and participate in the good-enough life. I have argued that individuals can flourish without the burdens of perfection, becoming creative, adaptable, humble, and open to others; that we can lead more meaningful lives by focusing less on getting the best for ourselves and more on becoming the kinds of people who can promote and participate in a good-enough world. I have argued that in our relationships the desire for perfection in fact makes us worse lovers, parents, and friends, and that the most miraculous aspects of being together shine forth once we appreciate both our similarities and our differences from each other. I have argued that our political structures do tremendous damage by working to reward the few—even when they do it in the name of the many—and that by developing policies to directly promote decency and sufficiency for all we can achieve a just and vibrant society. And now I have argued that we are good enough by nature, and that nature itself is good enough for us. We are not destined to greatness, and nature is not an endlessly great resource for us to exploit. So while I can't offer you the powerful feeling of greatness, I hope I have expressed some of the profound, sublime feeling earned in the effort of coming together to make a good-enough life for all.

Conclusion

A unifying theme cuts across much that troubles us in life. We can call this unifying theme greatness: a method of ordering the world so that some humans are considered better than others, humanity as a whole is considered greater than nature, and our task as individuals should be to prove ourselves worthy of possessing power and privilege. This vision of the world has given us an epidemic of stress, anxiety, inequality, and ecological damage. Many people who subscribe to this worldview, or some parts of it, do not view it as being in contradiction with good-enoughness for all. Indeed, many people believe that promoting the talents of the few is the best way to achieve decency and sufficiency for everyone. I have tried to show why systems of privileging the few make it difficult, if not impossible, to provide enough for everyone to live decently, and to truly respect and appreciate the complex and plural values of human lives and the planet we share.

We cannot eliminate all hierarchy or create perfect equalities, and we probably should not. Humans are too different and varied and complex to try to do so, and non-oppressive hierarchies—especially ones that allow for rotation into leadership positions—can let people who are good at leading or organizing explore that talent without malice. But having a different talent than others, or having no particular talent, should not mean that your voice in society is limited to a vote once every few years, if that. There are ways to organize the world that enable all of us to meaning-fully share the burdens and joys of life. And doing so not only uplifts those otherwise voiceless; it also reduces the pressure and anxiety on those who presently have too much.

Achieving the good-enough life for all is not easy. It is an evolving and uneven process, one that different individuals and social groups have been working toward for the history of our species. We can continue that progress by changing how we treat ourselves, each other, and our planet. And we can maintain a healthy understanding that we won't be perfect along the way. We may still slip into greatness. We may demand too much of each other. We may want more for ourselves. We may make poor political choices. I know that I do all of these things. Good-enoughness reminds us not to be too hard on ourselves. None of us are perfect, and none of us can be perfectly good enough in a world that is still largely driven by greatness and the competitive demands of the modern economy. At the same time, good-enoughness refuses to let us capitulate to these im-perfections. Adopting the good-enough worldview means doing a little better each day to orient ourselves toward making a world that is good and decent and sufficient for all.

Some might find my points utopian and unrealistic; others, dystopian and frighteningly similar to failed social experiments in the past. Some might doubt that greatness for some is incom-patible with good-enoughness for everyone else. Others will simply continue to maintain that some people really are greater than the rest of us. Some will say that I am confusing an eco-nomic problem with a social one, and that equality in the econ-omy is all that matters. Others will say that I am confusing a social problem with an economic one, and that what matters is that everyone has dignity and basic necessities, no matter how much more others may have. I have done my best throughout this book to refute each of these objections and show the logic of my positions, why I think they would work, and why greatness in any sphere of our lives is a problem in all spheres of our lives. So long as some have vastly more wealth and power than others, they will have too much control over the lives of others, and the perceived desirability of their lives will create the kinds of competitive contests that distort our appreciation of each other's plural values and abilities. Furthermore, as we have seen, people who believe in social hierarchies tend also to believe in human domination over nature, or at least in their own ability to escape the ravages of climate change while the rest of the world may suffer.

Moving beyond the regime of greatness would free us up to enjoy more leisure, more complexity, and more of the values of the world that get obscured in narrow competitive processes. This revision does not mean removing the vitality and joy of civil competition, acquiring skills, or developing talents and interests. But it does mean that being great at writing or basketball should not lead you to enjoy corollary rewards in the positional or material economy. We need systems of cooperative economic governance and means of distributing esteem and political voice in society to ensure that no one gets left out or excluded solely because their talents—whatever they might be—are not fully recognizable in competition alone. While this might seem a diminution to some, in fact it registers a remarkable possibility for progress, as many billions of otherwise overlooked humans become recognized and appreciated.

None of this, however, is meant to imagine some new path to perfection. People will continue to wish they were talented at things they are not good at. Diseases will still take away our loved ones and hurricanes will still strike. The person we love might still fall for someone else. Great inventions will still get lost because people's talents go unrecognized or emerge too late in life. Not everyone will get to have their voice heard on a decision that really matters to them. We need to stop imagining that we can innovate our way—in our minds or in our economies—out of the suffering that is part of our condition. And we need to recognize that this impossibility does not justify trying to get the most for ourselves in the brief time of our lives. Rather, it gives us cause to work as best as we can to ensure that everyone shares in the imperfections and joys of being human.

That, at least, is the argument I have tried to make. I hope I have managed to connect with you and encourage or deepen your appreciation of a good-enough life for all. No book can answer all our questions or speak equally powerfully to everyone, and no individual writer understands the world so perfectly that they can solve all our problems. Things are just too interdependent, complex, and replete with differences. This is not cause to lament, but to celebrate our necessary humility. I have offered my arguments here with as much confidence and clarity as I can muster, but also with a sense that they are not perfect, that they will require emendation and engagement from others, just as I have tried to emend and engage with others myself. I certainly don't have all the answers, but I believe that the idea of the good-enough life is a powerful and important way of thinking about our collective lives. Learning to live a good-enough life on this good-enough planet is a path not only to our survival, but to our flourishing as a species that provides decency, sufficiency, and imperfection for all.

ACKNOWLEDGMENTS

More than any other book I have written, this one draws from a lifetime of experiences. It is impossible for me to properly acknowledge all the people that have made it possible for me to write this book, let alone those who influenced my thinking. I will just offer here brief acknowledgments to those who directly helped in the process of writing. Rebecca Alpert read about as many drafts of this book as I did, always helping it get a little clearer and more focused in its message. Jodi Roseman, Eric Angles, and Barry Schwartz read drafts of this book cover to cover and offered incisive feedback. Barry was a guide and mentor throughout the publishing process. Three remarkable research assistants, hired with special assistance funding from Princeton University, also read through this book and provided invaluable feedback and perspective: Jayson Badal, Thea Dimapeles, and Michael Kim. Steve Forguson and Rit Premnath helped guide the introduction. Long conversations with Shadi Harouni, Nick Keys, Zach Luck, Mashinka Firunts, Danny Snelson, Umrao Sethi, and Rit Premnath helped me to articulate and shape my vision. A reading group primarily with Nick Siena and Nikil Saval a few years ago prompted some of the big questions about political economy that I sought answers to in this book. Joel Whitney and Peter Catapano gave me the first platform for this project at the Brooklyn Public Library and in the pages of the *New York Times*. Readers near and far sent letters and comments that helped me keep refining the argument. A second night at the Brooklyn Public Library—this time speaking around 1 am at the Night of Philosophy—helped me to really shape the argument. Miranda Samuels, Grayson Earle, and Daniel Benson came, and kept talking with me about this through the early morning. Lisa Godfrey at CBC heard about my work and engaged me in a long conversation that presented an early opportunity to explain my claims in more depth. Anne Savarese at Princeton University Press has shepherded this project along from day one, providing regular, constructive feedback on new drafts, and also secured several very helpful anonymous reviews. Many thanks are also due to the rest of the team at the Press who worked to make this book a reality and bring it to readers, including James Collier in editorial, Terri O'Prey, David Campbell, and Erin Suydam in production, and Jodi Price and Carmen Jimenez in publicity. Thanks also to Karl Spurzem for the design, Derek Gottlieb for the index, and Jodi Beder for her invaluable copyediting. Rich Balka and Paula Jones gave me a room with a view to read and write, and Paula Behm let me take over her dining room for a mini writer's retreat as I finished the manuscript. My parents—Rebecca, Christie, Joel, and Jodi—and my sister, Lynn, gave me a view on life that shaped all that I have said. I don't know if I could write at all without Anthea Behm there every day by my side.

NOTES

Introduction

1. Anthony Shorrocks, James Davies, and Rodrigo Lluberas, "Global Wealth Report 2020" (Credit Suisse: Research Institute, October 2020), https://www.credit -suisse.com/media/assets/corporate/docs/about-us/research/publications/global -wealth-report-2020-en.pdf; World Bank, "Nearly Half the World Lives on Less than $5.50 a Day," October 17, 2018, https://www.worldbank.org/en/news/press-release /2018/10/17/nearly-half-the-world-lives-on-less-than-550-a-day; Ramon Martinez et al., "Trends in Premature Avertable Mortality from Non-Communicable Diseases for 195 Countries and Territories, 1990–2017: A Population-Based Study," *The Lancet Global Health* 8, no. 4 (April 1, 2020): e511–23, https://doi.org/10.1016/S2214 -109X(20)30035–8; The World Counts, "How Many People Die from Hunger Each Year?," https://www.theworldcounts.com/challenges/people-and-poverty/hunger -and-obesity/how-many-people-die-from-hunger-each-year/story, accessed March 22, 2021.

2. Spencer L. James et al., "Global, Regional, and National Incidence, Prevalence, and Years Lived with Disability for 354 Diseases and Injuries for 195 Countries and Territories, 1990–2017: A Systematic Analysis for the Global Burden of Disease Study 2017," *The Lancet* 392, no. 10159 (November 10, 2018): 1789–1858, https://doi.org/10 .1016/S0140-6736(18)32279-7; Anne Helen Petersen, "How Millennials Became the Burnout Generation," *BuzzFeed News*, January 5, 2019, https://www.buzzfeednews .com/article/annehelenpetersen/millennials-burnout-generation-debt-work; Shannon Palus, "Burnout Is Real, but It's Not an Exclusively Millennial Condition," *Slate*, January 8, 2019, https://slate.com/human-interest/2019/01/burnout-millennials -capitalism-buzzfeed-essay.html; American Psychiatric Association, "Americans Say They Are More Anxious than a Year Ago; Baby Boomers Report Greatest Increase in Anxiety," May 7, 2018, https://www.psychiatry.org/newsroom/news-releases /americans-say-they-are-more-anxious-than-a-year-ago-baby-boomers-report -greatest-increase-in-anxiety.

3. David Lin et al., "Calculating Earth Overshoot Day 2020: Estimates Point to August 22nd" (Global Footprint Network, June 5, 2020), https://www.overshootday .org/content/uploads/2020/06/Earth-Overshoot-Day-2020-Calculation-Research -Report.pdf; Partha Dasgupta, "The Economics of Biodiversity: The Dasgupta Review" (London: HM Treasury, February 2021), 123, https://assets.publishing.service .gov.uk/government/uploads/system/uploads/attachment_data/file/962785/The _Economics_of_Biodiversity_The_Dasgupta_Review_Full_Report.pdf.

4. I say "including" because the list of what constitutes goodness is vast, and because what we need will continue to evolve and change across time and place. In some places with high smog, for example, air purifiers may be necessary.

5. The evidence that this is not only desirable but feasible continues to grow. See the helpful overview of recent research in: Bryce Covert, "8 Hours a Day, 5 Days a Week Is Not Working for Us," *The New York Times*, July 20, 2021, sec. Opinion, https:// www.nytimes.com/2021/07/20/opinion/covid-return-to-office.html.

6. Avram Alpert, "The Good-Enough Life," *The New York Times*, February 20, 2019, sec. Opinion, https://www.nytimes.com/2019/02/20/opinion/the-good -enough-life-philosophy.html.

7. Edith Zimmerman, "I'm Calling Hypocrisy on These 'Good-Enough Life' Advocates," The Cut, February 20, 2019, https://www.thecut.com/2019/02/calling -hypocrisy-on-these-good-enough-life-advocates.html.

8. It was particularly remarkable to see this admission in the editorial pages of the *Financial Times*, previously one of the big champions of the current global order. Financial Times Editorial Board, "Virus Lays Bare the Frailty of the Social Contract," April 3, 2020, https://www.ft.com/content/7eff769a-74dd-11ea-95fe-fcd274e920ca. For other examples, see Amina Mohammed, "COVID-19 Pandemic Exposes Global 'Frailties and Inequalities': UN Deputy Chief," UN News, May 3, 2020, https://news .un.org/en/story/2020/05/1063022; Keeanga-Yamahtta Taylor, "Reality Has Endorsed Bernie Sanders," *The New Yorker*, March 30, 2020, https://www.newyorker .com/news/our-columnists/reality-has-endorsed-bernie-sanders; New York Times Editorial Board, "The America We Need," *The New York Times*, April 17, 2020, sec. Opinion, https://www.nytimes.com/interactive/2020/opinion/america-inequality -coronavirus.html; Jeffrey Sachs et al., "Letter from Economists: To Rebuild Our World, We Must End the Carbon Economy," *The Guardian*, August 4, 2020, sec. Opinion, https://www.theguardian.com/commentisfree/2020/aug/04/economists -letter-carbon-economy-climate-change-rebuild.

9. Walter Benjamin, *Illuminations: Essays and Reflections*, ed. Hannah Arendt, trans. Harry Zohn (New York: Schocken, 2019), 257.

10. I'll discuss this more in the fourth chapter, but for a brief overview and references to key sources in the debate, see Hélène Landemore, *Open Democracy: Reinventing Popular Rule for the Twenty-First Century* (Princeton, NJ: Princeton

University Press, 2020), 42. The point is not that there is absolute empirical proof that this is necessarily better, but that there is enough evidence to suggest it is, at least, no worse. The real power of the idea is its normative force: allowing more, and more diverse, people to participate is a good in itself.

11. Geoff Mulgan, *Big Mind: How Collective Intelligence Can Change Our World* (Princeton, NJ: Princeton University Press, 2017).

12. In the words of Simon Rawidowicz, "Our soul has tired of that imaginary *realism* that governs relations between the nations and brings us, in every generation, to human slaughter and pushes us into the abyss of loss—of life and land alike. There is a kind of Realpolitik of the hour, which turns out to be a total disaster the next day." Simon Rawidowicz, "Between Arab and Jew," in *Between Jew and Arab: The Lost Voice of Simon Rawidowicz*, by David N. Myers (Waltham, MA: Brandeis University Press, 2009), 135–80.

13. Jester D (@JustMeTurtle). "I'm a garbageman, I can't work from home and my job is an essential city service that must get done," Twitter, March 14, 2020. https://twitter.com/JustMeTurtle/status/1238682510579478528.

Chapter 1: Why Greatness Is Not Good Enough

1. As a somewhat general example, see W. G. de Burgh, "Greatness and Goodness: The Presidential Address," *Proceedings of the Aristotelian Society* 32 (1932): 1–18.

2. John Milton, *Paradise Lost*, ed. David Scott Kastan (Indianapolis: Hackett Publishing, 2005), 91 (3.310–311).

3. On the history of this phrase, see Michael J. Sandel, *The Tyranny of Merit: What's Become of the Common Good?* (New York: Farrar, Straus and Giroux, 2020), 49–50.

4. On the challenges this poses for the future, and how increasing inequalities in power may in fact undo any material progress, see Pedro Conceição et al., "Human Development Report 2019: Beyond Income, Beyond Averages, Beyond Today: Inequalities in Human Development in the 21st Century" (New York: United Nations Human Development Programme, 2019), http://hdr.undp.org/sites/default/files/hdr2019.pdf.

5. Michael Young, *The Rise of the Meritocracy, 1870–2033: An Essay on Education and Equality* (Harmondsworth: Penguin Books, 1961), 179.

6. The term reflects certain prejudices not only of his time, but also, since he did not think it had to be the infant's "own mother"—presumably instead it could be a paid caretaker—of his own particular class background. Winnicott also writes, though less famously, about the "good-enough facilitating environment," showing the connections between interpersonal and political ideals. D. W. Winnicott, *Playing and Reality*, second edition (London: Routledge, 2005), 187.

7. The temptation to greatness is a recurring theme. For example, the three temptations of Christ were to be recognized as the greatest: to be more powerful than natural law, to have infinite glory and authority, and to defy death. But as Milton noted, Christ was chosen for being good, not great. *The Holy Bible: New Revised Standard Version*, Luke 4.1–13; Milton, *Paradise Lost*, 91 (3.310–311).

8. Winnicott, *Playing and Reality*, 14.

9. Roy F. Baumeister and Mark R. Leary, "The Need to Belong: Desire for Interpersonal Attachments as a Fundamental Human Motivation," *Psychological Bulletin* 117, no. 3 (May 1995): 497, https://doi.org/10.1037/0033-2909.117.3.497.

10. Baumeister and Leary, 498.

11. Martha C. Nussbaum, *Creating Capabilities: The Human Development Approach* (Cambridge, MA: Harvard University Press, 2013), 33–34. See also Katharina Lima de Miranda and Dennis J. Snower, "Recoupling Economic and Social Prosperity," *Global Perspectives* 1, no. 1 (February 20, 2020): 1–34, https://doi.org/10.1525/001c .11867.

12. I should say that I still deeply appreciate how these accounts push back against the relentless movements for self-perfection. For an enjoyable skewering of these trends, see Carl Cederström and André Spicer, *Desperately Seeking Self-Improvement: A Year inside the Optimization Movement* (New York: OR Books, 2017).

13. Ada Calhoun, *Why We Can't Sleep: Women's New Midlife Crisis* (New York: Grove Press, 2020), 219; Mark Manson, *The Subtle Art of Not Giving a F*ck: A Counterintuitive Approach to Living a Good Life* (New York: Harper, 2016).

14. The Danish psychologist and philosopher Svend Brinkmann does a better job of contextualizing the economic pressures driving us to pursue greatness. While his early work encouraged solutions that fell back on the cultivation of a personal ethic, his more recent work has taken a more political turn. Svend Brinkmann, *Stand Firm: Resisting the Self-Improvement Craze*, trans. Tam McTurk (Cambridge: Polity, 2017); Svend Brinkmann, *The Joy of Missing Out: The Art of Self-Restraint in an Age of Excess*, trans. Tam McTurk (Cambridge: Polity, 2019). I began reading Brinkmann's work on the advice of Barry Schwartz, whose own writings on the politics and psychology of being good enough helped shape my arguments throughout this book. See especially Barry Schwartz, *The Battle for Human Nature: Science, Morality, and Modern Life* (New York: Norton, 1986); Barry Schwartz, "Top Colleges Should Select Randomly from a Pool of 'Good Enough,'" *The Chronicle of Higher Education*, February 25, 2005, https://www.chronicle.com/article/Top-Colleges-Should-Select/14215/; Barry Schwartz, *The Paradox of Choice*, revised edition (New York: Ecco Press, 2016).

15. Elsie Chen, "These Chinese Millennials Are 'Chilling,' and Beijing Isn't Happy," *The New York Times*, July 3, 2021, sec. World, https://www.nytimes.com /2021/07/03/world/asia/china-slackers-tangping.html.

16. On the tendency of popular self-help writers to avoid questions of politics and governance, see Anand Giridharadas, *Winners Take All: The Elite Charade of Changing the World* (New York: Vintage, 2018), 87–128.

17. Robert Michels, *Political Parties: A Sociological Study of the Oligarchical Tendencies of Modern Democracy*, trans. Eden and Cedar Paul (New York: Dover Publications, 1959).

18. Christopher Boehm, *Hierarchy in the Forest: The Evolution of Egalitarian Behavior* (Cambridge, MA: Harvard University Press, 1999), vii.

19. Adam Smith, *The Theory of Moral Sentiments*, ed. Ryan Patrick Hanley (New York: Penguin Classics, 2010), 136. I have for the sake of clarity kept the gendered language in direct citations.

20. Smith, 64.

21. Smith, 73.

22. Smith, 215.

23. An historical account that dispels any idea of benevolent motivations for the economic origins of globalization can be found in Quinn Slobodian, *Globalists: The End of Empire and the Birth of Neoliberalism* (Cambridge, MA: Harvard University Press, 2018). For critical overviews of the problems of neoliberal globalization, see Ha-Joon Chang, *Bad Samaritans: The Myth of Free Trade and the Secret History of Capitalism* (New York: Bloomsbury Press, 2007); Vijay Prashad, *The Poorer Nations: A Possible History of the Global South* (New York: Verso, 2014).

24. Donald Justice, *Oblivion: On Writers and Writing* (Ashland, OR: Story Line Press, 1998), 55.

25. Thomas Piketty, *Capital and Ideology*, trans. Arthur Goldhammer (Cambridge, MA: Belknap Press, 2020), 584–85.

26. Aristotle, *The Politics*, trans. Ernest Barker, reissue edition (New York: Oxford University Press, 1998), 58.

27. Fred Hirsch, *Social Limits to Growth* (Cambridge, MA: Harvard University Press, 1978), 6.

28. Hirsch, 26.

29. Hirsch, 6. There is a certain parallel with what the cultural theorist Lauren Berlant more recently called "cruel optimism," or a system in which pursuing our desires is in fact a detriment to our own flourishing. Lauren Berlant, *Cruel Optimism* (Durham, NC: Duke University Press, 2011).

30. W.E.B. Du Bois, *Black Reconstruction in America, 1860–1880* (New York: Free Press, 1998), 700.

31. Hirsch, *Social Limits to Growth*, 190.

32. Mathias Döpfner and Jeff Bezos, "Jeff Bezos Reveals What It's Like to Build an Empire and Become the Richest Man in the World—and Why He's Willing to Spend

$1 Billion a Year to Fund the Most Important Mission of His Life," *Business Insider*, April 30, 2018, https://www.businessinsider.com/jeff-bezos-interview-axel-springer-ceo-amazon-trump-blue-origin-family-regulation-washington-post-2018-4.

33. Karen Weise, "Jeff Bezos Commits $10 Billion to Address Climate Change," *The New York Times*, February 17, 2020, sec. Technology, https://www.nytimes.com/2020/02/17/technology/jeff-bezos-climate-change-earth-fund.html.

34. Tim Fernholz, "How to Build a Space Economy That Avoids the Mistakes of Terrestrial Capitalism," *Quartz*, December 20, 2019, https://qz.com/work/1767415/can-nasa-build-a-space-economy-that-leaves-capitalisms-problems-behind/.

35. Döpfner and Bezos, Bezos interview.

36. Raj Chetty et al., "Who Becomes an Inventor in America? The Importance of Exposure to Innovation" (The Equality of Opportunity Project, 2018), http://www.equality-of-opportunity.org/assets/documents/inventors_paper.pdf.

37. Stephen Jay Gould, *The Panda's Thumb: More Reflections in Natural History* (New York: W. W. Norton & Company, 1992), 151.

38. Albert Einstein, "Reprise: Why Socialism?," *Monthly Review*, May 1, 2009, https://monthlyreview.org/2009/05/01/why-socialism/.

39. I owe the recognition of the need to address this concern upfront especially to my research assistants—Jayson Badal, Michael Kim, and Thea Dimapeles. They all expressed some concern with an early draft of the book that it did not fully appreciate the possibility of benefits from people genuinely seeking justice through great measures. I think this is a very fair point, and I have tried to explain why I agree yet remain hesitant here.

40. Marie Solis, "When Dismantling Power Dismantles You Instead," Vice, December 7, 2018, https://www.vice.com/en_us/article/3k95kk/when-dismantling-power-dismantles-you-instead-v25n4.

41. adrienne maree brown, "Stagger," June 12, 2017, http://adriennemareebrown.net/2017/06/12/stagger/.

42. Charles M. Payne, *I've Got the Light of Freedom: The Organizing Tradition and the Mississippi Freedom Struggle, with a New Preface*, second edition (Berkeley: University of California Press, 2007), 101.

43. Barbara Ransby, *Ella Baker and the Black Freedom Movement: A Radical Democratic Vision* (Chapel Hill: University of North Carolina Press, 2003), chapter 6; Payne, *I've Got the Light of Freedom*, 76.

44. Smith, *The Theory of Moral Sentiments*, 215.

45. Isaiah Berlin, *The Crooked Timber of Humanity: Chapters in the History of Ideas*, ed. Henry Hardy, second edition (Princeton, NJ: Princeton University Press, 1990), 15.

46. James Baldwin, "Notes of a Native Son," in *James Baldwin: Collected Essays*, ed. Toni Morrison (New York: Library of America, 1998), 84.

Chapter 2: For Our Selves

1. For a sophisticated articulation of this problem, see Albena Azmanova, *Capitalism on Edge: How Fighting Precarity Can Achieve Radical Change without Crisis or Utopia* (New York: Columbia University Press, 2020), 50–59.

2. This may also change with automation, where the challenge will become ensuring that all the gains from the elimination of unpleasant labor do not go to a tiny sliver of the population, while the rest of the world is just meant to be grateful for technological revolutions, even if we are disempowered and frustrated. For an interesting recent conversation about this, see Ezra Klein and Sam Altman, "Transcript: Ezra Klein Interviews Sam Altman," *The New York Times*, June 11, 2021, sec. Podcasts, https://www.nytimes.com/2021/06/11/podcasts/transcript-ezra-klein-interviews -sam-altman.html.

3. Manson, *The Subtle Art of Not Giving a F*ck*, 8.

4. Manson, 16.

5. Laurie Santos, "Laurie Santos, Yale Happiness Professor, on 5 Things That Will Make You Happier," Newsweek, December 20, 2020, https://www.newsweek.com /2021/01/08/laurie-santos-yale-happiness-professor-5-things-that-will-make-you -happier-1556182.html. For the research behind Santos's claims, see Jane Allyn Piliavin, "Doing Well by Doing Good: Benefits for the Benefactor," in *Flourishing: Positive Psychology and the Life Well-Lived* (Washington, DC: American Psychological Association, 2003), 227–47, https://doi.org/10.1037/10594-010; Elizabeth W. Dunn, Lara B. Aknin, and Michael I. Norton, "Spending Money on Others Promotes Happiness," *Science* 319, no. 5870 (2008): 1687–88.

6. *The Holy Bible*, NRSV, Genesis 1.

7. Sandor Goodhart, "Opening Genesis 1," *Prose Studies* 34, no. 1 (April 2012): 23, https://doi.org/10.1080/01440357.2012.686209. In *Isaiah* 41.7, the phrase "it is good" is spoken in a similar manner with respect to soldering: "the one who smooths with the hammer encourages the one who strikes the anvil, saying of the soldering, 'It is good.'"

8. Marshall Sahlins, *Stone Age Economics* (New York: Routledge, 2004). For recent work aligned with Sahlins's claims, see James Scott, *Against the Grain: A Deep History of the Earliest States* (New Haven, CT: Yale University Press, 2017). For a critical perspective, see Daniel Immerwahr, "Paleo Con," *The New Republic*, March 24, 2021, https://newrepublic.com/article/161593/prehistoric-myth-work -james-suzman.

9. Scott, *Against the Grain*, 10, 75.

10. *The Holy Bible*, NRSV, Genesis 3:17.

11. Scott, *Against the Grain*, 10, 75.

12. This is in reference to the famous quip about how to win an election—"It's the economy, stupid"—by James Carville, an advisor to President Clinton.

13. Kenneth E. Boulding, "Economics as a Moral Science," *The American Economic Review* 59, no. 1 (1969): 8.

14. Wendy Brown, *Undoing the Demos: Neoliberalism's Stealth Revolution* (New York: Zone Books, 2015).

15. Binyamin Appelbaum, *The Economists' Hour: False Prophets, Free Markets, and the Fracture of Society* (New York: Little, Brown and Company, 2019), 199.

16. Appelbaum, chapter 7.

17. Max Weber, *The Protestant Ethic and the "Spirit" of Capitalism and Other Writings*, trans. Peter Baehr and Gordon C. Wells (New York: Penguin Classics, 2002), 11–28.

18. See chapter 4 of this book. Smith and Franklin were not alone here. As A.O. Hirschman has shown, for example, earlier writers such as Montesquieu had argued that we could create a better political order by counterposing our rational "interests" (in material benefits and commerce) against our unruly "passions" (such as violence and the lust for power). Hirschman notes that whereas Montesquieu had focused on the potential political benefits of self-interest, Smith's writings narrowed in on economic growth as a good in itself. Albert O. Hirschman, *The Passions and the Interests: Political Arguments for Capitalism before Its Triumph* (Princeton: Princeton University Press, 2013).

19. Christine Hauser, "West Virginia Teachers, Protesting Low Pay, Walk Out," *The New York Times*, February 23, 2018, sec. U.S., https://www.nytimes.com/2018/02/23/us/west-virginia-teachers-strike.html.

20. Sylvia Allegretto and Lawrence Mishel, "The Teacher Pay Penalty Has Hit a New High" (Economic Policy Institute, September 5, 2018).

21. E. Tammy Kim, "Can Arizona's Teachers Still Consider Themselves Middle Class?," *The New Yorker*, May 2, 2018, https://www.newyorker.com/news/dispatch/can-arizonas-teachers-still-consider-themselves-middle-class.

22. Ironically, from a long-term perspective, this is also bad for the economy, since widely available public education has been a major factor in the past two centuries of economic growth. Piketty, *Capital and Ideology*, 517–23.

23. National Center on Education and the Economy, "Finland: Teacher and Principal Quality," Top Performing Countries, 2018, http://ncee.org/what-we-do/center-on-international-education-benchmarking/top-performing-countries/finland-overview/finland-teacher-and-principal-quality/; Dick Startz, "Teacher Pay around the World," Brookings (blog), June 20, 2016, https://www.brookings.edu/blog/brown-center-chalkboard/2016/06/20/teacher-pay-around-the-world/; Anu Partanen, *The Nordic Theory of Everything: In Search of a Better Life* (New York: Harper Paperbacks, 2017).

24. Ilari Kaila and Tuomas Kaila, "Finland, We Hardly Knew Ye," *Jacobin*, August 16, 2017, https://jacobinmag.com/2017/08/finland-welfare-state-true-finns-centennial.

25. See, for example, Alasdair MacIntyre, *After Virtue*, second edition (South Bend, IN: University of Notre Dame Press, 1984); Michael Walzer, *Spheres of Justice: A Defense of Pluralism and Equality* (New York: Basic Books, 1983); Michael Sandel, *Justice: What's the Right Thing to Do?* (New York: Farrar, Straus and Giroux, 2009). I learned to appreciate virtue ethics as a response to "economics imperialism" through reading Schwartz, *The Battle for Human Nature*, 268, 274–75, 301–4.

26. Aristotle, *The Nicomachean Ethics*, ed. Lesley Brown, trans. David Ross (Oxford: Oxford University Press, 2009), 23.

27. Aristotle, 25.

28. Aristotle, 36.

29. Aristotle, 195.

30. Walzer, *Spheres of Justice*; MacIntyre, *After Virtue*.

31. Walzer, *Spheres of Justice*, 319.

32. Sandel, *Justice*, 186–95.

33. Walzer, *Spheres of Justice*, 320.

34. Brooke N. Macnamara, David Moreau, and David Z. Hambrick, "The Relationship between Deliberate Practice and Performance in Sports: A Meta-Analysis," *Perspectives on Psychological Science* 11, no. 3 (May 1, 2016): 333–50, https://doi.org/10.1177/1745691616635591.

35. Alfie Kohn, *No Contest: The Case against Competition* (Boston: Houghton Mifflin, 1986). Although this book is a few decades old, it remains one of the most compelling accounts of the problems with competition. Kohn has since written many books that continue to advance his case against competition with new evidence. Two recent critics of Kohn have suggested that he is right about win-lose contests, but wrong about competitions that can encourage kids to excel in meaningful relation to each other. I think there is some merit to this argument, but its narrow focus on individual competitions rather than the role of competition in society at large misses a lot of the point. They think we can just get rid of unhealthy winner-based attitudes through pedagogy, but, while worthy, this won't live up to the challenges of refashioning a competitive society. David Light Shields and Brenda Light Bredemeier, "Competition: Was Kohn Right?," *The Phi Delta Kappan* 91, no. 5 (2010): 62–67.

36. Kohn, *No Contest*, 54.

37. Ralph Waldo Emerson, *Essays and Poems* (New York: Library of America, 1996), 263.

38. Jane E. Brody, "How to Avoid Burnout in Youth Sports," *The New York Times*, May 7, 2018, sec. Well, https://www.nytimes.com/2018/05/07/well/how-to-avoid-burnout-in-youth-sports.html.

39. See Daniel Markovits, *The Meritocracy Trap: How America's Foundational Myth Feeds Inequality, Dismantles the Middle Class, and Devours the Elite* (New York: Penguin Press, 2019), 111–56. Markovits's colleague at Yale Law, Anthony Kronman, has written one of the most transparent arguments for why virtue ethics is linked to aristocracy. Kronman laments the loss of the "Aristocratic tradition of respect for human greatness." While Kronman views his book as a defense of expertise and the value of higher learning, he does not see the profound connection traced by his colleague: that the search for an aristocracy to reward and promote has the effect of diminishing rather than unearthing human potential. Expertise is devalued in an aristocratic culture, because such a culture cannot but create invidious distinctions that undermine the pursuit of knowledge to serve the common good. Anthony T. Kronman, *The Assault on American Excellence* (New York: Free Press, 2019), 9.

40. As Fred Hirsch put it decades ago, "Clearly once the concept of equality of opportunity is taken seriously, it expands without natural barrier toward equality of outcome." Hirsch, *Social Limits to Growth*, 162–63n2. And as Hirsch points out, any honest economic libertarian will agree. He cites Friedrich Hayek's critique of "equality of opportunity" as evidence.

41. Karina Limburg et al., "The Relationship between Perfectionism and Psychopathology: A Meta-Analysis," *Journal of Clinical Psychology* 73, no. 10 (2017): 1301–26, https://doi.org/10.1002/jclp.22435; Martin M. Smith et al., "Perfectionism and the Five-Factor Model of Personality: A Meta-Analytic Review," *Personality and Social Psychology Review*, January 6, 2019, https://doi.org/10.1177/1088868318814973.

42. Andrew P. Hill and Thomas Curran, "How Perfectionism Became a Hidden Epidemic among Young People," The Conversation, January 3, 2018, http://theconversation.com/how-perfectionism-became-a-hidden-epidemic-among-young-people-89405.

43. Christie Aschwanden, "Perfectionism Is Killing Us," Vox, November 27, 2019, https://www.vox.com/the-highlight/2019/11/27/20975989/perfect-mental-health-perfectionism.

44. Tiana Clark, "This Is What Black Burnout Feels Like," *BuzzFeed News*, January 11, 2019, https://www.buzzfeednews.com/article/tianaclarkpoet/millennial-burnout-black-women-self-care-anxiety-depression.

45. Sandel, *The Tyranny of Merit*, 155.

46. Sandel, 208. For his sources on the term, see Sandel, 256n39.

47. Sandel, 224.

48. Oren Cass, *The Once and Future Worker: A Vision for the Renewal of Work in America* (New York: Encounter Books, 2018), chapters 5 and 7.

49. For an argument that Sandel does not focus enough on profound economic transformations, see Elizabeth Anderson, "What Comes after Meritocracy?," *The*

Nation, February 23, 2021, https://www.thenation.com/article/society/sandel -tyranny-merit/. While Anderson argues that Sandel focuses too much on meritoc- racy as the problem, I think she may focus too much on capitalism as the problem. Both of these share ideals of what I am calling greatness, and it is this underlying logic across various systems that I argue needs to be addressed.

50. Sandel, *The Tyranny of Merit*, 227.

51. Young, *The Rise of the Meritocracy, 1870–2033*, 169.   .

52. Kwame Anthony Appiah, *The Lies That Bind: Rethinking Identity* (New York: Liveright, 2019), 177.

53. Appiah, 178.

54. Appiah, 180.

55. Appiah, 182.

56. Appiah, 183–84.

57. Justice, *Oblivion*, 55.

58. Landemore, *Open Democracy*, 89.

59. Jeremy Egner, "'The Good Place' Finale Finds the Meaning of Life: 'Yep, Nailed It,'" *The New York Times*, January 28, 2020, sec. Arts, https://www.nytimes .com/2020/01/28/arts/television/the-good-place-michael-schur.html.

60. As an aside I would also note that sports do not have to be organized as competitions. There are also cooperative games that could have a more expansive role in our lives. The competitive focus excludes people with different body types, and it can even lead people who enjoy sports but not competition to burn out and quit. Alfie Kohn, "Fun and Fitness without Competition," July 3, 1990, https://www .alfiekohn.org/article/fun-fitness-without-competition/; Jane E. Brody, "How to Avoid Burnout in Youth Sports."

61. Adam Harris, "Who Do You Have to Know to Get a Coronavirus Test?," *The Atlantic*, March 15, 2020, https://www.theatlantic.com/politics/archive/2020/03 /coronavirus-testing-rich-people/608062/.

62. Mychal Denzel Smith, "LeBron James Is No Socialist, But His New Nike Ad Makes a Good Case for Socialism," Esquire, December 23, 2019, https://www.esquire .com/news-politics/a30316187/lebron-james-nike-ad-humble-beginnings-i-promise -school-socialism/.

63. Mariana Mazzucato, *The Entrepreneurial State: Debunking Public vs. Private Sector Myths*, revised edition (New York: PublicAffairs, 2015), 93–119.

64. Eliza Barclay, "The Growth of Yoga and Meditation in the US since 2012 Is Remarkable," Vox, November 8, 2018, https://www.vox.com/2018/11/8/18073422 /yoga-meditation-apps-health-anxiety-cdc.

65. Erik Braun, *The Birth of Insight: Meditation, Modern Buddhism, and the Burmese Monk Ledi Sayadaw* (Chicago: University of Chicago Press, 2013).

66. Alan W. Watts, *The Wisdom of Insecurity: A Message for an Age of Anxiety*, second edition (New York: Vintage Books, 2011), 9.

67. Manson, *The Subtle Art of Not Giving a F*ck*, 10.

68. Manson, 10–11.

69. Slavoj Žižek, *On Belief* (New York: Routledge, 2001), 13.

70. For a helpful overview, see Greg Bailey, "Buddhism and Caste," in *Oxford Bibliographies* (Oxford: Oxford University Press, 2014), DOI: 10.1093/OBO/978019 5393521–0191.

71. Johannes Bronkhorst, *Buddhism in the Shadow of Brahmanism* (Leiden: Brill, 2011), 36.

72. Bhikkhu Ñāṇamoli and Bhikkhu Bodhi, trans., *The Middle Length Discourses of the Buddha: A New Translation of the Majjhima Nikaya*, Teachings of the Buddha (Boston: Wisdom Publications, 1995), 763–70.

73. Steven Collins, *Selfless Persons: Imagery and Thought in Theravada Buddhism* (Cambridge: Cambridge University Press, 1990), 191. See also Steven Collins, *Nirvana and Other Buddhist Felicities: Utopias of the Pali Imaginaire* (Cambridge: Cambridge University Press, 1998), 249–50. Collins concludes: "Buddhist dramas of humankind as a whole are never-ending: only privatized, individual time can end, not public" (250).

74. Aristotle, *The Nicomachean Ethics*, 187.

75. Aristotle, 189.

76. Bhikkhu Bodhi, trans., *The Connected Discourses of the Buddha: A New Translation of the Saṃyutta Nikāya* (Somerville: Wisdom Publications, 2000), 98.

77. Maurice O'C. Walshe, trans., *The Long Discourses of the Buddha: A Translation of the Dīgha Nikāya*, The Teachings of the Buddha (Boston: Wisdom Publications, 1995), 346–47.

78. Robert Wright, *Why Buddhism Is True: The Science and Philosophy of Meditation and Enlightenment* (New York: Simon and Schuster, 2017). For a criticism of Wright's book, see Evan Thompson, *Why I Am Not a Buddhist* (New Haven, CT: Yale University Press, 2020), 56–85.

79. David McMahan, "How Meditation Works: Theorizing the Role of Cultural Context in Buddhist Contemplative Practices," in *Meditation, Buddhism, and Science*, ed. David McMahan and Erik Braun (New York: Oxford University Press, 2017), 21–46. For a more skeptical take, see Thompson, *Why I Am Not a Buddhist*, 118–39.

80. Walshe, *The Long Discourses of the Buddha*, 349.

81. Collins, *Selfless Persons*, 191–92.

82. bell hooks and Helen Tworkov, "Agent of Change: Helen Tworkov Interviews bell hooks," in *Tricycle*, Fall 1992, https://tricycle.org/magazine/bell-hooks -buddhism/.

83. Harris's phrase derives from Fredrick Douglass: "The whole history of the progress of human liberty shows that all concessions yet made to her august claims, have been born of earnest struggle." Leonard Harris, *A Philosophy of Struggle: The Leonard Harris Reader*, ed. Lee A. McBride III (London: Bloomsbury Academic, 2020), 13.

84. bell hooks, *Belonging: A Culture of Place* (New York: Routledge, 2009), 5.

85. W.E.B. Du Bois, "Criteria of Negro Art," *The Crisis*, October 1926.

86. W.E.B. Du Bois, "The Talented Tenth," in *The Negro Problem: A Series of Articles by Representative American Negroes of Today* (New York: James Pott & Company, 1903), 75.

87. W.E.B. Du Bois, "The Talented Tenth Memorial Address," in *The Future of the Race*, by Henry Louis Gates Jr. and Cornel West (New York: Knopf Doubleday Publishing Group, 2011), 174.

88. Du Bois, 177, 174.

89. My research assistant Thea Dimapeles, my editor Anne Savarese, and my mother Rebecca Alpert helped me hear this point.

90. Ta-Nehisi Coates, "Black Pathology and the Closing of the Progressive Mind," *The Atlantic*, March 21, 2014, https://www.theatlantic.com/politics/archive/2014/03/black-pathology-and-the-closing-of-the-progressive-mind/284523/. Cited in: Keeanga-Yamahtta Taylor, *From #BlackLivesMatter to Black Liberation* (Chicago: Haymarket Books, 2016), 28.

91. Heather McGhee, *The Sum of Us: What Racism Costs Everyone and How We Can Prosper Together* (New York: One World, 2021), 26.

92. James Baldwin, "The Fire Next Time," in *Collected Essays*, ed. Toni Morrison (New York: Library of America, 1998), 342.

93. Anna Julia Cooper, *The Voice of Anna Julia Cooper: Including "A Voice from the South" and Other Important Essays, Papers, and Letters*, ed. Charles Lemert and Esme Bhan (Lanham, MD: Rowman & Littlefield, 1998), 63.

94. Ella Baker, "Gerda Lerner Interview with Ella Baker," in *Black Women in White America: A Documentary History*, ed. Gerda Lerner (New York: Vintage Books, 1973), 351.

95. Baker, 351.

96. Baker, 352.

97. adrienne maree brown, *Emergent Strategy: Shaping Change, Changing Worlds* (Oakland: AK Press, 2017), 101.

98. brown, 99.

99. brown, 54.

100. Dr. Martin Luther King Jr., *Where Do We Go from Here: Chaos or Community?* (Boston: Beacon Press, 2010), 174. It is somewhat remarkable today to read King

saying in 1968 that ideas about meritocracy still prevalent in our time had already been overcome in his: "Earlier in the century this proposal would have been greeted with ridicule and denunciation as destructive of initiative and responsibility. At that time economic status was considered the measure of the individual's ability and talents. In the simplistic thinking of that day the absence of worldly goods indicated a want of industrious habits and moral fiber" (171).

101. I was also struck recently by how many themes in this book resonated in an interview by Ezra Klein with political scientist Jamila Michener. Michener articulates a worldview very much aligned with this tradition, in which the imperfections of life should lead us not to struggle against each other, but to work in solidarity with each other. Ezra Klein and Jamila Michener, "Transcript: Ezra Klein Interviews Jamila Michener," *The New York Times*, June 8, 2021, sec. Podcasts, https://www.nytimes.com/2021/06/08/podcasts/transcript-ezra-klein-interviews-jamila-michener.html.

Chapter 3: For Our Relationships

1. Kimberley Brownlee, *Being Sure of Each Other: An Essay on Social Rights and Freedoms, Being Sure of Each Other* (Oxford: Oxford University Press, 2020), 2.

2. Brownlee, 125–32.

3. For a strong argument to this effect, see Brownlee, especially chapters 4–6.

4. On how the meritocracy can thus "devour" even the winners, see Markovits, *The Meritocracy Trap*.

5. This is not just a hypothetical experience. For accounts along these lines, see Sandel, *The Tyranny of Merit*, chapter 6.

6. Benjamin, *Illuminations*, 30.

7. Alain de Botton, "Why You Will Marry the Wrong Person," *The New York Times*, May 28, 2016, sec. Opinion, https://www.nytimes.com/2016/05/29/opinion/sunday/why-you-will-marry-the-wrong-person.html.

8. Plato, *The Symposium*, trans. Alexander Nehamas and Paul Woodruff (Indianapolis: Hackett, 1989), 25–31.

9. Ovid, *Metamorphoses*, ed. E. J. Kenney, trans. A. D. Melville (Oxford: Oxford University Press, 2008), 190–93.

10. Lori Gottlieb, "Marry Him! The Case for Settling for Mr. Good Enough," *The Atlantic*, March 1, 2008, https://www.theatlantic.com/magazine/archive/2008/03/marry-him/306651/.

11. Lori Gottlieb, *Marry Him: The Case for Settling for Mr. Good Enough* (New York: Dutton, 2011), 273–82.

12. Gottlieb, "Marry Him! The Case for Setting for Mr. Good Enough."

13. Richard Schwartz and Jacqueline Olds, *Marriage in Motion: The Natural Ebb and Flow of Lasting Relationships* (Cambridge, MA: Da Capo Lifelong Books, 2002).

14. Erich Auerbach, *Mimesis: The Representation of Reality in Western Literature*, trans. Willard Trask (Princeton, NJ: Princeton University Press, 1953), 19.

15. A relationship here does not necessarily mean a couple. For some people, monogamy may very well not be good enough. But that does not mean, as it is sometimes suggested, that polygamous people live a life freed from the burdens of relationships and always filled with pleasure. They, too, have to find a form of good-enoughness.

16. Todd May, *A Decent Life: Morality for the Rest of Us* (Chicago: University of Chicago Press, 2019).

17. Amy Chua, *Battle Hymn of the Tiger Mother* (New York: Penguin, 2012), 4.

18. John Morreall, "Philosophy of Humor," in *The Stanford Encyclopedia of Philosophy*, ed. Edward N. Zalta, Winter 2016 (Metaphysics Research Lab, Stanford University, 2016), https://plato.stanford.edu/archives/win2016/entries/humor/.

19. Sigmund Freud, *Jokes and Their Relation to the Unconscious: The Standard Edition*, trans. James Strachey (New York: W. W. Norton & Company, 1990), 286.

20. Naomi Shihab Nye, *Words under the Words: Selected Poems* (Portland, OR: Eighth Mountain Press, 1995), 80.

21. Daniel Batson and John Darley, "From Jerusalem to Jericho: A Study of Situational and Dispositional Variables in Helping Behaviour," *Journal of Personality and Social Psychology* 27, no. 1 (1973): 101.

22. Batson and Darley, 105.

23. Hirsch, *Social Limits to Growth*, 77; Paul K. Piff et al., "Having Less, Giving More: The Influence of Social Class on Prosocial Behavior," *Journal of Personality and Social Psychology* 99, no. 5 (2010): 771–84, https://doi.org/10.1037/a0020092.

24. See Hirsch, *Social Limits to Growth*, chapter 5.

25. Schwartz, *The Paradox of Choice*.

26. Hirsch, *Social Limits to Growth*, 79.

27. Hirsch, 79.

28. Some conservatives like Ross Douthat are aware of this problem. Douthat wonders, however, if this is a more general problem of dynamic change and doubts if anyone, regardless of their political affiliation, has an adequate response. I believe that a cooperative economy such as outlined in the next chapter is the most obvious answer. Ross Douthat, "Is Capitalism Killing Conservatism?," *The New York Times*, May 8, 2021, sec. Opinion, https://www.nytimes.com/2021/05/08/opinion/sunday/capitalism-conservatism.html.

29. Henry David Thoreau, *Walden* (Princeton, NJ: Princeton University Press, 2004), 224.

30. Thoreau, 134.

31. Thoreau.

32. Zhuangzi, *Zhuangzi: The Essential Writings with Selections from Traditional Commentaries*, trans. Brook Ziporyn (Indianapolis: Hackett Publishing, 2009), 76.

33. Zhuangzi, 8.

34. Brook Ziporyn, "Introduction," in *Zhuangzi: The Essential Writings with Selections from Traditional Commentaries*, by Zhuangzi, trans. Brook Ziporyn (Indianapolis: Hackett Publishing, 2009), xv–xvi.

35. Zhuangzi, *Zhuangzi*, 124. Confucius is ridiculed throughout *Zhuangzi*, and their ideas are *very* different. But perhaps the critique is in this same spirit of dialogue.

36. Ziporyn, "Introduction," xvi.

37. Botton, "Why You Will Marry the Wrong Person."

38. The *Huainanzi* version is less about contingency of knowledge and more about the surprising skill of a family of diviners who keep seeing how seemingly good or bad things turn into their opposite. The story still arrives at a similar moral: "good fortune becoming calamity, calamity becoming good fortune; their transformations are limitless, so profound they cannot be fathomed." Liu An, *The Huainanzi: A Guide to the Theory and Practice of Government in Early Han China*, trans. John S. Major (New York: Columbia University Press, 2010), 729.

39. Heather Lanier, "'Good' and 'Bad' Are Incomplete Stories We Tell Ourselves," TED@BCG Milan, October 2017, https://www.ted.com/talks/heather_lanier_good_and_bad_are_incomplete_stories_we_tell_ourselves.

40. Primo Levi, *Survival in Auschwitz*, trans. Stuart Woolf (New York: Simon and Schuster, 1996), 86.

41. Levi, 86.

42. Levi, 88.

43. Levi, 121.

44. Levi, 121–22.

45. David Treuer, *The Heartbeat of Wounded Knee: Native America from 1890 to the Present* (New York: Riverhead Books, 2019), 1.

46. Treuer, 13.

47. Treuer, 404.

48. Cedric J. Robinson, *Black Marxism: The Making of the Black Radical Tradition*, second edition (Chapel Hill: University of North Carolina Press, 2000), 123–66.

49. Vincent Brown, "Social Death and Political Life in the Study of Slavery," *The American Historical Review* 114, no. 5 (2009): 1249.

50. See also Clint Smith's essay on discovering an archive of stories from the formerly enslaved. Smith notes, "While many of these narratives vividly portray the horror of slavery—of families separated, of backs beaten, of bones crushed—embedded within them are stories of enslaved people dancing together on Saturday evenings as respite from their work; of people falling in love, creating pockets of time to see each other when the threat of violence momentarily ceased; of children skipping rocks in a creek or playing hide-and-seek amid towering oak trees, finding moments when the movement of their bodies was not governed by anything other than

their own sense of wonder. These small moments—the sort that freedom allows us to take for granted—have stayed with me." Clint Smith, "Stories of Slavery, From Those Who Survived It," *The Atlantic*, March 2021, https://www.theatlantic.com /magazine/archive/2021/03/federal-writers-project/617790/.

51. Payne, *I've Got the Light of Freedom*, 79–80; Ransby, *Ella Baker and the Black Freedom Movement*, 21–22.

52. See also Imani Perry, "Racism Is Terrible. Blackness Is Not," *The Atlantic*, June 15, 2020, https://www.theatlantic.com/ideas/archive/2020/06/racism-terrible -blackness-not/613039/.

53. Saidiya Hartman, *Wayward Lives, Beautiful Experiments: Intimate Histories of Social Upheaval* (New York: W. W. Norton & Company, 2019), xv.

54. Hartman, *Wayward Lives, Beautiful Experiments*, 31–32.

55. Hartman, 33.

56. Hartman, 347.

57. Hartman, 348.

58. Barack Obama, *Dreams from My Father: A Story of Race and Inheritance* (New York: Crown, 2007), 120.

59. Obama, 120–21.

60. Obama, 303.

61. Barack Obama, *We Are the Change We Seek: The Speeches of Barack Obama*, ed. E. J. Dionne Jr and Joy-Ann Reid (New York: Bloomsbury, 2017), 7.

62. Obama, 7.

63. Obama, 98–99.

64. Mugambi Jouet, "The Real Story behind 'Make America Great Again,'" *Mother Jones*, January 2017, https://www.motherjones.com/politics/2017/01 /american-exceptionalism-maga-trump-obama/.

65. Sandel, *The Tyranny of Merit*, 89–91.

66. Adam Tooze, *Crashed: How a Decade of Financial Crises Changed the World* (New York: Viking, 2018), 291–301. For critiques of Obama's policies, see also Eddie S. Glaude Jr., *Democracy in Black: How Race Still Enslaves the American Soul* (New York: Broadway Books, 2017), chapter 7; Taylor, *From #BlackLivesMatter to Black Liberation*, chapter 5.

67. Paul Krugman, *Arguing with Zombies: Economics, Politics, and the Fight for a Better Future* (New York: W. W. Norton & Company, 2020), 115–17.

68. Cited in: Sandel, *The Tyranny of Merit*, 90–91.

69. Michael D. Shear and Gardiner Harris, "With High-Profile Help, Obama Plots Life after Presidency," *The New York Times*, August 16, 2015, sec. U.S., https:// www.nytimes.com/2015/08/17/us/politics/with-high-profile-help-obama-plots -life-after-presidency.html; Giridharadas, *Winners Take All*, 32–33.

70. Krugman, *Arguing with Zombies*, 120.

Chapter 4: For Our World

1. A good overview in Kate Raworth, *Doughnut Economics: Seven Ways to Think Like a 21st-Century Economist* (White River Junction, VT: Chelsea Green Publishing, 2018), 144–45.

2. For a fair overview of general issues in capitalism, see Erik Olin Wright, *Envisioning Real Utopias* (New York: Verso, 2010), chapter 3.

3. Martin Gilens and Benjamin I. Page, "Testing Theories of American Politics: Elites, Interest Groups, and Average Citizens," *Perspectives on Politics* 12, no. 3 (September 2014): 564–81, https://doi.org/10.1017/S1537592714001595; Ganesh Sitaraman, *The Crisis of the Middle-Class Constitution: Why Economic Inequality Threatens Our Republic* (New York: Knopf Doubleday, 2017), chapter 5.

4. For visions of a more just capitalism, see Mariana Mazzucato, *Mission Economy: A Moonshot Guide to Changing Capitalism* (New York: Harper Business, 2021); Joseph E. Stiglitz, *People, Power, and Profits: Progressive Capitalism for an Age of Discontent* (New York: W. W. Norton & Company, 2019).

5. For a sweeping overview of the "the Soviet experiment" that deals with both successes and failures, see Ronald Suny, *The Soviet Experiment: Russia, the USSR, and the Successor States*, second edition (New York: Oxford University Press, 2010). For a briefer account that evades the most polarizing positions, see Piketty, *Capital and Ideology*, chapter 12.

6. Rosa Luxemburg, *The Russian Revolution and Leninism or Marxism?* (Ann Arbor: University of Michigan Press, 1961), 23.

7. Bertrand Russell, *The Practice and Theory of Bolshevism* (London: George Allen & Unwin Limited, 1921), 6.

8. On the potentials of the Russian Revolution without this dictatorial setup, see Massimiliano Tomba, *Insurgent Universality: An Alternative Legacy of Modernity* (Oxford: Oxford University Press, 2019), chapter 4. For an extended criticism similar to what I have offered here, see James C. Scott, *Seeing like a State: How Certain Schemes to Improve the Human Condition Have Failed* (New Haven, CT: Yale University Press, 1999), chapter 5.

9. Piketty, *Capital and Ideology*, 584–85.

10. As Gareth Stedman Jones has explored in his recent biography, this occurred in the deification of Marx himself, a process that led followers to focus on the "illusion" of his "greatness," rather than the complexity of his struggles to understand the world. Gareth Stedman Jones, *Karl Marx: Greatness and Illusion* (Cambridge, MA: Belknap Press, 2016).

11. Jeanna Smialek and Jim Tankersley, "Black Workers, Already Lagging, Face Big Economic Risks," *The New York Times*, sec. Business, June 1, 2020 https://www .nytimes.com/2020/06/01/business/economy/black-workers-inequality

-economic-risks.html; Richard A. Oppel Jr et al., "The Fullest Look Yet at the Racial Inequity of Coronavirus," *The New York Times*, July 5, 2020, sec. U.S., https://www.nytimes.com/interactive/2020/07/05/us/coronavirus-latinos-african-americans-cdc-data.html; Kate Conger, Robert Gebeloff, and Richard A. Oppel Jr., "Native Americans Feel Devastated by the Virus Yet Overlooked in the Data," *The New York Times*, July 30, 2020, sec. U.S., https://www.nytimes.com/2020/07/30/us/native-americans-coronavirus-data.html.

12. Tony Kirby, "Evidence Mounts on the Disproportionate Effect of COVID-19 on Ethnic Minorities," *The Lancet. Respiratory Medicine* 8, no. 6 (May 10, 2020): 547–48, https://doi.org/10.1016/s2213-2600(20)30228-9; Benjamin Berteau, Barbara Wojazer, and Emma Reynolds, "From Private Testing for the Rich to Unrest in Banlieues, Coronavirus Is Highlighting France's Stark Divide," CNN, April 26, 2020, https://www.cnn.com/2020/04/26/europe/coronavirus-france-inequality-intl/index.html; BBC Wales Investigates, "Coronavirus: 'Institutional Racism Left Minorities Exposed,'" *BBC News*, August 3, 2020, sec. Wales, https://www.bbc.com/news/uk-wales-53539577.

13. John Geddie, Joe Brock, and Koustav Samanta, "Singapore's Migrant Workers Fear Financial Ruin after Virus Ordeal," *Reuters*, June 9, 2020, https://www.reuters.com/article/us-health-coronavirus-singapore-migrants-idUSKBN23G1PG; Rima Kalush, "In the Gulf, Migrant Workers Bear the Brunt of the Pandemic," June 1, 2020, https://www.aljazeera.com/indepth/opinion/gulf-migrant-workers-bear-brunt-pandemic-200529102238233.html.

14. Neeta Lal, "The COVID-19 Economic Crash Could Set Indian Women Back Decades," *Foreign Policy* (blog), August 4, 2020, https://foreignpolicy.com/2020/08/04/covid-19-economic-crash-india-jobless-women/; Amanda Holpuch, "The 'She-cession': Why Economic Crisis Is Affecting Women More than Men," *The Guardian*, August 4, 2020, sec. Business, https://www.theguardian.com/business/2020/aug/04/shecession-coronavirus-pandemic-economic-fallout-women; Talha Burki, "The Indirect Impact of COVID-19 on Women," *The Lancet Infectious Diseases* 20, no. 8 (August 1, 2020): 904–5, https://doi.org/10.1016/S1473-3099(20)30568-5.

15. Robinson, *Black Marxism*, 26–28.

16. Robinson, 74–80.

17. South African intellectuals writing around the same time as Robinson, for example, argued that "racial capitalism" was a phenomenon unique to the apartheid state. Peter James Hudson, "Racial Capitalism and the Dark Proletariat," Text, Boston Review, February 20, 2018, http://bostonreview.net/forum/remake-world-slavery-racial-capitalism-and-justice/peter-james-hudson-racial-capitalism-and. See also Adolph L. Reed Jr., "The Surprising Cross-Racial Saga of Modern Wealth Inequality," *The New Republic*, June 29, 2020, https://newrepublic.com/article/158059/racial-wealth-gap-vs-racial-income-gap-modern-economic-inequality;

Matt Bruenig, "The Racial Wealth Gap Is about the Upper Classes," June 29, 2020, https://www.peoplespolicyproject.org/2020/06/29/the-racial-wealth-gap-is-about -the-upper-classes/; Julian Go, "Three Tensions in the Theory of Racial Capitalism," *Sociological Theory*, December 24, 2020, https://doi.org/10.1177/0735275120979822.

18. Walter Johnson, "'To Remake the World: Slavery, Racial Capitalism, and Justice," Text, Boston Review, February 20, 2018, http://bostonreview.net/forum/walter -johnson-to-remake-the-world.

19. Silvia Federici, *Caliban and the Witch: Women, the Body and Primitive Accumulation* (New York: Autonomedia, 2004), 8.

20. Nina Banks, "Black Women in the United States and Unpaid Collective Work: Theorizing the Community as a Site of Production," *The Review of Black Political Economy* 47, no. 4 (December 1, 2020): 343–62, https://doi.org/10.1177 /0034644620962811.

21. Michael Oliver, *The Politics of Disablement: A Sociological Approach* (New York: St. Martin's Press, 1990), 27–29.

22. Marta Russell and Ravi Malhotra, "Capitalism and Disability," *Socialist Register* 38 (2002): 215, https://socialistregister.com/index.php/srv/article/view/5784.

23. Russell and Malhotra, 212.

24. Teodor Mladenov, "From State Socialist to Neoliberal Productivism: Disability Policy and Invalidation of Disabled People in the Postsocialist Region," *Critical Sociology* 43, no. 7–8 (2017): 1109–23.

25. Russell and Malhotra, "Capitalism and Disability," 223.

26. Adam Smith, *The Wealth of Nations* (New York: Modern Library, 2000), 12.

27. For a brief overview of the literature and an argument that centers on energy usage, see Raworth, *Doughnut Economics*, 222–24. For a complex summary of the various debates that arrives at no specific conclusion, except to see growth as a product of a hard-to-specify system of feedbacks, see Vaclav Smil, *Growth: From Microorganisms to Megacities* (Cambridge, MA: MIT Press, 2019), 419–36. Missing from Smil's account is any deep understanding of where gender, ableism, colonialism and slavery may factor in. On this, see previous section, as well as Jason Hickel, *The Divide: A Brief Guide to Global Inequality and Its Solutions* (New York: Norton, 2018), chapter 3. For an attempt to quantify and explain the earth's contribution, see Dasgupta, "The Economics of Biodiversity: The Dasgupta Review."

28. Smith, *The Wealth of Nations*, 93–94.

29. Smith, 75–76.

30. Smith, 90.

31. Smith, 483.

32. Smith, 485.

33. Smith, *The Theory of Moral Sentiments*, 13.

34. Smith, 31.

35. Smith, 52.

36. Smith, 74.

37. Smith, 73.

38. Smith, 213–14.

39. Smith, 214.

40. Smith's claim has been widely criticized by some historians of capitalism. After all, those who did the most toiling were not the wealthy but the poor who were driven into factory work after the commons on which they sustained themselves were privatized and their lands were confiscated. There is a helpful overview in Jason Hickel, "Degrowth: A Theory of Radical Abundance," no. 87 (2019): 59–61.

41. Smith, *The Theory of Moral Sentiments*, 215.

42. Smith, 215.

43. Smith, 215.

44. Smith, *The Wealth of Nations*, 500.

45. See the account in Giridharadas, *Winners Take All*, 201–44. Some economists, of course, did register these issues, but were often ignored by their colleagues. See Dani Rodrik, *Straight Talk on Trade: Ideas for a Sane World Economy* (Princeton, NJ: Princeton University Press, 2017), ix–xiii.

46. Andrea Cerrato, Francesco Ruggieri, and Federico Maria Ferrara, "Trump Won in Counties That Lost Jobs to China and Mexico," *Washington Post*, December 2, 2016, https://www.washingtonpost.com/news/monkey-cage/wp/2016/12/02/trump-won-where-import-shocks-from-china-and-mexico-were-strongest/.

47. Polanyi is not alone here. The link between inequality and political unrest has been known since at least Aristotle, and John Maynard Keynes also made an extensive analysis of this in the twentieth century. Keynes believed inequality *had* created general prosperity, but he thought that was more an historical coincidence than an economic law. Aristotle, *The Nicomachean Ethics*, 58–59; John Maynard Keynes, *The Economic Consequences of the Peace*, ed. Elizabeth Johnson and Donald Moggridge, vol. 2, The Collected Writings of John Maynard Keynes (Cambridge: Cambridge University Press for the Royal Economic Society, 2013), 11–13.

48. Karl Polanyi, *The Great Transformation: The Political and Economic Origins of Our Time* (Boston: Beacon Press, 2001), 224.

49. Sheri Berman, *The Primacy of Politics: Social Democracy and the Making of Europe's Twentieth Century* (Cambridge: Cambridge University Press, 2006); Frederick Solt, "The Social Origins of Authoritarianism," *Political Research Quarterly* 65, no. 4 (2012): 703–13.

50. Nicholas Wapshott, *Keynes Hayek: The Clash That Defined Modern Economics* (New York: W. W. Norton & Company, 2012), 258. I am indebted to this book for my overview of Hayek's life and influence.

51. Wapshott, 251.

52. For an overview of the book's reception see Wapshott, 198–205.

53. Orwell raised Polanyi's concern: "But he [Hayek] does not see, or will not admit, that a return to 'free' competition means for the great mass of people a tyranny probably worse, because more irresponsible, than that of the State. The trouble with competitions is that somebody wins them. Professor Hayek denies that free capitalism necessarily leads to monopoly, but in practice that is where it has led, and since the vast majority of people would far rather have State regimentation than slumps and unemployment, the drift towards collectivism is bound to continue if popular opinion has any say in the matter." George Orwell, *George Orwell: As I Please, 1943–1946* (Boston: Nonpareil, 2000), 118.

54. Bruce Caldwell, "Introduction," in *The Road to Serfdom: Text and Documents—The Definitive Edition*, by Friedrich Hayek, ed. Bruce Caldwell (Chicago: University of Chicago Press, 2007), 18–23.

55. Wapshott, *Keynes Hayek*, 256.

56. Gabriel Söderberg and Avner Offer, *The Nobel Factor: The Prize in Economics, Social Democracy, and the Market Turn* (Princeton, NJ: Princeton University Press, 2016).

57. Söderberg and Offer, 127–31.

58. Friedrich Hayek, *The Road to Serfdom: Text and Documents—The Definitive Edition*, ed. Bruce Caldwell (Chicago: University of Chicago Press, 2007), 165.

59. Hayek, 165–66.

60. Wapshott, *Keynes Hayek*, 221–23.

61. Hayek, *The Road to Serfdom*, 71.

62. Hayek, 90.

63. Hayek, 86–87.

64. Corey Robin makes this case convincingly: Corey Robin, *The Reactionary Mind: Conservatism from Edmund Burke to Donald Trump*, second edition (New York: Oxford University Press, 2017), 157–64.

65. Friedrich August Hayek, *The Constitution of Liberty: The Definitive Edition* (Chicago: The University of Chicago Press, 2011), 96.

66. As I was finishing this book, I also read a brilliant account of the problem in Mark Bittman's history of food production. Across his book, Bittman shows how technological innovations that are not *explicitly* implemented with a goal to equality and general well-being not only don't make most people better off (they tend to create cycles of debt and impoverishment as small farmers try to keep up with big producers), but they also become unhinged from environmental concerns and are part of what is endangering us today. Anyone who wants to understand why capital-friendly progress is bad for all and why egalitarian development can save us should read Bittman's book cover to cover. Mark Bittman, *Animal, Vegetable, Junk: A History of Food, from Sustainable to Suicidal* (Boston: Houghton Mifflin Harcourt, 2021).

67. Hayek, *The Constitution of Liberty*, 152–54.

68. Hayek, 154.

69. Friedrich Hayek, *Nobel Prize-Winning Economist Oral History Transcript* ([Los Angeles]: Oral History Program, University of California, Los Angeles, 1983), 11, http://archive.org/details/nobelprizewinnin00haye.

70. Federico Cingano, "Trends in Income Inequality and Its Impact on Economic Growth," *OECD Social, Employment and Migration Working Papers*, no. 163 (2014), https://doi.org/10.1787/5jxrjncwxv6j-en; Piketty, *Capital and Ideology*, 543–47. For an accessible, book-length overview, see Heather Boushey, *Unbound: How Inequality Constricts Our Economy and What We Can Do about It* (Cambridge, MA: Harvard University Press, 2019). There are some arguments that suggest that, regardless of inequality, growth itself is becoming less possible. One might then defend Hayek here by saying that inequality is not what is impeding growth. But all that move does is take the floor out from under the argument for why there has to be inequality. If there is no growth in either case, then this becomes a normative issue. See Robert J. Gordon, *The Rise and Fall of American Growth: The U.S. Standard of Living since the Civil War* (Princeton, NJ: Princeton University Press, 2017).

71. Piketty, *Capital and Ideology*, 544. There are of course other possible causes of declining growth, and there are defenders of Hayek's general position here. Ruchir Sharma of Morgan Stanley, for example, has argued that the real problem in this era was increased government intervention in the economy in the money supply. Sharma does have a legitimate point that easy money may prop up equities and create inequality. But it's a little hard to wrap one's mind around the broader claim that the years 1980–2020, the very era of the Reagan and Thatcher revolution, is when government is somehow *more* active than during the New Deal era that preceded it. To arrive at this claim, one has to ignore all other contributing factors to inequality, such as the decreasing tax rates. And sluggish growth may also be traced to poor allocation of what resources the state does have—such as fighting wars rather than shoring up public education. Or to the fact that I've mentioned with Mazzucato: that though the state funded much of the research behind the tech boom, it has largely let all the benefits be privatized. Ruchir Sharma, "Dear Joe Biden, Deficits Still Matter," *Financial Times*, January 20, 2021, https://www.ft.com/content/d49b537a-95f8-4e1a-b4b1-19f0c44d751e.

72. Heather Boushey, "Unbound: Releasing Inequality's Grip on Our Economy," *Review of Radical Political Economics* 52, no. 4 (December 2020): 602, https://doi.org/10.1177/0486613420938187.

73. Boushey, "Unbound," 604–5.

74. Piketty, *Capital and Ideology*, 499; Barry Schwartz, *Why We Work* (New York: Simon & Schuster/ TED, 2015); Arash Kolahi, "A Participatory Workplace Is a More Fulfilling One, Too," Inequality.org, March 2, 2020, https://inequality.org/research/participatory-workplace-more-fulfilling/.

75. For some critiques of GDP, see Ronald Colman, *What Really Counts: The Case for a Sustainable and Equitable Economy* (New York: Columbia University Press, 2021); Raworth, *Doughnut Economics*.

76. Malcolm Gladwell, *Outliers: The Story of Success* (New York: Back Bay Books, 2011), 50–68.

77. Mazzucato, *The Entrepreneurial State*.

78. As Mazzucato points out, there is an important "discursive battle" to show everyone just how important our collective investments have been in creating what are often seen as purely private initiatives. Mazzucato, 2–4.

79. And even this mantra, according to some Black women historians, may wind up creating invidious hierarchies between those climbing and those being lifted. There is a helpful, brief discussion of the debate around this and the relevant scholarly literature in Ransby, *Ella Baker and the Black Freedom Movement*, 379n22.

80. Morton Deutsch's research shows that if the task doesn't require cooperation (just independent tasks like data-crunching), it doesn't really matter how rewards are distributed (egalitarian, merit-based, or winner-take-all). But if the task requires working together (for example, three independent contractors designing the best routes for their garbage-collection companies so as to pick up the most trash), then winner-take-all and merit-based rewards lead to less productivity and/or poorer results than simple equality. Morton Deutsch, *Distributive Justice: A Social-Psychological Perspective* (New Haven, CT: Yale University Press, 1985), 151–63.

81. Daniel Immerwahr, *How to Hide an Empire: A History of the Greater United States* (New York: Farrar, Straus and Giroux, 2019), 269.

82. On the vaccine, see Matt Apuzzo and David D. Kirkpatrick, "Covid-19 Changed How the World Does Science, Together," *The New York Times*, April 1, 2020, sec. World, https://www.nytimes.com/2020/04/01/world/europe/coronavirus-science-research-cooperation.html. For more examples of where cooperation is helping but being ignored, see Heather Hurlburt, "The World Is Helping Americans Who Don't Always See It," *The New York Times*, May 4, 2020, sec. Opinion, https://www.nytimes.com/2020/05/04/opinion/coronavirus-global-cooperation-cities.html. On the economy: Adam Tooze, "In This Together: Global Cooperation on a Global Crisis," April 6, 2020, in *Reason to Be Cheerful*, podcast, https://www.cheerfulpodcast.com/rtbc-episodes/in-this-together; Peterson Institute for Economics, "How the G20 Can Hasten Recovery from COVID-19," PIIE, April 13, 2020, https://www.piie.com/publications/piie-briefings/how-g20-can-hasten-recovery-covid-19.

83. Jennifer Kahn, "How Scientists Could Stop the Next Pandemic Before It Starts," *The New York Times*, April 21, 2020, sec. Magazine, https://www.nytimes.com/2020/04/21/magazine/pandemic-vaccine.html.

84. Sharon LaFraniere et al., "Scientists Worry About Political Influence over Coronavirus Vaccine Project," *The New York Times*, August 2, 2020, sec. U.S., https://www.nytimes.com/2020/08/02/us/politics/coronavirus-vaccine.html.

85. World Health Organization, "More than 150 Countries Engaged in COVID-19 Vaccine Global Access Facility," July 15, 2020, https://www.who.int/news-room/detail/15-07-2020-more-than-150-countries-engaged-in-covid-19-vaccine-global-access-facility.

86. Ilara Kaila and Joona-Hermanni Makinen, "Finland Had a Patent-Free COVID-19 Vaccine Nine Months Ago—But Still Went with Big Pharma," *Jacobin*, February 28, 2021, https://jacobinmag.com/2021/02/finland-vaccine-covid-patent-ip; Alexander Zaitchik, "How Bill Gates Impeded Global Access to Covid Vaccines," *The New Republic*, April 12, 2021, https://newrepublic.com/article/162000/bill-gates-impeded-global-access-covid-vaccines; Jay Hancock, "They Pledged to Donate Rights to Their COVID Vaccine, Then Sold Them to Pharma," *Kaiser Health News* (blog), August 25, 2020, https://khn.org/news/rather-than-give-away-its-covid-vaccine-oxford-makes-a-deal-with-drugmaker/.

87. Selam Gebrekidan and Matt Apuzzo, "Rich Countries Signed Away a Chance to Vaccinate the World," *The New York Times*, March 21, 2021, sec. World, https://www.nytimes.com/2021/03/21/world/vaccine-patents-us-eu.html.

88. Jane Mayer, *Dark Money: The Hidden History of the Billionaires behind the Rise of the Radical Right* (New York: Doubleday, 2016), 27–28.

89. For global implications, see Adam Tooze, "Shockwave," *London Review of Books*, April 4, 2020, https://www.lrb.co.uk/the-paper/v42/n08/adam-tooze/shockwave; Adam Tooze, "How Coronavirus Almost Brought Down the Global Financial System," *The Guardian*, April 14, 2020, sec. Business, https://www.theguardian.com/business/2020/apr/14/how-coronavirus-almost-brought-down-the-global-financial-system.

90. Polanyi, *The Great Transformation*, 242.

91. Emily Ekins and Joy Pullman, "Why So Many Millennials Are Socialists," Cato Institute, February 15, 2016, https://www.cato.org/publications/commentary/why-so-many-millennials-are-socialists; Andreas Kluth, "OK Boomer, We're Gonna Socialize You," *Bloomberg.Com*, July 25, 2020, https://www.bloomberg.com/opinion/articles/2020-07-25/ok-boomer-coronavirus-is-turning-millennials-into-socialists.

92. Richard D. Wolff, "Socialism Means Abolishing the Distinction between Bosses and Employees," Truthout, June 27, 2015, https://truthout.org/articles/socialism-means-abolishing-the-distinction-between-bosses-and-employees/.

93. On the complexities of defining socialism, democratic socialism, and social democracy from an author who has a slightly different (more utopian) definition

than I do, see Nathan J. Robinson, *Why You Should Be a Socialist* (New York: All Points Books, 2019), 133–42.

94. George F. Will, "Freedom vs. Equality," *Washington Post*, February 1, 2004, https://www.washingtonpost.com/archive/opinions/2004/02/01/freedom-vs -equality/63bddf0b-6089-4bab-8663-f61571578e57/.

95. David Harvey, "Anti-Capitalist Politics in the Time of COVID-19," *Jacobin*, March 20, 2020, https://jacobinmag.com/2020/03/david-harvey-coronavirus -political-economy-disruptions; Corey Robin, "The New Socialists," *The New York Times*, August 24, 2018, sec. Opinion, https://www.nytimes.com/2018/08/24 /opinion/Sunday/what-socialism-looks-like-in-2018.html; Partanen, *The Nordic Theory of Everything*, 320–27.

96. Polanyi, *The Great Transformation*, 264.

97. David Graeber, *Bullshit Jobs* (New York: Simon & Schuster, 2019); Azmanova, *Capitalism on Edge*.

98. Piketty, *Capital and Ideology*, 979–91.

99. Polanyi, *The Great Transformation*, 268.

100. Andrew Carnegie, "The Gospel of Wealth," Carnegie Corporation of New York, June 1889, https://www.carnegie.org/about/our-history/gospelofwealth/.

101. This is also true on an international level, in which "aid" functions in the same way philanthropy does: as a Band-Aid over the damages caused by foreign ownership and control of resources. As Jason Hickel puts it, "Poor countries don't need . . . aid; they need [rich countries] to stop impoverishing them." Hickel, *The Divide*, 31.

102. Piketty, *Capital and Ideology*.

103. John Kenneth Galbraith, *The Affluent Society* (Boston: Houghton Mifflin, 1958), 69.

104. Carnegie, "The Gospel of Wealth."

105. Karl Marx and Friedrich Engels, "The German Ideology," 1845, https://www .marxists.org/archive/marx/works/1845/german-ideology/ch01b.htm.

106. Quoted in Rob Reich, *Just Giving: Why Philanthropy Is Failing Democracy and How It Can Do Better* (Princeton, NJ: Princeton University Press, 2018), 4.

107. George Soros, *The Crisis of Global Capitalism: Open Society Endangered* (New York: PublicAffairs, 1998).

108. Michael Steinberger, "George Soros Bet Big on Liberal Democracy. Now He Fears He Is Losing," *The New York Times*, July 17, 2018, sec. Magazine, https://www .nytimes.com/2018/07/17/magazine/george-soros-democrat-open-society.html.

109. Randall Smith, "As His Foundation Has Grown, Gates Has Slowed His Do-nations," DealBook, 1401155300, https://dealbook.nytimes.com/2014/05/26/as-his -foundation-has-grown-gates-has-slowed-his-donations/. See also Rob Larson, "Bill Gates's Philanthropic Giving Is a Racket," *Jacobin*, April 5, 2020, https://jacobinmag .com/2020/04/bill-gates-foundation-philanthropy-microsoft.

110. As of 2016, Gates's foundations controlled a fortune so vast that it would have around the 65th highest GDP in the world if it were a country. Reich, *Just Giving*, 9.

111. Zaitchik, "How Bill Gates Impeded Global Access to Covid Vaccines."

112. Reich, *Just Giving*, 5.

113. Reich, 1–7.

114. For more extensive discussions of the issues in philanthropy, see Mayer, *Dark Money*; Giridharadas, *Winners Take All*; Reich, *Just Giving*.

115. Peter Singer, *The Most Good You Can Do: How Effective Altruism Is Changing Ideas about Living Ethically* (New Haven, CT: Yale University Press, 2016), 50.

116. Stiglitz, *People, Power, and Profits*; Mazzucato, *Mission Economy*.

117. If the point isn't entirely clear, see the extensive detail in Thomas Piketty, *Capital in the Twenty-First Century*, trans. Arthur Goldhammer (Cambridge, MA: Belknap Press, 2014).

118. Berman, *The Primacy of Politics*; Söderberg and Offer, *The Nobel Factor*.

119. A robust overview in Piketty, *Capital and Ideology*, 486–577.

120. For a rebuttal to these concerns, see Adolph Reed Jr., "The New Deal Wasn't Intrinsically Racist," *The New Republic*, November 26, 2019, https://newrepublic.com /article/155704/new-deal-wasnt-intrinsically-racist.

121. Ira Katznelson, *When Affirmative Action Was White: An Untold History of Racial Inequality in Twentieth-Century America* (New York: W. W. Norton, 2005), 42–49.

122. Ta-Nehisi Coates, "The Case for Reparations," *The Atlantic*, June 2014, http:// www.theatlantic.com/magazine/archive/2014/06/the-case-for-reparations/361631/. *Inclusion*, in the form of predatory lending, was also a major problem. See Keeanga-Yamahtta Taylor, *Race for Profit: How Banks and the Real Estate Industry Undermined Black Homeownership* (Chapel Hill: University of North Carolina Press, 2019).

123. See the narrative history of the many ways the West has underdeveloped the rest of the world in Hickel, *The Divide*, 99–239. For more on this moment in time, see Prashad, *The Poorer Nations*, chapter 1.

124. Vincent Bevins, *The Jakarta Method: Washington's Anticommunist Crusade and the Mass Murder Program That Shaped Our World* (New York: PublicAffairs, 2020).

125. Hickel, *The Divide*, chapter 5.

126. Bevins, *The Jakarta Method*; Hickel, *The Divide*.

127. Noel Maurer, *The Empire Trap: The Rise and Fall of U.S. Intervention to Protect American Property Overseas, 1893–2013* (Princeton, NJ: Princeton University Press, 2013).

128. Göran Hugo Olsson, *Concerning Violence: Nine Scenes from the Anti-Imperialistic Self-Defense* (New York: Kino Lorber, Inc, 2014).

129. For some history of this particular event as well as an overview of scholarship on Sweden's global role in this period, see Karl Bruno, "The Technopolitics of Swedish Iron Mining in Cold War Liberia, 1950–1990," *The Extractive Industries and Society*

7, no. 1 (January 1, 2020): 39–49, https://doi.org/10.1016/j.exis.2019.06.008. For some positive remarks on Scandinavia in the context of a general history of this era, see Prashad, *The Poorer Nations*, 26, 29, 49.

130. Emmanuel Saez and Gabriel Zucman, *The Triumph of Injustice: How the Rich Dodge Taxes and How to Make Them Pay* (New York: W. W. Norton & Company, 2019).

131. Much of what we know about these conditions comes from the grassroots movements fighting against them. See the classic account in Naomi Klein, *No Logo: 10th Anniversary Edition with a New Introduction by the Author* (New York: Picador, 2009). There are some debates about whether there is any advantage to just having a job, and whether the disruptive force of globalization may have impacts on those who face other oppressions, especially women. See the nuanced discussion (if not nuanced article title) in Hester Eisenstein, "The Sweatshop Feminists," *Jacobin*, June 17, 2015, https://jacobinmag.com/2015/06/kristof-globalization-development -third-world/.

132. Chris Giles, Ralph Atkins, and Krishna Guha, "The Undeniable Shift to Keynes," December 29, 2008, https://www.ft.com/content/8a3d8122-d5da-11dd -a9cc-000077b07658; Paul Samuelson, "An Interview with Paul Samuelson, Part One," interview by Derek Thompson, June 17, 2009, https://www.theatlantic.com /business/archive/2009/06/an-interview-with-paul-samuelson-part-one/19586/.

133. Financial Times Editorial Board, "Virus Lays Bare the Frailty of the Social Contract." For carefully considered thoughts on how to move past both Keynesian and neoliberal economics in a manner aligned with the global transformations of the present, see James K. Galbraith, "The Death of Neoliberalism Is Greatly Exaggerated," *Foreign Policy* (blog), April 6, 2021, https://foreignpolicy.com/2021/04/06 /death-neoliberalism-larry-summers-biden-pandemic/.

134. Cited in: Zachary D. Carter, *The Price of Peace: Money, Democracy, and the Life of John Maynard Keynes* (New York: Random House, 2020), xvii.

135. Gary Dorrien, *Social Democracy in the Making: Political and Religious Roots of European Socialism* (New Haven, CT: Yale University Press, 2019); Berman, *The Primacy of Politics*.

136. According to a recent biography, Marx himself may have agreed. Jones, *Karl Marx*.

137. Berman, *The Primacy of Politics*.

138. Dorrien, *Social Democracy in the Making*, 1.

139. I've taken these names from Robert Alan Dahl, *A Preface to Economic Democracy* (Berkeley: University of California Press, 1986); Gary Dorrien, *The Democratic Socialist Vision* (Baltimore: Rowman & Littlefield, 1986); Gar Alperovitz, *Principles of a Pluralist Commonwealth* (Washington, DC: The Democracy Collaborative, 2017); Richard Wolff, *Democracy at Work: A Cure for Capitalism* (Chicago: Haymarket Books, 2012); Piketty, *Capital and Ideology*. There is much exciting work being

done to show the diversity of these practices. See Jessica Gordon Nembhard, *Collective Courage: A History of African American Cooperative Economic Thought and Practice* (University Park: The Pennsylvania State University Press, 2014); brown, *Emergent Strategy*. There is also wonderful ongoing work on these topics by the Democracy Collaborative, The Next System Project, the Institute for Policy Studies, and others. Many good ideas are out there.

140. Henry J. Kaye, "FDR's Second Bill of Rights: 'Necessitous Men Are Not Free Men,'" *Roosevelt Institute* (blog), January 11, 2011, https://rooseveltinstitute.org/fdrs -second-bill-rights-necessitous-men-are-not-free-men/.

141. See, for example, the very interesting collection The Next System Project, "New Systems: Possibilities and Proposals," TheNextSystem.org, June 28, 2017, https:// thenextsystem.org/learn/collections/new-systems-possibilities-and-proposals.

142. Piketty, *Capital and Ideology*, 493–513.

143. Labour Party, UK, "Alternative Models of Ownership," 2017, https://labour .org.uk/wp-content/uploads/2017/10/Alternative-Models-of-Ownership.pdf; "Corporate Accountability and Democracy," Bernie Sanders—Official Campaign Website, accessed May 24, 2020, https://berniesanders.com/issues/corporate -accountability-and-democracy/; "Empowering Workers through Accountable Capitalism: Elizabeth Warren," Warren Democrats, accessed May 24, 2020, https:// elizabethwarren.com/plans/accountable-capitalism.

144. Joe Guinan, "Socialising Capital: Looking Back on the Meidner Plan," *International Journal of Public Policy* 15, no. 1/2 (2019): 38.

145. Matthew Brown, "Preston Is a Lesson for Labour: Show Communities You Can Deliver Change," *The Guardian*, May 18, 2021, http://www.theguardian.com /commentisfree/2021/may/18/preston-labour-communities-change-voters-uk.

146. Gar Alperovitz, Thad Williamson, and Ted Howard, "The Cleveland Model," February 11, 2010, https://www.thenation.com/article/archive/cleveland-model/.

147. Matt Bruenig, "Social Wealth Fund for America," People's Policy Project, accessed May 7, 2020, https://peoplespolicyproject.org/projects/social-wealth-fund.

148. Gar Alperovitz, *What Then Must We Do? Straight Talk about the Next American Revolution* (White River Junction, VT: Chelsea Green Publishing, 2013), 58.

149. Alperovitz, 58.

150. Raworth, *Doughnut Economics*, chapter 6.

151. Deutsch, *Distributive Justice*, 114–16.

152. Riane Eisler, "Whole Systems Change," TheNextSystem.org, 2020, https:// thenextsystem.org/whole-systems-change; brown, *Emergent Strategy*.

153. Gordon Nembhard, *Collective Courage*; Michaela Haas, "'When Someone Hires Me, They Get the Boss Herself,'" *The New York Times*, July 7, 2020, sec. Opinion, https://www.nytimes.com/2020/07/07/opinion/gig-economy-immigrants -fair-wage.html.

154. Kolahi, "A Participatory Workplace Is a More Fulfilling One, Too"; Schwartz, *Why We Work*.

155. Paul Keegan, "Here's What Really Happened at That Company That Set a $70,000 Minimum Wage," Inc.com, October 21, 2015, https://www.inc.com /magazine/201511/paul-keegan/does-more-pay-mean-more-growth.html.

156. Dan Price, Twitter, August 23, 2020, https://twitter.com/DanPriceSeattle /status/1297583024587104262.

157. Lydia DePillis, "For Amazon HQ2 Hopefuls, Seattle Serves as a Cautionary Tale," CNNMoney, May 13, 2018, https://money.cnn.com/2018/05/13/news /companies/amazon-hq2-seattle/index.html; Paul Roberts, "This Is What Really Happens When Amazon Comes to Your Town," POLITICO Magazine, October 19, 2017, https://www.politico.com/magazine/story/2017/10/19/amazon -headquarters-seattle-215725.

158. Alec MacGillis, "Amazon and the Breaking of Baltimore," *The New York Times*, March 9, 2021, sec. Opinion, https://www.nytimes.com/2021/03/09 /opinion/amazon-baltimore-dc.html.

159. James Jacoby, *Amazon Empire: The Rise and Reign of Jeff Bezos*, Documentary (PBS, 2020), https://www.pbs.org/wgbh/frontline/film/amazon-empire/.

160. It is also important that powerful interests have continually worked against the development of such enterprises. See Alperovitz, *What Then Must We Do?*, 28–32.

161. Alperovitz, *Principles of a Pluralist Commonwealth*.

162. Djaffar Shalchi, "The American Dream Is Now in Denmark," interview by Anand Giridharadas, February 23, 2021, https://the.ink/p/the-american-dream-is -now-in-denmark.

163. And most people, I think, recognize this. For example, Bhaskar Sunkara, the editor of the socialist magazine *Jacobin*, writes: "Even if we can't solve the human condition, we can turn a world filled with excruciating misery into one where ordinary unhappiness [in Freud's phrase] reigns." Bhaskar Sunkara, *The Socialist Manifesto: The Case for Radical Politics in an Era of Extreme Inequality* (New York: Basic Books, 2019), 29.

164. On why achieving economic justice is difficult, but why such difficulty does not exclude the ideal of pursuing it, see G. A. Cohen, *Why Not Socialism?* (Princeton, NJ: Princeton University Press, 2009), 53–82.

165. Deutsch, *Distributive Justice*, 246.

166. King, *Where Do We Go from Here?*; Bernard Friot, "Le salaire universel: Un déjà-là considérable à généraliser," *Mouvements* 73, no. 1 (March 14, 2013): 60–69.

167. This discussion is not at all to countenance the absurd critiques of worker-run enterprises that one finds in works like Robert Nozick's *Anarchy, State, and Utopia*. Nozick's argument is refutable line by line if one moves from his theoretical assumptions about how such enterprises work to actual empirical study. To see this, one can easily compare his arguments with Deutsch's summary of the literature from the

same era. Robert Nozick, *Anarchy, State, and Utopia* (New York: Basic Books, 2013), 250–53; Deutsch, *Distributive Justice*, 222–33.

168. See, for example, Mary Pattillo, *Black Picket Fences: Privilege and Peril among the Black Middle Class*, second edition (Chicago: University of Chicago Press, 2013); Karyn Lacy, *Blue-Chip Black: Race, Class, and Status in the New Black Middle Class* (Berkeley: University of California Press, 2007).

169. Nozick, *Anarchy, State, and Utopia*, 243.

170. Sigmund Freud, *Civilization and Its Discontents*, trans. James Strachey (New York: Norton, 1962), 60–61.

171. Peter Frase, "Four Futures," *Jacobin*, December 13, 2011, https://jacobinmag .com/2011/12/four-futures.

172. William Shakespeare, *Timon of Athens*, ed. Anthony Dawson and Gretchen E. Minton, third edition (London: The Arden Shakespeare, 2008), 275.

173. Samuel Stebbins, "Here's How Rich Every US Senator Is," MSN, September 12, 2019, https://www.msn.com/en-us/money/markets/heres-how-rich-every -us-senator-is/ss-AAH9wWI.

174. Robert K. Merton, "The Matthew Effect in Science," *Science* 159, no. 3810 (January 5, 1968): 57.

175. Margit Osterloh and Bruno S. Frey, "How to Avoid Borrowed Plumes in Academia," *Research Policy* 49, no. 1 (February 1, 2020): 103831, https://doi.org/10.1016 /j.respol.2019.103831; David Adam, "Science Funders Gamble on Grant Lotteries," *Nature* 575, no. 7784 (November 20, 2019): 574–75, https://doi.org/10.1038/d41586 -019-03572-7; Ferrie Fang and Arturo Casadevall, "Grant Funding: Playing the Odds," *Science* 352, no. 6282 (April 2016): 158.

176. Osterloh and Frey, "How to Avoid Borrowed Plumes in Academia."

177. One exception was the 2020 Sobey Art Awards in Canada, which, in response to COVID-19, granted twenty-five awards to everyone on the long list, rather than one grand winner and four runners-up. "Canada's 2020 Sobey Art Award to Divide Grand Prize among Longlisted Artists," April 16, 2020, https://www.artforum.com /news/canada-s-2020-sobey-art-award-to-divide-grand-prize-among-longlisted -artists-82748.

178. Danielle L. Herbert et al., "The Impact of Funding Deadlines on Personal Workloads, Stress and Family Relationships: A Qualitative Study of Australian Researchers," *BMJ Open* 4, no. 3 (March 1, 2014): e004462, https://doi.org/10.1136 /bmjopen-2013-004462.

179. Krist Vaesen and Joel Katzav, "How Much Would Each Researcher Receive If Competitive Government Research Funding Were Distributed Equally among Researchers?," *PLOS ONE* 12, no. 9 (September 8, 2017): e0183967, https://doi.org /10.1371/journal.pone.0183967; John P. A. Ioannidis, "Fund People Not Projects," *Nature* 477, no. 7366 (September 2011): 529–31, https://doi.org/10.1038/477529a.

180. Matt Ford, "Rebuilding the Constitution," *The New Republic*, May 15, 2020, https://newrepublic.com/article/157690/rebuilding-constitution.

181. Alexander Guerrero, "Forget Voting—It's Time to Start Choosing Our Leaders by Lottery," *Aeon*, January 23, 2014, https://aeon.co/essays/forget-voting-it-s-time-to-start-choosing-our-leaders-by-lottery.

182. Landemore, *Open Democracy*, 89.

183. Landemore, 42.

184. Osterloh and Frey, "How to Avoid Borrowed Plumes in Academia," 6.

185. Schwartz, "Top Colleges Should Select Randomly from a Pool of 'Good Enough.'"

186. Sandel makes an excellent case for the lottery system in greater detail: Sandel, *The Tyranny of Merit*, 184–89.

187. Sandel, 184.

188. Hirsch, *Social Limits to Growth*, 182–85.

189. McGhee, *The Sum of Us*, 38–39.

190. McGhee, 289.

191. John Rawls, *A Theory of Justice*, revised edition (Cambridge, MA: Belknap Press, 1999).

Chapter 5: For Our Planet

1. David Wallace-Wells, *The Uninhabitable Earth: Life after Warming* (New York: Tim Duggan Books, 2019), 20.

2. World Meteorological Organization (WMO), *WMO Statement on the State of the Global Climate in 2019*, WMO (Geneva: WMO, 2020), 4.

3. Wallace-Wells, *The Uninhabitable Earth*, 1–40.

4. Thomas Wiedmann et al., "Scientists' Warning on Affluence," *Nature Communications* 11, no. 1 (June 19, 2020): 3107, https://doi.org/10.1038/s41467-020-16941-y.

5. Somini Sengupta and Julfikar Ali Manik, "A Quarter of Bangladesh Is Flooded. Millions Have Lost Everything," *The New York Times*, July 30, 2020, sec. Climate, https://www.nytimes.com/2020/07/30/climate/bangladesh-floods.html; Hickel, *The Divide*, 137–73.

6. Rubén O. Martínez, "Environmental Racism," in *The Oxford Encyclopedia of Latinos and Latinas in the United States* (Oxford University Press, 2005), http://www.oxfordreference.com/view/10.1093/acref/9780195156003.001.0001/acref-9780195156003-e-277.

7. McGhee, *The Sum of Us*, 193–218; Rob Nixon, *Slow Violence and the Environmentalism of the Poor* (Cambridge, MA: Harvard University Press, 2013).

8. McGhee, *The Sum of Us*, 198.

9. Mark Z. Jacobson et al., "100% Clean and Renewable Wind, Water, and Sunlight All-Sector Energy Roadmaps for 139 Countries of the World," *Joule* 1, no. 1 (September 6, 2017): 108–21, https://doi.org/10.1016/j.joule.2017.07.005. See also the engaging remarks on this in Vaclav Smil, "Want Not, Waste Not," interview by Nathan Gardels, *Noema*, February 25, 2021, https://www.noemamag.com/want-not-waste-not.

10. Max Horkheimer and Theodor W. Adorno, *Dialectic of Enlightenment*, ed. Gunzelin Schmid Noerr, trans. Edmund Jephcott (Palo Alto, CA: Stanford University Press, 2007).

11. For a helpful overview of White's thesis and the controversies that have surrounded it, see Elspeth Whitney, "Lynn White Jr.'s 'The Historical Roots of Our Ecologic Crisis' After 50 Years," *History Compass* 13, no. 8 (August 2015): 396–410, https://doi.org/10.1111/hic3.12254.

12. McGhee, *The Sum of Us*, 201–3. See also Taciano L. Milfont et al., "On the Relation between Social Dominance Orientation and Environmentalism: A 25-Nation Study," *Social Psychological and Personality Science* 9, no. 7 (September 1, 2018): 811, https://doi.org/10.1177/1948550617722832.

13. McGhee, *The Sum of Us*, 205.

14. Ronald Wright, *A Short History of Progress*, CBC Massey Lectures (Toronto: House of Anansi Press, 2004), 57–64.

15. Wright, 5.

16. I do not know if there is evidence to refute this based on the paleoethnobotany of the island. On the Amazon, see Thomas E. Lovejoy and Carlos Nobre, "Amazon Tipping Point," *Science Advances* 4, no. 2 (February 1, 2018): eaat2340, https://doi.org/10.1126/sciadv.aat2340.

17. Steven Pinker, *The Better Angels of Our Nature: Why Violence Has Declined* (New York: Penguin Books, 2012).

18. Rutger Bregman, *Humankind: A Hopeful History*, trans. Elizabeth Manton and Erica Moore (New York: Little, Brown and Company, 2020).

19. Immanuel Kant, *"Religion within the Boundaries of Mere Reason" and Other Writings*, ed. and trans. George di Giovanni and Allen Wood (Cambridge; New York: Cambridge University Press, 1998), 58.

20. I have written extensively about Rousseau and Kant on human nature in Avram Alpert, *Global Origins of the Modern Self, from Montaigne to Suzuki* (Albany: SUNY Press, 2019), chapter 2.

21. Frans de Waal, *Our Inner Ape: A Leading Primatologist Explains Why We Are Who We Are* (New York: Penguin, 2005), 249–50.

22. Waal, 250.

23. Edwin Hutchins, "Cognitive Ecology," *Topics in Cognitive Science* 2, no. 4 (2010): 705–15, https://doi.org/10.1111/j.1756-8765.2010.01089.x.

24. Albert Newen, Leon de Bruin, and Shaun Gallagher, *The Oxford Handbook of 4E Cognition*, Oxford Handbooks Online (Oxford: Oxford University Press, 2018), http://dx.doi.org/10.1093/oxfordhb/9780198735410.001.0001.

25. Hayek, *The Constitution of Liberty*, 154.

26. Thomas Sowell, *A Conflict of Visions: Ideological Origins of Political Struggles* (New York: Basic Books, 1987), 34.

27. David Brooks, "The Tipping System Is Immoral," *The New York Times*, October 24, 2019, sec. Opinion, https://www.nytimes.com/2019/10/24/opinion/tipping .html.

28. Charles Darwin, "The Origin of the Species," in *Charles Darwin: An Anthology*, ed. Marston Bates and Philip S. Humphrey (New Brunswick, NJ: Transaction Publishers, 2009), 146.

29. Herbert Spencer, *Principles of Biology* (New York, 1893), 444, http://hdl .handle.net/2027/nyp.33433010812422; Darwin, "The Origin of the Species," 132.

30. Stephen Jay Gould, "Darwin's Untimely Burial," *Natural History* 85, no. 8 (October 1976): 26.

31. Erin Fry et al., "Functional Architecture of Deleterious Genetic Variants in the Genome of a Wrangel Island Mammoth," *Genome Biology and Evolution* 12, no. 3 (March 1, 2020): 48–58, https://doi.org/10.1093/gbe/evz279; Russell W. Graham et al., "Timing and Causes of Mid-Holocene Mammoth Extinction on St. Paul Island, Alaska," *Proceedings of the National Academy of Sciences* 113, no. 33 (August 16, 2016): 9313, https://doi.org/10.1073/pnas.1604903113.

32. Darwin, "The Origin of the Species," 143.

33. Apoorva Mandavilli, "The Coronavirus Patients Betrayed by Their Own Immune Systems," *The New York Times*, April 1, 2020, sec. Health, https://www.nytimes .com/2020/04/01/health/coronavirus-cytokine-storm-immune-system.html.

34. Daniel S. Milo, *Good Enough: The Tolerance for Mediocrity in Nature and Society* (Cambridge, MA: Harvard University Press, 2019), 51.

35. Jerry A. Coyne, *Why Evolution Is True* (New York: Penguin Books, 2010), 85.

36. Coyne, 120–21.

37. Coyne, 218.

38. Darwin, "The Origin of the Species," 132.

39. Darwin, 132.

40. Milo, *Good Enough*, 5; Stephen Jay Gould, "Kropotkin Was No Crackpot," *Natural History*, July 1988.

41. Timothy W. Ryback, "A Disquieting Book from Hitler's Library," *The New York Times*, December 7, 2011, sec. Opinion, https://www.nytimes.com/2011/12/08 /opinion/a-disquieting-book-from-hitlers-library.html. For more details on this history, see the extensive documentation in James Q. Whitman, *Hitler's American*

Model: The United States and the Making of Nazi Race Law (Princeton, NJ: Princeton University Press, 2017).

42. Roger Griffin, ed., "General Introduction," in *Fascism*, Oxford Readers (Oxford: Oxford University Press, 1995), 3.

43. David A. Graham et al., "An Oral History of Trump's Bigotry," *The Atlantic*, June 2019, https://www.theatlantic.com/magazine/archive/2019/06/trump-racism -comments/588067/.

44. Vanessa Williamson and Isabella Gelfand, "Trump and Racism: What Do the Data Say?," *Brookings* (blog), August 14, 2019, https://www.brookings.edu/blog /fixgov/2019/08/14/trump-and-racism-what-do-the-data-say/.

45. For further context on the phrase, see Jouet, "The Real Story behind 'Make America Great Again.'"

46. Khalil Gibran Muhammad, *The Condemnation of Blackness: Race, Crime, and the Making of Modern Urban America*, second edition (Cambridge, MA: Harvard University Press, 2019).

47. For a further exploration of how "racial habits" in both individuals and institutions create a "value gap" in how Black and White lives are valued in the United States in many aspects of life (not just the criminal justice system), see Glaude, *Democracy in Black*.

48. Milo, *Good Enough*, 13.

49. Milo, 197.

50. Milo, 236.

51. Milo, 244.

52. Milo, 247.

53. Will Steffen et al., "Planetary Boundaries: Guiding Human Development on a Changing Planet," *Science* 347, no. 6223 (February 13, 2015), https://doi.org/10.1126 /science.1259855.

54. Ted Nordhaus, "The Earth's Carrying Capacity for Human Life Is Not Fixed," *Aeon*, July 5, 2018, https://aeon.co/ideas/the-earths-carrying-capacity-for-human -life-is-not-fixed; Katrina Brown, "Global Environmental Change II: Planetary Boundaries—A Safe Operating Space for Human Geographers?," *Progress in Human Geography* 41, no. 1 (February 1, 2017): 118–30, https://doi.org/10.1177/03091325 15604429.

55. Fridolin Krausmann et al., "Long-Term Trajectories of the Human Appropriation of Net Primary Production: Lessons from Six National Case Studies," *Ecological Economics* 77 (May 1, 2012): 129–38, https://doi.org/10.1016/j.ecolecon.2012.02.019.

56. Dasgupta, "The Economics of Biodiversity: The Dasgupta Review"; Partha Dasgupta, "Include the True Value of Nature When Rebuilding Economies after Coronavirus," *Nature* 581, no. 7807 (May 12, 2020): 119, https://doi.org/10.1038/d41586-020 -01390-w.

57. Dasgupta, "The Economics of Biodiversity: The Dasgupta Review"; Inger Andersen, "First Person: COVID-19 Is Not a Silver Lining for the Climate, Says UN Environment Chief," UN News, April 5, 2020, https://news.un.org/en/story/2020/04/1061082; United Nations Environment Programme, *UNEP Frontiers 2016 Report: Emerging Issues of Environment Concern*, 2016, 18–31; Inger Andersen, "Preventing the Next Pandemic: Zoonotic Diseases and How to Break the Chain of Transmission," UN Environment, July 6, 2020, http://www.unenvironment.org/news-and-stories/statement/preventing-next-pandemic-zoonotic-diseases-and-how-break-chain.

58. "Cyclone Amphan Live Updates: Storm Strikes Coast as India and Bangladesh Take Shelter," *The New York Times*, May 20, 2020, sec. World, https://www.nytimes.com/2020/05/20/world/asia/cyclone-amphan.html.

59. Graham W. Prescott et al., "Quantitative Global Analysis of the Role of Climate and People in Explaining Late Quaternary Megafaunal Extinctions," *Proceedings of the National Academy of Sciences* 109, no. 12 (March 20, 2012): 4527–31, https://doi.org/10.1073/pnas.1113875109. See also the helpful overview in Yuval N. Harari, *Sapiens: A Brief History of Humankind* (New York: Harper Perennial, 2015), 63–74.

60. Pamela McElwee et al., "Indigenous Ecologies," *Oxford Bibliographies*, 2018, https://www.oxfordbibliographies.com/view/document/obo-9780199830060/obo-9780199830060-0199.xml.

61. Paul Nadasdy, "Transcending the Debate over the Ecologically Noble Indian: Indigenous Peoples and Environmentalism," *Ethnohistory* 52, no. 2 (April 1, 2005): 291–331, https://doi.org/10.1215/00141801-52-2-291.

62. Naomi Klein, *This Changes Everything: Capitalism vs. the Climate* (New York: Simon & Schuster, 2015), 269–76.

63. This is, I take it, the recurring theme of Elizabeth Kolbert, *Under a White Sky: The Nature of the Future* (New York: Crown, 2021).

64. Krausmann et al., "Long-Term Trajectories of the Human Appropriation of Net Primary Production."

65. Prabhu L. Pingali, "Green Revolution: Impacts, Limits, and the Path Ahead," *Proceedings of the National Academy of Sciences* 109, no. 31 (July 31, 2012): 12302–8, https://doi.org/10.1073/pnas.0912953109.

66. Bittman, *Animal, Vegetable, Junk*, 206.

67. Bittman, 205.

68. Akshat Rathi, "Bill Gates-Led Energy Fund Is Expanding Its Portfolio of Startups Fighting Climate Change," *Quartz*, August 23, 2019, https://qz.com/1402301/bill-gatess-1-billion-energy-fund-is-expanding-its-portfolio-of-startups-fighting-climate-change/.

69. Akshat Rathi, "In Search of Clean Energy, Investments in Nuclear-Fusion Startups Are Heating Up," *Quartz*, June 29, 2019, https://qz.com/1402282/in-search-of-clean-energy-investments-in-nuclear-fusion-startups-are-heating-up/.

70. Bill Gates, *How to Avoid a Climate Disaster: The Solutions We Have and the Break-throughs We Need* (New York: Knopf, 2021), 48–49. On Gates's general evasion of politics and how it limits his solutions, see Bill McKibben, "How Does Bill Gates Plan to Solve the Climate Crisis?," *The New York Times*, February 15, 2021, sec. Books, https://www.nytimes.com/2021/02/15/books/review/bill-gates-how-to-avoid-a-climate-disaster.html. On how technological advance in the name of global good has historically benefited the rich at the expense of the poor, see Bittman, *Animal, Vegetable, Junk*, 105.

71. Klein, *This Changes Everything*, 447.

72. Hickel, "Degrowth: A Theory of Radical Abundance."

73. "An Ecomodernist Manifesto," accessed May 21, 2020, http://www.ecomodernism.org.

74. Ted Nordhaus, "Decarbonization and Its Discontents," The Breakthrough Institute, May 5, 2020, https://thebreakthrough.org/issues/energy/decarbonization-and-discontents. Some socialists also agree about nuclear power. Bhaskar Sunkara, "If We Want to Fight the Climate Crisis, We Must Embrace Nuclear Power," *The Guardian*, June 21, 2021, sec. Opinion, http://www.theguardian.com/commentisfree/2021/jun/21/fight-climate-crisis-clean-energy-nuclear-power.

75. Andrew McAfee, *More from Less: The Surprising Story of How We Learned to Prosper Using Fewer Resources—and What Happens Next* (New York: Scribner, 2019).

76. McAfee, 4.

77. McAfee, 4.

78. McAfee, 243.

79. McAfee, 75–86.

80. Andy Fitch, "Much Lighter: Talking to Andrew McAfee," *BLARB* (blog), November 1, 2019, https://blog.lareviewofbooks.org/interviews/much-lighter-talking-andrew-mcafee/.

81. For a detailed critique of his work, see Jason Hickel, "The Myth of America's Green Growth," *Foreign Policy* (blog), June 18, 2020, https://foreignpolicy.com/2020/06/18/more-from-less-green-growth-environment-gdp/. Their debate has continued: Andrew McAfee, "Why Degrowth Is the Worst Idea on the Planet," *Wired*, October 6, 2020, https://www.wired.com/story/opinion-why-degrowth-is-the-worst-idea-on-the-planet/; Jason Hickel, "A Response to McAfee: No, the 'Environmental Kuznets Curve' Won't Save Us," Jason Hickel, October 10, 2020, https://www.jasonhickel.org/blog/2020/10/9/response-to-mcafee.

82. Vaclav Smil, *Making the Modern World: Materials and Dematerialization* (West Sussex: John Wiley & Sons, 2014), 131.

83. Smil, 136.

84. Smil, 136.

85. Drew Harwell, "How America's Truck, the Ford F-150, Became a Plaything for the Rich," *Washington Post*, July 30, 2015, https://www.washingtonpost.com/news

/wonk/wp/2015/07/30/how-americas-truck-the-ford-f-150-became-a-plaything
-for-the-rich/.

86. Smil, *Making the Modern World*, 132–35.

87. Smil, "Want Not, Waste Not."

88. Smil, *Making the Modern World*, 82.

89. McAfee, *More from Less*, 107.

90. Polanyi, *The Great Transformation*, 3. It is interesting that McAfee admits the social failures here, devoting a whole chapter to the rise in "social disconnection." Sadly, he says, economics has not yet worked out a good "playbook" for dealing with this. It's surprising to read these words, because even rather traditional economics *has* worked this out. Social disconnection is almost universally found to be related to declines in social trust precipitated by corruption and inequality. Scandinavian countries thus have the world's highest social cohesion. See, for example, Organization for Economic Co-operation and Development, *Perspectives on Global Development 2012*, 2011, https://doi.org/10.1787/persp_glob_dev-2012-en.

91. This has led to some strong debates among socialists. See, for example, the heated response to *Jacobin* issue 26: "Earth, Wind, And Fire" (2017) in John Bellamy Foster, "The Long Ecological Revolution," *Monthly Review* 69, no. 6 (November 1, 2017), https://monthlyreview.org/2017/11/01/the-long-ecological-revolution/.

92. Fredric Jameson, *Representing Capital: A Commentary on Volume One* (London; New York: Verso, 2011), 90.

93. Klein, *This Changes Everything*, 178–79; Alperovitz, *Principles of a Pluralist Commonwealth*, 95.

94. Smil, *Growth*, 498.

95. Thomas Princen, *The Logic of Sufficiency* (Cambridge, MA: MIT Press, 2005); James Traub, "Our 'Pursuit of Happiness' Is Killing the Planet," *The New York Times*, March 6, 2020, sec. Opinion, https://www.nytimes.com/2020/03/06/opinion/our-pursuit-of-happiness-is-killing-the-planet.html.

96. Smil, "Want Not, Waste Not."

97. Paul Robbins, "Is Less More . . . or Is More Less? Scaling the Political Ecologies of the Future," *Political Geography* 76 (January 1, 2020): 102018, https://doi.org/10.1016/j.polgeo.2019.04.010; Alperovitz, *Principles of a Pluralist Commonwealth*, 94–95.

98. Wiedmann et al., "Scientists' Warning on Affluence."

99. Narasimha D. Rao and Jihoon Min, "Decent Living Standards: Material Prerequisites for Human Wellbeing," *Social Indicators Research* 138, no. 1 (July 1, 2018): 225–44, https://doi.org/10.1007/s11205-017-1650-0; Joel Millward-Hopkins et al., "Providing Decent Living with Minimum Energy: A Global Scenario," *Global Environmental Change* 65 (November 1, 2020): 102168, https://doi.org/10.1016/j.gloenvcha.2020.102168.

100. As Mazzucato argues, this is why government financing is inevitably part of the solution, and this is in turn why everyone should more equally benefit both from the technology and from the economic growth it creates. Mazzucato, *Mission Economy*.

101. Jacobson et al., "100% Clean and Renewable Wind, Water, and Sunlight All-Sector Energy Roadmaps for 139 Countries of the World."

102. Umair Irfan, "Democratic Candidates Want to Use Trade to Make Other Countries Act on Climate Change," Vox, February 7, 2020, https://www.vox.com /2020/2/7/21128928/2020-democratic-debate-new-hampshire-climate-change -trade-sanders-steyer-warren.

103. Immanuel Kant, *Critique of the Power of Judgment*, ed. Paul Guyer, trans. Paul Guyer and Eric Matthews (Cambridge: Cambridge University Press, 2000), 145.

BIBLIOGRAPHY

Adam, David. "Science Funders Gamble on Grant Lotteries." *Nature* 575, no. 7784 (November 20, 2019): 574–75. https://doi.org/10.1038/d41586-019-03572-7.

Allegretto, Sylvia, and Lawrence Mishel. "The Teacher Pay Penalty Has Hit a New High." Economic Policy Institute, September 5, 2018.

Alperovitz, Gar. *Principles of a Pluralist Commonwealth*. Washington, DC: The Democracy Collaborative, 2017.

———. *What Then Must We Do? Straight Talk about the Next American Revolution*. White River Junction, VT: Chelsea Green Publishing, 2013.

Alperovitz, Gar, Thad Williamson, and Ted Howard. "The Cleveland Model," February 11, 2010. https://www.thenation.com/article/archive/cleveland-model/.

Alpert, Avram. *Global Origins of the Modern Self, from Montaigne to Suzuki*. Albany: SUNY Press, 2019.

———. "The Good-Enough Life." *The New York Times*, February 20, 2019, sec. Opinion. https://www.nytimes.com/2019/02/20/opinion/the-good-enough-life-philosophy.html.

American Psychiatric Association. "Americans Say They Are More Anxious than a Year Ago; Baby Boomers Report Greatest Increase in Anxiety," May 7, 2018. https://www.psychiatry.org/newsroom/news-releases/americans-say-they-are-more-anxious-than-a-year-ago-baby-boomers-report-greatest-increase-in-anxiety.

"An Ecomodernist Manifesto." Accessed May 21, 2020. http://www.ecomodernism.org.

Andersen, Inger. "First Person: COVID-19 Is Not a Silver Lining for the Climate, Says UN Environment Chief." UN News, April 5, 2020. https://news.un.org/en/story/2020/04/1061082.

———. "Preventing the Next Pandemic: Zoonotic Diseases and How to Break the Chain of Transmission." UN Environment, July 6, 2020. http://www.unenvironment.org/news-and-stories/statement/preventing-next-pandemic-zoonotic-diseases-and-how-break-chain.

Anderson, Elizabeth. "What Comes After Meritocracy?" *The Nation*, February 23, 2021. https://www.thenation.com/article/society/sandel-tyranny-merit/.

Appelbaum, Binyamin. *The Economists' Hour: False Prophets, Free Markets, and the Fracture of Society*. New York: Little, Brown and Company, 2019.

Appiah, Kwame Anthony. *The Lies That Bind: Rethinking Identity*. New York: Liveright, 2019.

Apuzzo, Matt, and David D. Kirkpatrick. "Covid-19 Changed How the World Does Science, Together." *The New York Times*, April 1, 2020, sec. World. https://www.nytimes.com/2020/04/01/world/europe/coronavirus-science-research-cooperation.html.

Aristotle. *The Nicomachean Ethics*. Edited by Lesley Brown. Translated by David Ross. Oxford: Oxford University Press, 2009.

———. *The Politics*. Translated by Ernest Barker. Reissue edition. New York: Oxford University Press, 1998.

Aschwanden, Christie. "Perfectionism Is Killing Us." Vox, November 27, 2019. https://www.vox.com/the-highlight/2019/11/27/20975989/perfect-mental-health-perfectionism.

Auerbach, Erich. *Mimesis: The Representation of Reality in Western Literature*. Translated by Willard Trask. Princeton, NJ: Princeton University Press, 1953.

Azmanova, Albena. *Capitalism on Edge: How Fighting Precarity Can Achieve Radical Change without Crisis or Utopia*. New York: Columbia University Press, 2020.

Bailey, Greg. "Buddhism and Caste." In *Oxford Bibliographies*. Oxford: Oxford University Press, 2014. DOI: 10.1093/OBO/9780195393521–0191.

Baker, Ella. "Gerda Lerner Interview with Ella Baker." In *Black Women in White America: A Documentary History*, edited by Gerda Lerner. New York: Vintage Books, 1973.

Baldwin, James. "The Fire Next Time." In *Collected Essays*, edited by Toni Morrison, 291–347. New York: Library of America, 1998.

———. "Notes of a Native Son." In *James Baldwin: Collected Essays*, edited by Toni Morrison. New York: Library of America, 1998.

Banks, Nina. "Black Women in the United States and Unpaid Collective Work: Theorizing the Community as a Site of Production." *The Review of Black Political Economy* 47, no. 4 (December 1, 2020): 343–62. https://doi.org/10.1177/0034644620962811.

Barclay, Eliza. "The Growth of Yoga and Meditation in the US since 2012 Is Remarkable." Vox, November 8, 2018. https://www.vox.com/2018/11/8/18073422/yoga-meditation-apps-health-anxiety-cdc.

Batson, Daniel, and John Darley. "From Jerusalem to Jericho: A Study of Situational and Dispositional Variables in Helping Behaviour." *Journal of Personality and Social Psychology* 27, no. 1 (1973): 100–108.

Baumeister, Roy F., and Mark R. Leary. "The Need to Belong: Desire for Interpersonal Attachments as a Fundamental Human Motivation." *Psychological Bulletin* 117, no. 3 (May 1995): 497–529. https://doi.org/10.1037/0033-2909.117.3.497.

BBC Wales Investigates. "Coronavirus: 'Institutional Racism Left Minorities Exposed.'" *BBC News*, August 3, 2020, sec. Wales. https://www.bbc.com/news/uk-wales-53539577.

Benjamin, Walter. *Illuminations: Essays and Reflections*. Edited by Hannah Arendt. Translated by Harry Zohn. New York: Schocken, 2019.

Berlant, Lauren. *Cruel Optimism*. Durham, NC: Duke University Press, 2011.

Berlin, Isaiah. *The Crooked Timber of Humanity: Chapters in the History of Ideas*. Edited by Henry Hardy. Second edition. Princeton, NJ: Princeton University Press, 1990.

Berman, Sheri. *The Primacy of Politics: Social Democracy and the Making of Europe's Twentieth Century*. Cambridge: Cambridge University Press, 2006.

Berteau, Benjamin, Barbara Wojazer, and Emma Reynolds. "From Private Testing for the Rich to Unrest in Banlieues, Coronavirus Is Highlighting France's Stark Divide." *CNN*, April 26, 2020. https://www.cnn.com/2020/04/26/europe/coronavirus-france-inequality-intl/index.html.

Bevins, Vincent. *The Jakarta Method: Washington's Anticommunist Crusade and the Mass Murder Program That Shaped Our World*. New York: PublicAffairs, 2020.

Bittman, Mark. *Animal, Vegetable, Junk: A History of Food, from Sustainable to Suicidal*. Boston: Houghton Mifflin Harcourt, 2021.

Bodhi, Bhikkhu, trans. *The Connected Discourses of the Buddha: A New Translation of the Saṃyutta Nikāya*. Somerville: Wisdom Publications, 2000.

Boehm, Christopher. *Hierarchy in the Forest: The Evolution of Egalitarian Behavior*. Cambridge, MA: Harvard University Press, 1999.

Botton, Alain de. "Why You Will Marry the Wrong Person." *The New York Times*, May 28, 2016, sec. Opinion. https://www.nytimes.com/2016/05/29/opinion/sunday/why-you-will-marry-the-wrong-person.html.

Boulding, Kenneth E. "Economics as a Moral Science." *The American Economic Review* 59, no. 1 (1969): 1–12.

Boushey, Heather. *Unbound: How Inequality Constricts Our Economy and What We Can Do about It*. Cambridge, MA: Harvard University Press, 2019.

———. "Unbound: Releasing Inequality's Grip on Our Economy." *Review of Radical Political Economics* 52, no. 4 (December 2020): 597–609. https://doi.org/10.1177/0486613420938187.

Braun, Erik. *The Birth of Insight: Meditation, Modern Buddhism, and the Burmese Monk Ledi Sayadaw*. Chicago: University of Chicago Press, 2013.

Bregman, Rutger. *Humankind: A Hopeful History*. Translated by Elizabeth Manton and Erica Moore. New York: Little, Brown and Company, 2020.

Brinkmann, Svend. *The Joy of Missing Out: The Art of Self-Restraint in an Age of Excess*. Translated by Tam McTurk. Cambridge: Polity, 2019.

———. *Stand Firm: Resisting the Self-Improvement Craze*. Translated by Tam Mc-Turk. Cambridge: Polity, 2017.

Brody, Jane E. "How to Avoid Burnout in Youth Sports." *The New York Times*, May 7, 2018, sec. Well. https://www.nytimes.com/2018/05/07/well/how-to-avoid -burnout-in-youth-sports.html.

Bronkhorst, Johannes. *Buddhism in the Shadow of Brahmanism*. Leiden: Brill, 2011.

Brooks, David. "The Tipping System Is Immoral." *The New York Times*, October 24, 2019, sec. Opinion. https://www.nytimes.com/2019/10/24/opinion/tipping .html.

brown, adrienne maree. *Emergent Strategy: Shaping Change, Changing Worlds*. Oakland: AK Press, 2017.

———. "Stagger," June 12, 2017. http://adriennemareebrown.net/2017/06/12 /stagger/.

Brown, Katrina. "Global Environmental Change II: Planetary Boundaries—A Safe Operating Space for Human Geographers?" *Progress in Human Geography* 41, no. 1 (February 1, 2017): 118–30. https://doi.org/10.1177/0309132515604429.

Brown, Matthew. "Preston Is a Lesson for Labour: Show Communities You Can Deliver Change." *The Guardian*, May 18, 2021. http://www.theguardian.com /commentisfree/2021/may/18/preston-labour-communities-change-voters-uk.

Brown, Vincent. "Social Death and Political Life in the Study of Slavery." *The American Historical Review* 114, no. 5 (2009): 1231–49.

Brown, Wendy. *Undoing the Demos: Neoliberalism's Stealth Revolution*. New York: Zone Books, 2015.

Brownlee, Kimberley. *Being Sure of Each Other: An Essay on Social Rights and Freedoms*. *Being Sure of Each Other*. Oxford: Oxford University Press, 2020.

Bruenig, Matt. "The Racial Wealth Gap Is about the Upper Classes," June 29, 2020. https://www.peoplespolicyproject.org/2020/06/29/the-racial-wealth-gap-is -about-the-upper-classes/.

———. "Social Wealth Fund for America." People's Policy Project. Accessed May 7, 2020. . https://peoplespolicyproject.org/projects/social-wealth-fund.

Bruno, Karl. "The Technopolitics of Swedish Iron Mining in Cold War Liberia, 1950–1990." *The Extractive Industries and Society* 7, no. 1 (January 1, 2020): 39–49. https://doi.org/10.1016/j.exis.2019.06.008.

Burgh, W.G. de. "Greatness and Goodness: The Presidential Address." *Proceedings of the Aristotelian Society* 32 (1932): 1–18.

Burki, Talha. "The Indirect Impact of COVID-19 on Women." *The Lancet Infectious Diseases* 20, no. 8 (August 1, 2020): 904–5. https://doi.org/10.1016/S1473 -3099(20)30568-5.

Caldwell, Bruce. "Introduction." In *The Road to Serfdom: Text and Documents—The Definitive Edition*, by Friedrich Hayek, 1–33. edited by Bruce Caldwell. Chicago: University of Chicago Press, 2007.

Calhoun, Ada. *Why We Can't Sleep: Women's New Midlife Crisis*. New York: Grove Press, 2020.

"Canada's 2020 Sobey Art Award to Divide Grand Prize among Longlisted Artists." April 16, 2020. https://www.artforum.com/news/canada-s-2020-sobey-art-award-to-divide-grand-prize-among-longlisted-artists-82748.

Carnegie, Andrew. "The Gospel of Wealth." Carnegie Corporation of New York. June 1889. https://www.carnegie.org/about/our-history/gospelofwealth/.

Carter, Zachary D. *The Price of Peace: Money, Democracy, and the Life of John Maynard Keynes*. New York: Random House, 2020.

Cass, Oren. *The Once and Future Worker: A Vision for the Renewal of Work in America*. New York: Encounter Books, 2018.

Cederström, Carl, and André Spicer. *Desperately Seeking Self-Improvement: A Year inside the Optimization Movement*. New York: OR Books, 2017.

Cerrato, Andrea, Francesco Ruggieri, and Federico Maria Ferrara. "Trump Won in Counties That Lost Jobs to China and Mexico." *Washington Post*, December 2, 2016. https://www.washingtonpost.com/news/monkey-cage/wp/2016/12/02/trump-won-where-import-shocks-from-china-and-mexico-were-strongest/.

Chang, Ha-Joon. *Bad Samaritans: The Myth of Free Trade and the Secret History of Capitalism*. New York: Bloomsbury Press, 2007.

Chen, Elsie. "These Chinese Millennials Are 'Chilling,' and Beijing Isn't Happy." *The New York Times*, July 3, 2021, sec. World. https://www.nytimes.com/2021/07/03/world/asia/china-slackers-tangping.html.

Chetty, Raj, Xavier Jaravel, Neviana Petkova, John Van Reenen, and Alex Bell. "Who Becomes an Inventor in America? The Importance of Exposure to Innovation." The Equality of Opportunity Project, 2018. http://www.equality-of-opportunity.org/assets/documents/inventors_paper.pdf.

Chua, Amy. *Battle Hymn of the Tiger Mother*. New York: Penguin, 2012.

Cingano, Federico. "Trends in Income Inequality and Its Impact on Economic Growth." *OECD Social, Employment and Migration Working Papers*, no. 163 (2014). https://doi.org/10.1787/5jxrjncwxv6j-en.

Clark, Tiana. "This Is What Black Burnout Feels Like." *BuzzFeed News*, January 11, 2019. https://www.buzzfeednews.com/article/tianaclarkpoet/millennial-burnout-black-women-self-care-anxiety-depression.

Coates, Ta-Nehisi. "Black Pathology and the Closing of the Progressive Mind." *The Atlantic*, March 21, 2014. https://www.theatlantic.com/politics/archive/2014/03/black-pathology-and-the-closing-of-the-progressive-mind/284523/.

———. "The Case for Reparations." *The Atlantic*, June 2014. http://www.theatlantic
.com/magazine/archive/2014/06/the-case-for-reparations/361631/.

Cohen, G. A. *Why Not Socialism?* Princeton, NJ: Princeton University Press, 2009.

Collins, Steven. *Nirvana and Other Buddhist Felicities: Utopias of the Pali Imaginaire.*
Cambridge: Cambridge University Press, 1998.

———. *Selfless Persons: Imagery and Thought in Theravada Buddhism.* Cambridge:
Cambridge University Press, 1990.

Colman, Ronald. *What Really Counts: The Case for a Sustainable and Equitable Economy.* New York: Columbia University Press, 2021.

Conceição, Pedro, et al. "Human Development Report 2019: Beyond Income, Beyond Averages, Beyond Today: Inequalities in Human Development in the
21st Century." New York: United Nations Human Development Programme,
2019. http://hdr.undp.org/sites/default/files/hdr2019.pdf.

Conger, Kate, Robert Gebeloff, and Richard A. Oppel Jr. "Native Americans Feel
Devastated by the Virus Yet Overlooked in the Data." *The New York Times*, July 30,
2020, sec. U.S. https://www.nytimes.com/2020/07/30/us/native-americans
-coronavirus-data.html.

Cooper, Anna Julia. *The Voice of Anna Julia Cooper: Including "A Voice from the South"
and Other Important Essays, Papers, and Letters.* Edited by Charles Lemert and
Esme Bhan. Lanham, MD: Rowman & Littlefield, 1998.

"Corporate Accountability and Democracy." Bernie Sanders—Official Campaign
Website. Accessed May 24, 2020. https://berniesanders.com/issues/corporate
-accountability-and-democracy/.

Covert, Bryce. "8 Hours a Day, 5 Days a Week Is Not Working for Us." *The New York
Times*, July 20, 2021, sec. Opinion. https://www.nytimes.com/2021/07/20
/opinion/covid-return-to-office.html.

Coyne, Jerry A. *Why Evolution Is True.* New York: Penguin Books, 2010.

"Cyclone Amphan Live Updates: Storm Strikes Coast as India and Bangladesh Take
Shelter." *The New York Times*, May 20, 2020, sec. World. https://www.nytimes
.com/2020/05/20/world/asia/cyclone-amphan.html.

Dahl, Robert Alan. *A Preface to Economic Democracy.* Berkeley: University of California Press, 1986.

Darwin, Charles. "The Origin of the Species." In *Charles Darwin: An Anthology*, edited by Marston Bates and Philip S. Humphrey. New Brunswick, NJ: Transaction
Publishers, 2009.

Dasgupta, Partha. "The Economics of Biodiversity: The Dasgupta Review." London:
HM Treasury, February 2021. https://assets.publishing.service.gov.uk/government
/uploads/system/uploads/attachment_data/file/962785/The_Economics_of
_Biodiversity_The_Dasgupta_Review_Full_Report.pdf.

————. "Include the True Value of Nature When Rebuilding Economies after Coronavirus." *Nature* 581, no. 7807 (May 12, 2020): 119. https://doi.org/10.1038/d41586-020-01390-w.

DePillis, Lydia. "For Amazon HQ2 Hopefuls, Seattle Serves as a Cautionary Tale." *CNNMoney*, May 13, 2018. https://money.cnn.com/2018/05/13/news/companies/amazon-hq2-seattle/index.html.

Deutsch, Morton. *Distributive Justice: A Social-Psychological Perspective*. New Haven, CT: Yale University Press, 1985.

Döpfner, Mathias, and Jeff Bezos. "Jeff Bezos Reveals What It's Like to Build an Empire and Become the Richest Man in the World—and Why He's Willing to Spend $1 Billion a Year to Fund the Most Important Mission of His Life." *Business Insider*, April 30, 2018. https://www.businessinsider.com/jeff-bezos-interview-axel-springer-ceo-amazon-trump-blue-origin-family-regulation-washington-post-2018-4.

Dorrien, Gary. *The Democratic Socialist Vision*. Baltimore: Rowman & Littlefield, 1986.

————. *Social Democracy in the Making: Political and Religious Roots of European Socialism*. New Haven, CT: Yale University Press, 2019.

Douthat, Ross. "Is Capitalism Killing Conservatism?" *The New York Times*, May 8, 2021, sec. Opinion. https://www.nytimes.com/2021/05/08/opinion/sunday/capitalism-conservatism.html.

Du Bois, W.E.B. *Black Reconstruction in America, 1860–1880*. New York: Free Press, 1998.

————. "Criteria of Negro Art." *The Crisis*. October 1926.

————. "The Talented Tenth." In *The Negro Problem: A Series of Articles by Representative American Negroes of Today*, 31–75. New York: James Pott & Company, 1903.

————. "The Talented Tenth Memorial Address." In *The Future of the Race*, by Henry Louis Gates Jr and Cornel West. New York: Knopf Doubleday Publishing Group, 2011.

Dunn, Elizabeth W., Lara B. Aknin, and Michael I. Norton. "Spending Money on Others Promotes Happiness." *Science* 319, no. 5870 (2008): 1687–88.

Egner, Jeremy. "'The Good Place' Finale Finds the Meaning of Life: 'Yep, Nailed It.'" *The New York Times*, January 28, 2020, sec. Arts. https://www.nytimes.com/2020/01/28/arts/television/the-good-place-michael-schur.html.

Einstein, Albert. "Reprise: Why Socialism?" *Monthly Review* (blog), May 1, 2009. https://monthlyreview.org/2009/05/01/why-socialism/.

Eisenstein, Hester. "The Sweatshop Feminists." *Jacobin*, June 17, 2015. https://jacobinmag.com/2015/06/kristof-globalization-development-third-world/.

Eisler, Riane. "Whole Systems Change." TheNextSystem.org, 2020. https://thenextsystem.org/whole-systems-change.

Ekins, Emily, and Joy Pullman. "Why So Many Millennials Are Socialists." Cato Institute, February 15, 2016. https://www.cato.org/publications/commentary/why-so-many-millennials-are-socialists.

Emerson, Ralph Waldo. *Essays and Poems.* New York: Library of America, 1996.

Warren Democrats. "Empowering Workers through Accountable Capitalism: Elizabeth Warren." Accessed May 24, 2020. https://elizabethwarren.com/plans/accountable-capitalism.

Fang, Ferrie, and Arturo Casadevall. "Grant Funding: Playing the Odds." *Science* 352, no. 6282 (April 2016): 158.

Federici, Silvia. *Caliban and the Witch: Women, the Body and Primitive Accumulation.* New York: Autonomedia, 2004.

Fernholz, Tim. "How to Build a Space Economy That Avoids the Mistakes of Terrestrial Capitalism." *Quartz*, December 20, 2019. https://qz.com/work/1767415/can-nasa-build-a-space-economy-that-leaves-capitalisms-problems-behind/.

Financial Times Editorial Board. "Virus Lays Bare the Frailty of the Social Contract," April 3, 2020. https://www.ft.com/content/7eff769a-74dd-11ea-95fe-fcd274e920ca.

Fitch, Andy. "Much Lighter: Talking to Andrew McAfee." *BLARB* (blog), November 1, 2019. https://blog.lareviewofbooks.org/interviews/much-lighter-talking-andrew-mcafee/.

Ford, Matt. "Rebuilding the Constitution." *The New Republic*, May 15, 2020. https://newrepublic.com/article/157690/rebuilding-constitution.

Foster, John Bellamy. "The Long Ecological Revolution." *Monthly Review* 69, no. 6 (November 1, 2017). https://monthlyreview.org/2017/11/01/the-long-ecological-revolution/.

Frase, Peter. "Four Futures." *Jacobin*, December 13, 2011. https://jacobinmag.com/2011/12/four-futures.

Freud, Sigmund. *Civilization and Its Discontents.* Translated by James Strachey. New York: Norton, 1962.

———. *Jokes and Their Relation to the Unconscious: The Standard Edition.* Translated by James Strachey. New York: W. W. Norton & Company, 1990.

Friot, Bernard. "Le salaire universel: Un déjà-là considérable à généraliser." *Mouvements* 73, no. 1 (March 14, 2013): 60–69.

Fry, Erin, Sun K. Kim, Sravanthi Chigurapti, Katelyn M. Mika, Aakrosh Ratan, Alexander Dammermann, Brian J. Mitchell, Webb Miller, and Vincent J. Lynch. "Functional Architecture of Deleterious Genetic Variants in the Genome of a Wrangel Island Mammoth." *Genome Biology and Evolution* 12, no. 3 (March 1, 2020): 48–58. https://doi.org/10.1093/gbe/evz279.

Galbraith, James K. "The Death of Neoliberalism Is Greatly Exaggerated." *Foreign Policy* (blog), April 6, 2021. https://foreignpolicy.com/2021/04/06/death-neoliberalism-larry-summers-biden-pandemic/.

Galbraith, John Kenneth. *The Affluent Society*. Boston: Houghton Mifflin, 1958.

Gates, Bill. *How to Avoid a Climate Disaster: The Solutions We Have and the Break-throughs We Need*. New York: Knopf, 2021.

Gebrekidan, Selam, and Matt Apuzzo. "Rich Countries Signed Away a Chance to Vaccinate the World." *The New York Times*, March 21, 2021, sec. World. https://www.nytimes.com/2021/03/21/world/vaccine-patents-us-eu.html.

Geddie, John, Joe Brock, and Koustav Samanta. "Singapore's Migrant Workers Fear Financial Ruin after Virus Ordeal." *Reuters*, June 9, 2020. https://www.reuters.com/article/us-health-coronavirus-singapore-migrants-idUSKBN23G1PG.

Gilens, Martin, and Benjamin I. Page. "Testing Theories of American Politics: Elites, Interest Groups, and Average Citizens." *Perspectives on Politics* 12, no. 3 (September 2014): 564–81. https://doi.org/10.1017/S1537592714001595.

Giles, Chris, Ralph Atkins, and Krishna Guha. "The Undeniable Shift to Keynes," December 29, 2008. https://www.ft.com/content/8a3d8122-d5da-11dd-a9cc-000077b07658.

Giridharadas, Anand. *Winners Take All: The Elite Charade of Changing the World*. New York: Vintage, 2018.

Gladwell, Malcolm. *Outliers: The Story of Success*. New York: Back Bay Books, 2011.

Glaude, Eddie S., Jr. *Democracy in Black: How Race Still Enslaves the American Soul*. New York: Broadway Books, 2017.

Go, Julian. "Three Tensions in the Theory of Racial Capitalism." *Sociological Theory*, December 24, 2020. https://doi.org/10.1177/0735275120979822.

Goodhart, Sandor. "Opening Genesis 1." *Prose Studies* 34, no. 1 (April 2012): 18–31. https://doi.org/10.1080/01440357.2012.686209.

Gordon Nembhard, Jessica. *Collective Courage: A History of African American Cooperative Economic Thought and Practice*. University Park: The Pennsylvania State University Press, 2014.

Gordon, Robert J. *The Rise and Fall of American Growth: The U.S. Standard of Living since the Civil War*. Princeton, NJ: Princeton University Press, 2017.

Gottlieb, Lori. "Marry Him! The Case for Settling for Mr. Good Enough." *The Atlantic*, March 1, 2008. https://www.theatlantic.com/magazine/archive/2008/03/marry-him/306651/.

———. *Marry Him: The Case for Settling for Mr. Good Enough*. New York: Dutton, 2011.

Gould, Stephen Jay. "Darwin's Untimely Burial." *Natural History* 85, no. 8 (October 1976): 24–30.

———. "Kropotkin Was No Crackpot." *Natural History*, July 1988.

———. *The Panda's Thumb: More Reflections in Natural History*. New York: W. W. Norton & Company, 1992.

Graeber, David. *Bullshit Jobs*. New York: Simon & Schuster, 2019.

Graham, David A., Adrienne Green, Cullen Murphy, and Parker Richard. "An Oral History of Trump's Bigotry." *The Atlantic*, June 2019. https://www.theatlantic.com /magazine/archive/2019/06/trump-racism-comments/588067/.

Graham, Russell W., Soumaya Belmecheri, Kyungcheol Choy, Brendan J. Culleton, Lauren J. Davies, Duane Froese, Peter D. Heintzman, et al. "Timing and Causes of Mid-Holocene Mammoth Extinction on St. Paul Island, Alaska." *Proceedings of the National Academy of Sciences* 113, no. 33 (August 16, 2016): 9310–14. https:// doi.org/10.1073/pnas.1604903113.

Griffin, Roger, ed. "General Introduction." In *Fascism*, 1–14. Oxford Readers. Oxford: Oxford University Press, 1995.

Guerrero, Alexander. "Forget Voting—It's Time to Start Choosing Our Leaders by Lottery." *Aeon*, January 23, 2014. https://aeon.co/essays/forget-voting-it-s-time -to-start-choosing-our-leaders-by-lottery.

Guinan, Joe. "Socialising Capital: Looking Back on the Meidner Plan." *International Journal of Public Policy* 15, no. 1/2 (2019): 38.

Haas, Michaela. "'When Someone Hires Me, They Get the Boss Herself.'" *The New York Times*, July 7, 2020, sec. Opinion. https://www.nytimes.com/2020/07/07 /opinion/gig-economy-immigrants-fair-wage.html.

Hancock, Jay. "They Pledged to Donate Rights to Their COVID Vaccine, Then Sold Them to Pharma." *Kaiser Health News* (blog), August 25, 2020. https://khn.org /news/rather-than-give-away-its-covid-vaccine-oxford-makes-a-deal-with -drugmaker/.

Harari, Yuval N. *Sapiens: A Brief History of Humankind*. New York: Harper Perennial, 2015.

Harris, Adam. "Who Do You Have to Know to Get a Coronavirus Test?" *The Atlantic*, March 15, 2020. https://www.theatlantic.com/politics/archive/2020/03 /coronavirus-testing-rich-people/608062/.

Harris, Leonard. *A Philosophy of Struggle: The Leonard Harris Reader*. Edited by Lee A. McBride III. London: Bloomsbury Academic, 2020.

Hartman, Saidiya. *Wayward Lives, Beautiful Experiments: Intimate Histories of Social Upheaval*. New York: W. W. Norton & Company, 2019.

Harvey, David. "Anti-Capitalist Politics in the Time of COVID-19." *Jacobin*, March 20, 2020. https://jacobinmag.com/2020/03/david-harvey-coronavirus-political -economy-disruptions.

Harwell, Drew. "How America's Truck, the Ford F-150, Became a Plaything for the Rich." *Washington Post*, July 30, 2015. https://www.washingtonpost.com/news /wonk/wp/2015/07/30/how-americas-truck-the-ford-f-150-became-a -plaything-for-the-rich/.

Hauser, Christine. "West Virginia Teachers, Protesting Low Pay, Walk Out." *The New York Times*, February 23, 2018, sec. U.S. https://www.nytimes.com/2018/02/23 /us/west-virginia-teachers-strike.html.

Hayek, Friedrich August. *The Constitution of Liberty: The Definitive Edition*. Chicago: The University of Chicago Press, 2011.

———. *Nobel Prize-Winning Economist Oral History Transcript*. [Los Angeles]: Oral History Program, University of California, Los Angeles, 1983. http://archive.org/details/nobelprizewinnin00haye.

———. *The Road to Serfdom: Text and Documents—The Definitive Edition*. Edited by Bruce Caldwell. Chicago: University of Chicago Press, 2007.

Herbert, Danielle L., John Coveney, Philip Clarke, Nicholas Graves, and Adrian G. Barnett. "The Impact of Funding Deadlines on Personal Workloads, Stress and Family Relationships: A Qualitative Study of Australian Researchers." *BMJ Open* 4, no. 3 (March 1, 2014): e004462. https://doi.org/10.1136/bmjopen-2013-004462.

Hickel, Jason. "A Response to McAfee: No, the 'Environmental Kuznets Curve' Won't Save Us." Jason Hickel, October 10, 2020. https://www.jasonhickel.org/blog/2020/10/9/response-to-mcafee.

———. "Degrowth: A Theory of Radical Abundance." *Real-world Economics Review* no. 87 (2019): 54–68.

———. *The Divide: A Brief Guide to Global Inequality and Its Solutions*. New York: Norton, 2018.

———. "The Myth of America's Green Growth." *Foreign Policy* (blog), June 18, 2020. https://foreignpolicy.com/2020/06/18/more-from-less-green-growth-environment-gdp/.

Hill, Andrew P., and Thomas Curran. "How Perfectionism Became a Hidden Epidemic among Young People." The Conversation. January 4, 2018. http://theconversation.com/how-perfectionism-became-a-hidden-epidemic-among-young-people-89405.

Hirsch, Fred. *Social Limits to Growth*. Cambridge, MA: Harvard University Press, 1978.

Hirschman, Albert O. *The Passions and the Interests: Political Arguments for Capitalism before Its Triumph*. Princeton, NJ: Princeton University Press, 2013.

Holpuch, Amanda. "The 'Shecession': Why Economic Crisis Is Affecting Women More than Men." *The Guardian*, August 4, 2020, sec. Business. https://www.theguardian.com/business/2020/aug/04/shecession-coronavirus-pandemic-economic-fallout-women.

The Holy Bible: New Revised Standard Version. Edited by Michael D. Coogan, Marc Z. Brettler, and Carol Newsom. New York: Oxford University Press, 1989.

hooks, bell. *Belonging: A Culture of Place*. New York: Routledge, 2009.

hooks, bell, and Helen Tworkov. "Agent of Change: Helen Tworkov Interviews bell hooks." *Tricycle*, Fall 1992. https://tricycle.org/magazine/bell-hooks-buddhism/.

Horkheimer, Max, and Theodor W. Adorno. *Dialectic of Enlightenment*. Edited by Gunzelin Schmid Noerr. Translated by Edmund Jephcott. Palo Alto, CA: Stanford University Press, 2007.

Hudson, Peter James. "Racial Capitalism and the Dark Proletariat." Text. Boston Review, February 20, 2018. http://bostonreview.net/forum/remake-world-slavery-racial-capitalism-and-justice/peter-james-hudson-racial-capitalism-and.

Hurlburt, Heather. "The World Is Helping Americans Who Don't Always See It." The New York Times, May 4, 2020, sec. Opinion. https://www.nytimes.com/2020/05/04/opinion/coronavirus-global-cooperation-cities.html.

Hutchins, Edwin. "Cognitive Ecology." Topics in Cognitive Science 2, no. 4 (2010): 705–15. https://doi.org/10.1111/j.1756-8765.2010.01089.x.

Immerwahr, Daniel. How to Hide an Empire: A History of the Greater United States. New York: Farrar, Straus and Giroux, 2019.

———. "Paleo Con." The New Republic, March 24, 2021. https://newrepublic.com/article/161593/prehistoric-myth-work-james-suzman.

Ioannidis, John P. A. "Fund People Not Projects." Nature 477, no. 7366 (September 2011): 529–31. https://doi.org/10.1038/477529a.

Irfan, Umair. "Democratic Candidates Want to Use Trade to Make Other Countries Act on Climate Change." Vox, February 7, 2020. https://www.vox.com/2020/2/7/21128928/2020-democratic-debate-new-hampshire-climate-change-trade-sanders-steyer-warren.

Jacobson, Mark Z., Mark A. Delucchi, Zack A. F. Bauer, Savannah C. Goodman, William E. Chapman, Mary A. Cameron, Cedric Bozonnat, et al. "100% Clean and Renewable Wind, Water, and Sunlight All-Sector Energy Roadmaps for 139 Countries of the World." Joule 1, no. 1 (September 6, 2017): 108–21. https://doi.org/10.1016/j.joule.2017.07.005.

Jacoby, James. Amazon Empire: The Rise and Reign of Jeff Bezos. Documentary. PBS, 2020. https://www.pbs.org/wgbh/frontline/film/amazon-empire/.

James, Spencer L., Degu Abate, Kalkidan Hassen Abate, Solomon M. Abay, Cristiana Abbafati, Nooshin Abbasi, Hedayat Abbastabar, et al. "Global, Regional, and National Incidence, Prevalence, and Years Lived with Disability for 354 Diseases and Injuries for 195 Countries and Territories, 1990–2017: A Systematic Analysis for the Global Burden of Disease Study 2017." The Lancet 392, no. 10159 (November 10, 2018): 1789–1858. https://doi.org/10.1016/S0140-6736(18)32279-7.

Jameson, Fredric. Representing Capital: A Commentary on Volume One. London; New York: Verso, 2011.

Jester D (@JustMeTurtle). "I'm a garbageman, I can't work from home and my job is an essential city service that must get done." Twitter, March 14, 2020. https://twitter.com/JustMeTurtle/status/1238682510579478528.

Johnson, Walter. "To Remake the World: Slavery, Racial Capitalism, and Justice." Text. Boston Review, February 20, 2018. http://bostonreview.net/forum/walter-johnson-to-remake-the-world.

Jones, Gareth Stedman. *Karl Marx: Greatness and Illusion*. Cambridge, MA: Belknap Press, 2016.

Jouet, Mugambi. "The Real Story behind 'Make America Great Again.'" *Mother Jones*, January 2017. https://www.motherjones.com/politics/2017/01/american -exceptionalism-maga-trump-obama/.

Justice, Donald. *Oblivion: On Writers and Writing*. Ashland, OR: Story Line Press, 1998.

Kahn, Jennifer. "How Scientists Could Stop the Next Pandemic Before It Starts." *The New York Times*, April 21, 2020, sec. Magazine. https://www.nytimes.com/2020 /04/21/magazine/pandemic-vaccine.html.

Kaila, Ilara, and Joona-Hermanni Makinen. "Finland Had a Patent-Free COVID-19 Vaccine Nine Months Ago—But Still Went with Big Pharma." *Jacobin*, February 28, 2021. https://jacobinmag.com/2021/02/finland-vaccine-covid-patent-ip.

Kaila, Ilari, and Tuomas Kaila. "Finland, We Hardly Knew Ye." *Jacobin*, August 16, 2017. https://jacobinmag.com/2017/08/finland-welfare-state-true-finns -centennial.

Kalush, Rima. "In the Gulf, Migrant Workers Bear the Brunt of the Pandemic," June 1, 2020. https://www.aljazeera.com/indepth/opinion/gulf-migrant-workers -bear-brunt-pandemic-200529102238233.html.

Kant, Immanuel. *Critique of the Power of Judgment*. Edited by Paul Guyer. Translated by Paul Guyer and Eric Matthews. Cambridge: Cambridge University Press, 2000.

———. *"Religion within the Boundaries of Mere Reason" and Other Writings*. Edited and translated by George di Giovanni and Allen Wood. Cambridge; New York: Cambridge University Press, 1998.

Katznelson, Ira. *When Affirmative Action Was White: An Untold History of Racial In-equality in Twentieth-Century America*. New York: W. W. Norton, 2005.

Kaye, Henry J. "FDR's Second Bill of Rights: 'Necessitous Men Are Not Free Men.'" *Roosevelt Institute* (blog), January 11, 2011. https://rooseveltinstitute.org/fdrs -second-bill-rights-necessitous-men-are-not-free-men/.

Keegan, Paul. "Here's What Really Happened at That Company That Set a $70,000 Minimum Wage." Inc.com, October 21, 2015. https://www.inc.com/magazine /201511/paul-keegan/does-more-pay-mean-more-growth.html.

Keynes, John Maynard. *The Economic Consequences of the Peace*. Edited by Elizabeth Johnson and Donald Moggridge. Vol. 2. The Collected Writings of John Maynard Keynes. Cambridge: Cambridge University Press for the Royal Economic Society, 2013.

Kim, E. Tammy. "Can Arizona's Teachers Still Consider Themselves Middle Class?" *The New Yorker*, May 2, 2018. https://www.newyorker.com/news/dispatch/can -arizonas-teachers-still-consider-themselves-middle-class.

King, Dr. Martin Luther, Jr. *Where Do We Go from Here: Chaos or Community?* Boston: Beacon Press, 2010.

Kirby, Tony. "Evidence Mounts on the Disproportionate Effect of COVID-19 on Ethnic Minorities." *The Lancet. Respiratory Medicine* 8, no. 6 (May 10, 2020): 547–48. https://doi.org/10.1016/s2213-2600(20)30228-9.

Klein, Ezra, and Sam Altman. "Transcript: Ezra Klein Interviews Sam Altman." *The New York Times*, June 11, 2021, sec. Podcasts. https://www.nytimes.com/2021/06/11/podcasts/transcript-ezra-klein-interviews-sam-altman.html.

Klein, Ezra, and Jamila Michener. "Transcript: Ezra Klein Interviews Jamila Michener." *The New York Times*, June 8, 2021, sec. Podcasts. https://www.nytimes.com/2021/06/08/podcasts/transcript-ezra-klein-interviews-jamila-michener.html.

Klein, Naomi. *No Logo: 10th Anniversary Edition with a New Introduction by the Author.* New York: Picador, 2009.

———. *This Changes Everything: Capitalism vs. the Climate.* New York: Simon & Schuster, 2015.

Kluth, Andreas. "OK Boomer, We're Gonna Socialize You." *Bloomberg.Com*, July 25, 2020. https://www.bloomberg.com/opinion/articles/2020-07-25/ok-boomer-coronavirus-is-turning-millennials-into-socialists.

Kohn, Alfie. "Fun and Fitness without Competition." July 3, 1990. https://www.alfiekohn.org/article/fun-fitness-without-competition/.

———. *No Contest: The Case against Competition.* Boston: Houghton Mifflin, 1986.

Kolahi, Arash. "A Participatory Workplace Is a More Fulfilling One, Too." Inequality.org, March 2, 2020. https://inequality.org/research/participatory-workplace-more-fulfilling/.

Kolbert, Elizabeth. *Under a White Sky: The Nature of the Future.* New York: Crown, 2021.

Krausmann, Fridolin, Simone Gingrich, Helmut Haberl, Karl-Heinz Erb, Annabella Musel, Thomas Kastner, Norbert Kohlheb, Maria Niedertscheider, and Elmar Schwarzlmüller. "Long-Term Trajectories of the Human Appropriation of Net Primary Production: Lessons from Six National Case Studies." *Ecological Economics* 77 (May 1, 2012): 129–38. https://doi.org/10.1016/j.ecolecon.2012.02.019.

Kronman, Anthony T. *The Assault on American Excellence.* New York: Free Press, 2019.

Krugman, Paul. *Arguing with Zombies: Economics, Politics, and the Fight for a Better Future.* New York: W. W. Norton & Company, 2020.

Labour Party, UK. "Alternative Models of Ownership," 2017. https://labour.org.uk/wp-content/uploads/2017/10/Alternative-Models-of-Ownership.pdf.

Lacy, Karyn. *Blue-Chip Black: Race, Class, and Status in the New Black Middle Class.* Berkeley: University of California Press, 2007.

LaFraniere, Sharon, Katie Thomas, Noah Weiland, Peter Baker, and Annie Karni. "Scientists Worry About Political Influence over Coronavirus Vaccine Project." *The New York Times*, August 2, 2020, sec. U.S. https://www.nytimes.com/2020/08/02/us/politics/coronavirus-vaccine.html.

Lal, Neeta. "The COVID-19 Economic Crash Could Set Indian Women Back Decades." *Foreign Policy* (blog), August 4, 2020. https://foreignpolicy.com/2020/08/04/covid-19-economic-crash-india-jobless-women/.

Landemore, Hélène. *Open Democracy: Reinventing Popular Rule for the Twenty-First Century*. Princeton, NJ: Princeton University Press, 2020.

Lanier, Heather. "'Good' and 'Bad' Are Incomplete Stories We Tell Ourselves." TED@BCG Milan, October 2017. https://www.ted.com/talks/heather_lanier_good_and_bad_are_incomplete_stories_we_tell_ourselves.

Larson, Rob. "Bill Gates's Philanthropic Giving Is a Racket." *Jacobin*, April 5, 2020. https://jacobinmag.com/2020/04/bill-gates-foundation-philanthropy-microsoft.

Levi, Primo. *Survival In Auschwitz*. Translated by Stuart Woolf. New York: Simon and Schuster, 1996.

Lima de Miranda, Katharina, and Dennis J. Snower. "Recoupling Economic and Social Prosperity." *Global Perspectives* 1, no. 1 (February 20, 2020): 1–34. https://doi.org/10.1525/001c.11867.

Limburg, Karina, Hunna J. Watson, Martin S. Hagger, and Sarah J. Egan. "The Relationship Between Perfectionism and Psychopathology: A Meta-Analysis." *Journal of Clinical Psychology* 73, no. 10 (2017): 1301–26. https://doi.org/10.1002/jclp.22435.

Lin, David, Leopold Wambersie, Mathis Wackernagel, and Pat Hanscom. "Calculating Earth Overshoot Day 2020: Estimates Point to August 22nd." Global Footprint Network, June 5, 2020. https://www.overshootday.org/content/uploads/2020/06/Earth-Overshoot-Day-2020-Calculation-Research-Report.pdf.

Liu An. *The Huainanzi: A Guide to the Theory and Practice of Government in Early Han China*. Translated by John S. Major. New York: Columbia University Press, 2010.

Lovejoy, Thomas E., and Carlos Nobre. "Amazon Tipping Point." *Science Advances* 4, no. 2 (February 1, 2018): eaat2340. https://doi.org/10.1126/sciadv.aat2340.

Luxemburg, Rosa. *The Russian Revolution and Leninism or Marxism?* Ann Arbor: University of Michigan Press, 1961.

MacGillis, Alec. "Amazon and the Breaking of Baltimore." *The New York Times*, March 9, 2021, sec. Opinion. https://www.nytimes.com/2021/03/09/opinion/amazon-baltimore-dc.html.

MacIntyre, Alasdair. *After Virtue*. Second edition. South Bend, IN: University of Notre Dame Press, 1984.

Macnamara, Brooke N., David Moreau, and David Z. Hambrick. "The Relationship Between Deliberate Practice and Performance in Sports: A Meta-Analysis."

Perspectives on Psychological Science 11, no. 3 (May 1, 2016): 333–50. https://doi.org /10.1177/1745691616635591.

Mandavilli, Apoorva. "The Coronavirus Patients Betrayed by Their Own Immune Systems." *The New York Times*, April 1, 2020, sec. Health. https://www.nytimes .com/2020/04/01/health/coronavirus-cytokine-storm-immune-system.html.

Manson, Mark. *The Subtle Art of Not Giving a F*ck: A Counterintuitive Approach to Living a Good Life*. New York: Harper, 2016.

Markovits, Daniel. *The Meritocracy Trap: How America's Foundational Myth Feeds Inequality, Dismantles the Middle Class, and Devours the Elite*. New York: Penguin Press, 2019.

Martinez, Ramon, Peter Lloyd-Sherlock, Patricia Soliz, Shah Ebrahim, Enrique Vega, Pedro Ordunez, and Martin McKee. "Trends in Premature Avertable Mortality from Non-Communicable Diseases for 195 Countries and Territories, 1990–2017: A Population-Based Study." *The Lancet Global Health* 8, no. 4 (April 1, 2020): e511–23. https://doi.org/10.1016/S2214-109X(20)30035-8.

Martínez, Rubén O. "Environmental Racism." In *The Oxford Encyclopedia of Latinos and Latinas in the United States*. Oxford University Press, 2005. http://www .oxfordreference.com/view/10.1093/acref/9780195156003.001.0001/acref -9780195156003-e-277.

Marx, Karl, and Friedrich Engels. "The German Ideology," 1845. https://www .marxists.org/archive/marx/works/1845/german-ideology/ch01b.htm.

Maurer, Noel. *The Empire Trap: The Rise and Fall of U.S. Intervention to Protect American Property Overseas, 1893–2013*. Princeton, NJ: Princeton University Press, 2013.

May, Todd. *A Decent Life: Morality for the Rest of Us*. Chicago: University of Chicago Press, 2019.

Mayer, Jane. *Dark Money: The Hidden History of the Billionaires behind the Rise of the Radical Right*. New York: Doubleday, 2016.

Mazzucato, Mariana. *The Entrepreneurial State: Debunking Public vs. Private Sector Myths*. Revised edition. New York: PublicAffairs, 2015.

———. *Mission Economy: A Moonshot Guide to Changing Capitalism*. New York: Harper Business, 2021.

McAfee, Andrew. *More from Less: The Surprising Story of How We Learned to Prosper Using Fewer Resources—and What Happens Next*. New York: Scribner, 2019.

———. "Why Degrowth Is the Worst Idea on the Planet." *Wired*, October 6, 2020. https://www.wired.com/story/opinion-why-degrowth-is-the-worst-idea-on-the -planet/.

McElwee, Pamela, Álvaro Fernández-Llamazares, Marian Ahn Thorpe, Kyle Powys Whyte, Beth Rose Middleton, Kaitlin Reed, waaseyaa'sin Christine Sy, and Alysse Marie Moldawer. "Indigenous Ecologies." *Oxford Bibliographies*, 2018.

https://www.oxfordbibliographies.com/view/document/obo-9780199830060
/obo-9780199830060-0199.xml.

McGhee, Heather. *The Sum of Us: What Racism Costs Everyone and How We Can
Prosper Together.* New York: One World, 2021.

McKibben, Bill. "How Does Bill Gates Plan to Solve the Climate Crisis?" *The New
York Times,* February 15, 2021, sec. Books. https://www.nytimes.com/2021/02
/15/books/review/bill-gates-how-to-avoid-a-climate-disaster.html.

McMahan, David. "How Meditation Works: Theorizing the Role of Cultural Context
in Buddhist Contemplative Practices." In *Meditation, Buddhism, and Science,* edited by David McMahan and Erik Braun, 21–46. New York: Oxford University
Press, 2017.

Merton, Robert K. "The Matthew Effect in Science." *Science* 159, no. 3810 (January 5,
1968): 56–63.

Michels, Robert. *Political Parties: A Sociological Study of the Oligarchical Tendencies of
Modern Democracy.* Translated by Eden and Cedar Paul. New York: Dover Publications, 1959.

Milfont, Taciano L., Paul G. Bain, Yoshihisa Kashima, Victor Corral-Verdugo, Car-
lota Pasquali, Lars-Olof Johansson, Yanjun Guan, et al. "On the Relation between
Social Dominance Orientation and Environmentalism: A 25-Nation Study." *Social Psychological and Personality Science* 9, no. 7 (September 1, 2018): 802–14.
https://doi.org/10.1177/1948550617722832.

Millward-Hopkins, Joel, Julia K. Steinberger, Narasimha D. Rao, and Yannick Os-
wald. "Providing Decent Living with Minimum Energy: A Global Scenario."
Global Environmental Change 65 (November 1, 2020): 102168. https://doi.org/10
.1016/j.gloenvcha.2020.102168.

Milo, Daniel S. *Good Enough: The Tolerance for Mediocrity in Nature and Society.* Cambridge, MA: Harvard University Press, 2019.

Milton, John. *Paradise Lost.* Edited by David Scott Kastan. Indianapolis: Hackett
Publishing, 2005.

Mladenov, Teodor. "From State Socialist to Neoliberal Productivism: Disability
Policy and Invalidation of Disabled People in the Postsocialist Region." *Critical
Sociology* 43, no. 7–8 (2017): 1109–23.

Mohammed, Amina. "COVID-19 Pandemic Exposes Global 'Frailties and Inequalities': UN Deputy Chief." UN News, May 3, 2020. https://news.un.org/en/story
/2020/05/1063022.

Morreall, John. "Philosophy of Humor." In *The Stanford Encyclopedia of Philosophy,* edited by Edward N. Zalta, Winter 2016. Metaphysics Research Lab, Stanford University, 2016. https://plato.stanford.edu/archives/win2016/entries
/humor/.

Muhammad, Khalil Gibran. *The Condemnation of Blackness: Race, Crime, and the Making of Modern Urban America*. Second edition. Cambridge, MA: Harvard University Press, 2019.

Mulgan, Geoff. *Big Mind: How Collective Intelligence Can Change Our World*. Princeton, NJ: Princeton University Press, 2017.

Nadasdy, Paul. "Transcending the Debate over the Ecologically Noble Indian: Indigenous Peoples and Environmentalism." *Ethnohistory* 52, no. 2 (April 1, 2005): 291–331. https://doi.org/10.1215/00141801-52-2-291.

Ñāṇamoli, Bhikkhu, and Bhikkhu Bodhi, trans. *The middle Length Discourses of the Buddha: A New Translation of the Majjhima Nikaya*. Teachings of the Buddha. Boston: Wisdom Publications, 1995.

National Center on Education and the Economy. "Finland: Teacher and Principal Quality." Top Performing Countries, 2018. http://ncee.org/what-we-do/center-on-international-education-benchmarking/top-performing-countries/finland-overview/finland-teacher-and-principal-quality/.

TheNextSystem.org. "New Systems: Possibilities and Proposals." June 28, 2017. https://thenextsystem.org/learn/collections/new-systems-possibilities-and-proposals.

New York Times Editorial Board. "The America We Need." *The New York Times*, April 17, 2020, sec. Opinion. https://www.nytimes.com/interactive/2020/opinion/america-inequality-coronavirus.html.

Newen, Albert, Leon de Bruin, and Shaun Gallagher. *The Oxford Handbook of 4E Cognition*. Oxford Handbooks Online. Oxford: Oxford University Press, 2018. http://dx.doi.org/10.1093/oxfordhb/9780198735410.001.0001.

Nixon, Rob. *Slow Violence and the Environmentalism of the Poor*. Cambridge, MA: Harvard University Press, 2013.

Nordhaus, Ted. "Decarbonization and Its Discontents." The Breakthrough Institute, May 5, 2020. https://thebreakthrough.org/issues/energy/decarbonization-and-discontents.

———. "The Earth's Carrying Capacity for Human Life Is Not Fixed." *Aeon*, July 5, 2018. https://aeon.co/ideas/the-earths-carrying-capacity-for-human-life-is-not-fixed.

Nozick, Robert. *Anarchy, State, and Utopia*. New York: Basic Books, 2013.

Nussbaum, Martha C. *Creating Capabilities: The Human Development Approach*. Cambridge, MA: Harvard University Press, 2013.

Nye, Naomi Shihab. *Words under the Words: Selected Poems*. Eighth Mountain Press, 1995.

Obama, Barack. *Dreams from My Father: A Story of Race and Inheritance*. New York: Crown, 2007.

———. *We Are the Change We Seek: The Speeches of Barack Obama*. Edited by E. J. Dionne Jr and Joy-Ann Reid. New York: Bloomsbury, 2017.

Oliver, Michael. *The Politics of Disablement: A Sociological Approach*. New York: St. Martin's Press, 1990.

Olsson, Göran Hugo. *Concerning Violence: Nine Scenes from the Anti-Imperialistic Self-Defense*. New York: Kino Lorber, Inc, 2014.

Oppel, Richard A., Jr., Robert Gebeloff, K. K. Rebecca Lai, Will Wright, and Mitch Smith. "The Fullest Look Yet at the Racial Inequity of Coronavirus." *The New York Times*, July 5, 2020, sec. U.S. https://www.nytimes.com/interactive/2020 /07/05/us/coronavirus-latinos-african-americans-cdc-data.html.

Organization for Economic Co-operation and Development. *Perspectives on Global Development 2012*, 2011. https://doi.org/10.1787/persp_glob_dev-2012-en.

Orwell, George. *George Orwell: As I Please, 1943–1946*. Boston: Nonpareil, 2000.

Osterloh, Margit, and Bruno S. Frey. "How to Avoid Borrowed Plumes in Academia." *Research Policy* 49, no. 1 (February 1, 2020): 103831. https://doi.org/10.1016/j .respol.2019.103831.

Ovid. *Metamorphoses*. Edited by E. J. Kenney. Translated by A. D. Melville. Oxford: Oxford University Press, 2008.

Palus, Shannon. "Burnout Is Real, but It's Not an Exclusively Millennial Condition." *Slate Magazine*, January 8, 2019. https://slate.com/human-interest/2019/01 /burnout-millennials-capitalism-buzzfeed-essay.html.

Partanen, Anu. *The Nordic Theory of Everything: In Search of a Better Life*. New York: Harper Paperbacks, 2017.

Pattillo, Mary. *Black Picket Fences: Privilege and Peril among the Black Middle Class*. Second edition. Chicago: University of Chicago Press, 2013.

Payne, Charles M. *I've Got the Light of Freedom: The Organizing Tradition and the Mississippi Freedom Struggle, with a New Preface*. Second edition. Berkeley: University of California Press, 2007.

Perry, Imani. "Racism Is Terrible. Blackness Is Not." *The Atlantic*, June 15, 2020. https://www.theatlantic.com/ideas/archive/2020/06/racism-terrible-blackness-not /613039/.

Petersen, Anne Helen. "How Millennials Became the Burnout Generation." *BuzzFeed News*, January 5, 2019. https://www.buzzfeednews.com/article /annehelenpetersen/millennials-burnout-generation-debt-work.

Peterson Institute for Economics. "How the G20 Can Hasten Recovery from COVID-19." PIIE, April 13, 2020. https://www.piie.com/publications/piie-briefings/how -g20-can-hasten-recovery-covid-19.

Piff, Paul K., Michael W. Kraus, Stéphane Côté, Bonnie Hayden Cheng, and Dacher Keltner. "Having Less, Giving More: The Influence of Social Class on Prosocial

Behavior." *Journal of Personality and Social Psychology* 99, no. 5 (2010): 771–84. https://doi.org/10.1037/a0020092.

Piketty, Thomas. *Capital and Ideology*. Translated by Arthur Goldhammer. Cambridge, MA: Belknap Press, 2020.

———. *Capital in the Twenty-First Century*. Translated by Arthur Goldhammer. Cambridge, MA: Belknap Press, 2014.

Piliavin, Jane Allyn. "Doing Well by Doing Good: Benefits for the Benefactor." In *Flourishing: Positive Psychology and the Life Well-Lived*, 227–47. Washington, DC: American Psychological Association, 2003. https://doi.org/10.1037/10594-010.

Pingali, Prabhu L. "Green Revolution: Impacts, Limits, and the Path Ahead." *Proceedings of the National Academy of Sciences* 109, no. 31 (July 31, 2012): 12302–8. https://doi.org/10.1073/pnas.0912953109.

Pinker, Steven. *The Better Angels of Our Nature: Why Violence Has Declined*. New York: Penguin Books, 2012.

Plato. *The Symposium*. Translated by Alexander Nehamas and Paul Woodruff. Indianapolis: Hackett, 1989.

Polanyi, Karl. *The Great Transformation: The Political and Economic Origins of Our Time*. Boston: Beacon Press, 2001.

Prashad, Vijay. *The Poorer Nations: A Possible History of the Global South*. New York: Verso, 2014.

Prescott, Graham W., David R. Williams, Andrew Balmford, Rhys E. Green, and Andrea Manica. "Quantitative Global Analysis of the Role of Climate and People in Explaining Late Quaternary Megafaunal Extinctions." *Proceedings of the National Academy of Sciences* 109, no. 12 (March 20, 2012): 4527–31. https://doi.org/10.1073/pnas.1113875109.

Price, Dan (@DanPriceSeattle). "Since my company started a $70k min wage in 2015." Twitter, August 23, 2020. https://twitter.com/DanPriceSeattle/status/1297583024587104262.

Princen, Thomas. *The Logic of Sufficiency*. Cambridge, MA: MIT Press, 2005.

Ransby, Barbara. *Ella Baker and the Black Freedom Movement: A Radical Democratic Vision*. Chapel Hill: University of North Carolina Press, 2003.

Rao, Narasimha D., and Jihoon Min. "Decent Living Standards: Material Prerequisites for Human Wellbeing." *Social Indicators Research* 138, no. 1 (July 1, 2018): 225–44. https://doi.org/10.1007/s11205-017-1650-0.

Rathi, Akshat. "Bill Gates-Led Energy Fund Is Expanding Its Portfolio of Startups Fighting Climate Change." *Quartz*, August 23, 2019. https://qz.com/1402301/bill-gatess-1-billion-energy-fund-is-expanding-its-portfolio-of-startups-fighting-climate-change/.

———. "In Search of Clean Energy, Investments in Nuclear-Fusion Startups Are Heating Up." *Quartz*, June 29, 2019. https://qz.com/1402282/in-search-of-clean-energy-investments-in-nuclear-fusion-startups-are-heating-up/.

Rawidowicz, Simon. "Between Arab and Jew." In *Between Jew and Arab: The Lost Voice of Simon Rawidowicz*, by David N. Myers, 135–80. Waltham, MA: Brandeis University Press, 2009.

Rawls, John. *A Theory of Justice*. Revised edition. Cambridge, MA: Belknap Press, 1999.

Raworth, Kate. *Doughnut Economics: Seven Ways to Think Like a 21st-Century Economist*. White River Junction, VT: Chelsea Green Publishing, 2018.

Reed, Adolph, Jr. "The New Deal Wasn't Intrinsically Racist." *The New Republic*, November 26, 2019. https://newrepublic.com/article/155704/new-deal-wasnt-intrinsically-racist.

———. "The Surprising Cross-Racial Saga of Modern Wealth Inequality." *The New Republic*, June 29, 2020. https://newrepublic.com/article/158059/racial-wealth-gap-vs-racial-income-gap-modern-economic-inequality.

Reich, Rob. *Just Giving: Why Philanthropy Is Failing Democracy and How It Can Do Better*. Princeton, NJ: Princeton University Press, 2018.

Robbins, Paul. "Is Less More . . . or Is More Less? Scaling the Political Ecologies of the Future." *Political Geography* 76 (January 1, 2020): 102018. https://doi.org/10.1016/j.polgeo.2019.04.010.

Roberts, Paul. "This Is What Really Happens When Amazon Comes to Your Town." POLITICO Magazine, October 19, 2017. https://www.politico.com/magazine/story/2017/10/19/amazon-headquarters-seattle-215725.

Robin, Corey. "The New Socialists." *The New York Times*, August 24, 2018, sec. Opinion. https://www.nytimes.com/2018/08/24/opinion/sunday/what-socialism-looks-like-in-2018.html.

———. *The Reactionary Mind: Conservatism from Edmund Burke to Donald Trump*. Second edition. New York: Oxford University Press, 2017.

Robinson, Cedric J. *Black Marxism: The Making of the Black Radical Tradition*. Second edition. Chapel Hill: University of North Carolina Press, 2000.

Robinson, Nathan J. *Why You Should Be a Socialist*. New York: All Points Books, 2019.

Rodrik, Dani. *Straight Talk on Trade: Ideas for a Sane World Economy*. Princeton, NJ: Princeton University Press, 2017.

Russell, Bertrand. *The Practice and Theory of Bolshevism*. London: George Allen & Unwin Limited, 1921.

Russell, Marta, and Ravi Malhotra. "Capitalism and Disability." *Socialist Register* 38 (2002). https://socialistregister.com/index.php/srv/article/view/5784.

Ryback, Timothy W. "A Disquieting Book from Hitler's Library." *The New York Times*, December 7, 2011, sec. Opinion. https://www.nytimes.com/2011/12/08/opinion/a-disquieting-book-from-hitlers-library.html.

Sachs, Jeffrey, Joseph Stiglitz, Mariana Mazzucato, Clair Brown, Indivar Dutta-Gupta, Robert Reich, Gabriel Zucman, and others. "Letter from Economists: To Rebuild Our World, We Must End the Carbon Economy." *The Guardian*, August 4, 2020, sec. Opinion. https://www.theguardian.com/commentisfree/2020/aug/04/economists-letter-carbon-economy-climate-change-rebuild.

Saez, Emmanuel, and Gabriel Zucman. *The Triumph of Injustice: How the Rich Dodge Taxes and How to Make Them Pay*. New York: W. W. Norton & Company, 2019.

Sahlins, Marshall. *Stone Age Economics*. New York: Routledge, 2004.

Samuelson, Paul. "An Interview with Paul Samuelson, Part One." Interview by Derek Thompson, June 17, 2009. https://www.theatlantic.com/business/archive/2009/06/an-interview-with-paul-samuelson-part-one/19586/.

Sandel, Michael J. *Justice: What's the Right Thing to Do?* New York: Farrar, Straus and Giroux, 2009.

———. *The Tyranny of Merit: What's Become of the Common Good?* New York: Farrar, Straus and Giroux, 2020.

Santos, Laurie. "Laurie Santos, Yale Happiness Professor, on 5 Things That Will Make You Happier." Newsweek, December 20, 2020. https://www.newsweek.com/2021/01/08/laurie-santos-yale-happiness-professor-5-things-that-will-make-you-happier-1556182.html.

Schwartz, Barry. *The Battle for Human Nature: Science, Morality, and Modern Life*. New York: Norton, 1986.

———. *The Paradox of Choice*. Revised edition. New York: Ecco Press, 2016.

———. "Top Colleges Should Select Randomly from a Pool of 'Good Enough.'" *The Chronicle of Higher Education*, February 25, 2005. https://www.chronicle.com/article/Top-Colleges-Should-Select/14215/.

———. *Why We Work*. New York: Simon & Schuster/ TED, 2015.

Schwartz, Richard, and Jacqueline Olds. *Marriage in Motion: The Natural Ebb and Flow of Lasting Relationships*. Cambridge, MA: Da Capo Lifelong Books, 2002.

Scott, James. *Against the Grain: A Deep History of the Earliest States*. New Haven, CT: Yale University Press, 2017.

Scott, James C. *Seeing like a State: How Certain Schemes to Improve the Human Condition Have Failed*. New Haven, CT: Yale University Press, 1999.

Sengupta, Somini, and Julfikar Ali Manik. "A Quarter of Bangladesh Is Flooded. Millions Have Lost Everything." *The New York Times*, July 30, 2020, sec. Climate. https://www.nytimes.com/2020/07/30/climate/bangladesh-floods.html.

Shakespeare, William. *Timon of Athens*. Edited by Anthony Dawson and Gretchen E. Minton. Third edition. London: The Arden Shakespeare, 2008.

Shalchi, Djaffar. "The American Dream Is Now in Denmark." Interview by Anand Giridharadas, February 23, 2021. https://the.ink/p/the-american-dream-is-now-in-denmark.

Sharma, Ruchir. "Dear Joe Biden, Deficits Still Matter." *Financial Times*, January 20, 2021. https://www.ft.com/content/d49b537a-95f8-4e1a-b4b1-19f0c44d751e.

Shear, Michael D., and Gardiner Harris. "With High-Profile Help, Obama Plots Life after Presidency." *The New York Times*, August 16, 2015, sec. U.S. https://www.nytimes.com/2015/08/17/us/politics/with-high-profile-help-obama-plots-life-after-presidency.html.

Shields, David Light, and Brenda Light Bredemeier. "Competition: Was Kohn Right?" *The Phi Delta Kappan* 91, no. 5 (2010): 62–67.

Shorrocks, Anthony, James Davies, and Rodrigo Lluberas. "Global Wealth Report 2020." Credit Suisse: Research Institute, October 2020. https://www.credit-suisse.com/media/assets/corporate/docs/about-us/research/publications/global-wealth-report-2020-en.pdf.

Singer, Peter. *The Most Good You Can Do: How Effective Altruism Is Changing Ideas about Living Ethically*. New Haven, CT: Yale University Press, 2016.

Sitaraman, Ganesh. *The Crisis of the Middle-Class Constitution: Why Economic Inequality Threatens Our Republic*. New York: Knopf Doubleday, 2017.

Slobodian, Quinn. *Globalists: The End of Empire and the Birth of Neoliberalism*. Cambridge, MA: Harvard University Press, 2018.

Smialek, Jeanna, and Jim Tankersley. "Black Workers, Already Lagging, Face Big Economic Risks." *The New York Times*, sec. Business. June 1, 2020. https://www.nytimes.com/2020/06/01/business/economy/black-workers-inequality-economic-risks.html.

Smil, Vaclav. *Growth: From Microorganisms to Megacities*. Cambridge, MA: MIT Press, 2019.

———. *Making the Modern World: Materials and Dematerialization*. West Sussex: John Wiley & Sons, 2014.

———. "Want Not, Waste Not." Interview by Nathan Gardels. *Noema*, February 25, 2021. https://www.noemamag.com/want-not-waste-not.

Smith, Adam. *The Theory of Moral Sentiments*. Edited by Ryan Patrick Hanley. New York: Penguin Classics, 2010.

———. *The Wealth of Nations*. New York: Modern Library, 2000.

Smith, Clint. "Stories of Slavery, From Those Who Survived It." *The Atlantic*, March 2021. https://www.theatlantic.com/magazine/archive/2021/03/federal-writers-project/617790/.

Smith, Martin M., Simon B. Sherry, Vanja Vidovic, Donald H. Saklofske, Joachim Stoeber, and Aryn Benoit. "Perfectionism and the Five-Factor Model of Personality: A Meta-Analytic Review." *Personality and Social Psychology Review*, January 6, 2019. https://doi.org/10.1177/1088868318814973.

Smith, Mychal Denzel. "LeBron James Is No Socialist, But His New Nike Ad Makes a Good Case for Socialism." Esquire, December 23, 2019. https://www.esquire.com/news-politics/a30316187/lebron-james-nike-ad-humble-beginnings-i-promise-school-socialism/.

Smith, Randall. "As His Foundation Has Grown, Gates Has Slowed His Donations." DealBook, 1401155300. https://dealbook.nytimes.com/2014/05/26/as-his-foundation-has-grown-gates-has-slowed-his-donations/.

Söderberg, Gabriel, and Avner Offer. *The Nobel Factor: The Prize in Economics, Social Democracy, and the Market Turn*. Princeton, NJ: Princeton University Press, 2016.

Solis, Marie. "When Dismantling Power Dismantles You Instead." Vice, December 7, 2018. https://www.vice.com/en_us/article/3k95kk/when-dismantling-power-dismantles-you-instead-v25n4.

Solt, Frederick. "The Social Origins of Authoritarianism." *Political Research Quarterly* 65, no. 4 (2012): 703–13.

Soros, George. *The Crisis of Global Capitalism: Open Society Endangered*. New York: PublicAffairs, 1998.

Sowell, Thomas. *A Conflict of Visions: Ideological Origins of Political Struggles*. New York: Basic Books, 1987.

Startz, Dick. "Teacher Pay around the World." *Brookings* (blog), June 20, 2016. https://www.brookings.edu/blog/brown-center-chalkboard/2016/06/20/teacher-pay-around-the-world/.

Stebbins, Samuel. "Here's How Rich Every US Senator Is." MSN, September 12, 2019. https://www.msn.com/en-us/money/markets/heres-how-rich-every-us-senator-is/ss-AAH9wWI.

Steffen, Will, Katherine Richardson, Johan Rockström, Sarah E. Cornell, Ingo Fetzer, Elena M. Bennett, Reinette Biggs, et al. "Planetary Boundaries: Guiding Human Development on a Changing Planet." *Science* 347, no. 6223 (February 13, 2015). https://doi.org/10.1126/science.1259855.

Steinberger, Michael. "George Soros Bet Big on Liberal Democracy. Now He Fears He Is Losing." *The New York Times*, July 17, 2018, sec. Magazine. https://www.nytimes.com/2018/07/17/magazine/george-soros-democrat-open-society.html.

Stiglitz, Joseph E. *People, Power, and Profits: Progressive Capitalism for an Age of Discontent*. New York: W. W. Norton & Company, 2019.

Sunkara, Bhaskar. "If We Want to Fight the Climate Crisis, We Must Embrace Nuclear Power." *The Guardian*, June 21, 2021, sec. Opinion. http://www.theguardian.com/commentisfree/2021/jun/21/fight-climate-crisis-clean-energy-nuclear-power.

———. *The Socialist Manifesto: The Case for Radical Politics in an Era of Extreme Inequality*. New York: Basic Books, 2019.

Suny, Ronald. *The Soviet Experiment: Russia, the USSR, and the Successor States*. Second edition. New York: Oxford University Press, 2010.

Taylor, Keeanga-Yamahtta. *From #BlackLivesMatter to Black Liberation*. Chicago: Haymarket Books, 2016.

———. *Race for Profit: How Banks and the Real Estate Industry Undermined Black Homeownership*. Chapel Hill: University of North Carolina Press, 2019.

———. "Reality Has Endorsed Bernie Sanders." *The New Yorker*, March 30, 2020. https://www.newyorker.com/news/our-columnists/reality-has-endorsed-bernie-sanders.

Thompson, Evan. *Why I Am Not a Buddhist*. New Haven, CT: Yale University Press, 2020.

Thoreau, Henry David. *Walden*. Princeton, NJ: Princeton University Press, 2004.

Tomba, Massimiliano. *Insurgent Universality: An Alternative Legacy of Modernity*. Oxford: Oxford University Press, 2019.

Tooze, Adam. *Crashed: How a Decade of Financial Crises Changed the World*. New York: Viking, 2018.

———. "How Coronavirus Almost Brought Down the Global Financial System." *The Guardian*, April 14, 2020, sec. Business. https://www.theguardian.com/business/2020/apr/14/how-coronavirus-almost-brought-down-the-global-financial-system.

———. "In This Together: Global Cooperation on a Global Crisis." *Reason to Be Cheerful*, podcast, April 6, 2020. *https://www.cheerfulpodcast.com/rtbc-episodes/in-this-together*.

———. "Shockwave." *London Review of Books*, April 4, 2020. https://www.lrb.co.uk/the-paper/v42/n08/adam-tooze/shockwave.

Traub, James. "Our 'Pursuit of Happiness' Is Killing the Planet." *The New York Times*, March 6, 2020, sec. Opinion. https://www.nytimes.com/2020/03/06/opinion/our-pursuit-of-happiness-is-killing-the-planet.html.

Treuer, David. *The Heartbeat of Wounded Knee: Native America from 1890 to the Present*. New York: Riverhead Books, 2019.

United Nations Environment Programme. *UNEP Frontiers 2016 Report: Emerging Issues of Environment Concern*, 2016.

Vaesen, Krist, and Joel Katzav. "How Much Would Each Researcher Receive If Competitive Government Research Funding Were Distributed Equally among Researchers?" *PLOS ONE* 12, no. 9 (September 8, 2017): e0183967. https://doi.org/10.1371/journal.pone.0183967.

Waal, Frans de. *Our Inner Ape: A Leading Primatologist Explains Why We Are Who We Are*. New York: Penguin, 2005.

Wallace-Wells, David. *The Uninhabitable Earth: Life after Warming*. New York: Tim Duggan Books, 2019.

Walshe, Maurice O'C., trans. *The Long Discourses of the Buddha: A Translation of the Dīgha Nikāya*. The Teachings of the Buddha. Boston: Wisdom Publications, 1995.

Walzer, Michael. *Spheres of Justice: A Defense of Pluralism and Equality*. New York: Basic Books, 1983.

Wapshott, Nicholas. *Keynes Hayek: The Clash That Defined Modern Economics*. New York: W. W. Norton & Company, 2012.

Watts, Alan W. *The Wisdom of Insecurity: A Message for an Age of Anxiety*. Second edition. New York: Vintage Books, 2011.

Weber, Max. *The Protestant Ethic and the "Spirit" of Capitalism and Other Writings*. Translated by Peter Baehr and Gordon C. Wells. New York: Penguin Classics, 2002.

Weise, Karen. "Jeff Bezos Commits $10 Billion to Address Climate Change." *The New York Times*, February 17, 2020, sec. Technology. https://www.nytimes.com/2020/02/17/technology/jeff-bezos-climate-change-earth-fund.html.

Whitman, James Q. *Hitler's American Model: The United States and the Making of Nazi Race Law*. Princeton, NJ: Princeton University Press, 2017.

Whitney, Elspeth. "Lynn White Jr.'s 'The Historical Roots of Our Ecologic Crisis' after 50 Years." *History Compass* 13, no. 8 (August 2015): 396–410. https://doi.org/10.1111/hic3.12254.

Wiedmann, Thomas, Manfred Lenzen, Lorenz T. Keyßer, and Julia K. Steinberger. "Scientists' Warning on Affluence." *Nature Communications* 11, no. 1 (June 19, 2020): 3107. https://doi.org/10.1038/s41467-020-16941-y.

Will, George F. "Freedom vs. Equality." *Washington Post*, February 1, 2004. https://www.washingtonpost.com/archive/opinions/2004/02/01/freedom-vs-equality/63bddf0b-6089-4bab-8663-f61571578e57/.

Williamson, Vanessa, and Isabella Gelfand. "Trump and Racism: What Do the Data Say?" Brookings (blog), August 14, 2019. *https://www.brookings.edu/blog/fixgov/2019/08/14/trump-and-racism-what-do-the-data-say/*.

Winnicott, D. W. *Playing and Reality*. Second edition. London: Routledge, 2005.

Wolff, Richard D. *Democracy at Work: A Cure for Capitalism*. Chicago: Haymarket Books, 2012.

———. "Socialism Means Abolishing the Distinction between Bosses and Employees." Truthout, July 27, 2015. https://truthout.org/articles/socialism-means-abolishing-the-distinction-between-bosses-and-employees/.

World Bank. "Nearly Half the World Lives on Less than $5.50 a Day," October 17, 2018. https://www.worldbank.org/en/news/press-release/2018/10/17/nearly-half-the-world-lives-on-less-on-550-a-day.

The World Counts. "How Many People Die from Hunger Each Year?—TheWorldCounts." Accessed March 22, 2020. https://www.theworldcounts.com /challenges/people-and-poverty/hunger-and-obesity/how-many-people-die -from-hunger-each-year/story.

World Health Organization. "More than 150 Countries Engaged in COVID-19 Vaccine Global Access Facility," July 15, 2020. https://www.who.int/news-room /detail/15-07-2020-more-than-150-countries-engaged-in-covid-19-vaccine -global-access-facility.

World Meteorological Organization (WMO). *WMO Statement on the State of the Global Climate in 2019.* WMO. Geneva: WMO, 2020.

Wright, Erik Olin. *Envisioning Real Utopias.* New York: Verso, 2010.

Wright, Robert. *Why Buddhism Is True: The Science and Philosophy of Meditation and Enlightenment.* New York: Simon and Schuster, 2017.

Wright, Ronald. *A Short History of Progress.* CBC Massey Lectures. Toronto: House of Anansi Press, 2004.

Young, Michael. *The Rise of the Meritocracy, 1870–2033: An Essay on Education and Equality.* Harmondsworth: Penguin Books, 1961.

Zaitchik, Alexander. "How Bill Gates Impeded Global Access to Covid Vaccines." *The New Republic,* April 12, 2021. https://newrepublic.com/article/162000/bill -gates-impeded-global-access-covid-vaccines.

Zhuangzi. *Zhuangzi: The Essential Writings with Selections from Traditional Commentaries.* Translated by Brook Ziporyn. Indianapolis: Hackett Publishing, 2009.

Zimmerman, Edith. "I'm Calling Hypocrisy on These 'Good-Enough Life' Advocates." *The Cut,* February 20, 2019. https://www.thecut.com/2019/02/calling -hypocrisy-on-these-good-enough-life-advocates.html.

Ziporyn, Brook. "Introduction." In *Zhuangzi: The Essential Writings with Selections from Traditional Commentaries,* by Zhuangzi, translated by Brook Ziporyn. Indianapolis: Hackett Publishing, 2009.

Žižek, Slavoj. *On Belief.* New York: Routledge, 2001.

INDEX

environmental racism, 199

equality: and cooperation, 151, 178; and democracy, 151, 186; ecological, 229–31; economic, 222, 237; fight for, 90–92; and freedom, 164–65; and the good-enough life, 11, 22, 40; and the human condition, 20, 207; material, 184; moral, 67, 69; of opportunity, 15, 31, 59, 156, 252n40; political, 169; and progress, 155–56. *See also* inequality

Equality of Opportunity Project, 31

essential workers, 12, 75

ethical system, 44

ethics, 13–14, 19, 66–67, 87, 105, 166–67. *See also* Good Samaritan; morality; virtue ethics

eugenics, 210–11

Evergreen coops, 177

evolution, 10, 17, 40, 47, 197, 208–16, 218

excellence, pursuing, 57, 60, 74, 77–78

the excellence conspiracy, 215

excess, 130

exclusion, 96

expertise, 61–62, 185, 252n39

extinction, 198, 217

failure (coping with), 18, 38–39, 60, 73, 80, 195

The Fall, 47–48

fame: and greatness, 1, 25, 32, 61; laws of, 25–26, 69–70. *See also* success

family, 42

family, the author's, 23–24, 28–29, 95, 99

fascism, 151, 154, 175, 211. *See also* authoritarianism

Federici, Silvia, 141

feminism, 14, 141–43, 146. *See also* patriarchy; women

Ferrell, Will, 110

film, 102, 104, 110–11

Financial Times Editorial Board, 244n8

Finland, 52

Floyd, George, 9

food, 218–19, 264n66

Ford administration, 48

founder effects, 213

Four Noble Truths, 84

France (politics), 190–91

Franklin, Benjamin, 50–51, 250n18

Frase, Peter, 185

freedom, 139, 152, 155, 164–66, 176, 258n50

free speech, 49

Freud, Sigmund, 109–10, 184, 186, 194

friendship, 98–99, 101, 115–21, 126, 135. *See also* relationships

Galbraith, John Kenneth, 167

Garden of Eden, 47–48

Gates, Bill, 168–70, 219–21, 230, 269n110

Gates Foundation, 160

Gautama, Siddhartha, 47, 81–83, 86. *See also* Buddha

GDP, 157

Genesis, 46–48

genetic drift, 213

genius, 10, 14

geographic isolation, 213

global debt, 221

globalization, 24, 89, 150, 173, 270n131

global warming. *See* climate change

Goldwater, Barry, 152

"the good," 13–14

good elites, 200

good-enough individuals, 38–39

good-enough mother, 17

good-enoughness: and change, 6, 94, 229–30; criticisms of, 20; definition of, 4–5, 8, 38; and greatness, 8,